"*Ayo Gorkhali* takes us on a journey of the Gurkhas, starting with their induction into the British Indian Army. Impressed by their bravery in the Anglo-Nepal War, the British decided to recruit soldiers from Nepal, and the 1st Gorkha Rifles was raised in 1815. This was the beginning of a 200-year-old legacy that survives till today. ... As an officer who has worn the Gorkha badge for 40 years, I can relate to the passion and sentiment of Tim Gurung and his attempt in the book to go beyond the stories of valour and fighting skills of the Gurkhas. He has, therefore, covered a whole range of issues like Gurkha women, Gurkhas in literature, recruitment policy, etc." — *The Tribune*, India

"While the Gurkhas have been much celebrated, there is hardly a book written on them from within the community. Tim I. Gurung, who hails from mid-western Nepal and served in the British Army Gurkhas, should be given the credit to be one of the first to come out with the unfiltered voices of veteran Gurkhas. ... As an insider, Gurung has a clarity of thought about presenting the life struggles of the Gurkhas and the reasons for them to acquire war skills. To know the past, present and way forward on the Gurkhas, *Ayo Gorkhali* is an essential read."
— *The Kathmandu Post*

"*Ayo Gorkhali* is a timely narrative inclusive of many other battles fought by Gurkhas and their friends for securing, though belatedly, a level playing field for preserving the 200-year Gurkha legacy with Britain and shared with India. To the question Tim poses: were the British fair to the Gurkhas? – the answer comes out clearly. It is difficult not to love the Gurkhas especially if you have served with them. A must-read book of Gurkha valour and their fight for justice in the British Army."
— *Force Newsmagazine*, India

"*Ayo Gorkhali* by Tim I. Gurung, a former British Gurkha, is the first work of history by a member of the community and brings alive the story of a people who have served flags other than their own with honour, even as they have attempted to keep their native warrior traditions alive in letter and spirit." — *Hindustan Times*

"Very few Gurkhas have written and published their stories in the form of books. And less than a handful have done so in the English language. The scant stories written by retired Gurkha soldiers are generally in the Nepali language and have seldom reached a global audience. I cannot emphasize the importance of such writings enough. They help break the stereotype built by western authors who oftentimes present a skewed image of the Gurkhas by glamorizing and valorizing their bravery, martial prowess, and loyalty. Western authors seldom pick up on or highlight the harrowing experiences faced by the Gurkhas both on and off the battlefield. *Ayo Gorkhali* disrupts this one-sided narrative by offering a more comprehensive and multidimensional view of the recruitment, pre- and post-recruitment, and post-retirement facets of Gurkha life.

The author has done extensive fieldwork within Nepal and beyond, and talked to over a hundred veteran Gurkhas in order to bring forth many of their unheard stories. The book is also an important addition to migration scholarship as it closely examines the Gurkha diaspora within the context of the larger category of Nepali migrants. Overall, *Ayo Gorkhali* succeeds in shattering the myth that western authors generally create by romanticizing the Gurkha soldiers while presenting an alternative narrative whose strengths are a combination of personal introspection and rigorous research on Gurung's part."

— *The Record*, Nepal

Ayo Gorkhali

THE TRUE STORY OF THE GURKHAS

Tim I. Gurung

BLACKSMITH BOOKS

In memory of, and with respect for, those brave Gurkhas
who sacrificed their precious today for our tomorrows.

Ayo Gorkhali
The true story of the Gurkhas

ISBN 978-988-79639-0-5

Published by Blacksmith Books
Unit 26, 19/F, Block B, Wah Lok Industrial Centre,
37-41 Shan Mei Street, Fo Tan, Hong Kong
Tel: (+852) 2877 7899
www.blacksmithbooks.com

CONTENTS

Map 1: The Gurkhas in Nepal

(1) MAHAKALI
(2) DOTI
(3) MYAGDI
(4) GULMI
(5) PALPA
(6) JITGADHI (FORT 1814-1816)
(7) PAKLIHAWA
(8) SUNAULI
(9) GORAKHPUR (INDIA)
(10) POKHARA / KASKI
(11) LAMJUNG
(12) GORKHA
(13) SYANGJA
(14) TANAHU
(15) KATHMANDU
(16) RAMECHHAP
(17) SINDHULI GADHI (FORT 1767)
(18) OKHALDUNGA
(19) BHOJPUR
(20) TEHRATHUM
(21) DHANKUTA
(22) DHARAN
(23) ILAM
(24) DARJEELING (INDIA)
(25) MAKAWANPUR GADHI
     (FORT 1814-1816)

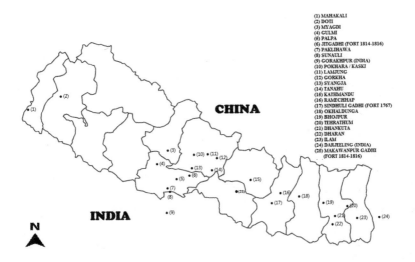

Map 2: Gurkha deployments from 1815-2018

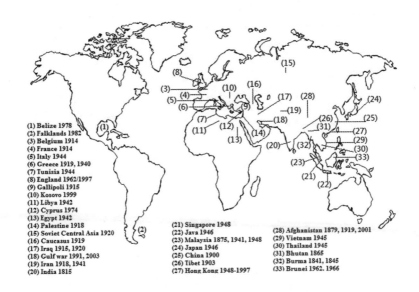

(1) Belize 1978
(2) Falklands 1982
(3) Belgium 1914
(4) France 1914
(5) Italy 1944
(6) Greece 1919, 1940
(7) Tunisia 1944
(8) England 1962/1997
(9) Gallipoli 1915
(10) Kosovo 1999
(11) Libya 1942
(12) Cyprus 1974
(13) Palestine 1918
(14) Palestine 1918
(15) Soviet Central Asia 1920
(16) Caucasus 1919
(17) Iraq 1915, 1920
(18) Gulf war 1991, 2003
(19) Iran 1918, 1941
(20) India 1815

(21) Singapore 1948
(22) Java 1946
(23) Malaysia 1875, 1941, 1948
(24) Japan 1946
(25) China 1900
(26) Tibet 1903
(27) Hong Kong 1948-1997

(28) Afghanistan 1879, 1919, 2001
(29) Vietnam 1945
(30) Thailand 1945
(31) Bhutan 1865
(32) Burma 1841, 1845
(33) Brunei 1962. 1966

MAP 3: THE GURKHAS IN HONG KONG

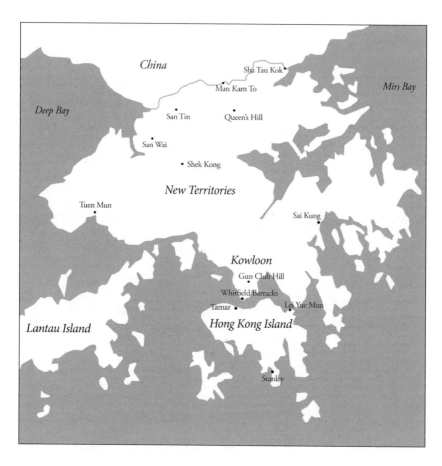

CHAPTER I

FIRST WORDS

'I prayed to 'Bhagawati Maai' for my safe return. She heard my prayers and I did puja after my safe return. It was just like yesterday, but so many years have passed. The saddest part of life today is that all of my friends from the old army days are gone.'

Rifleman Karna Bahadur Rai/Dewan (99) 1/10th GR, a WWII veteran from Ilam, East Nepal, who saw action in Burma. With no pension, he joined the police force as an instructor and then became a farmer.

It was late 2016 when I decided to write a book about the Gurkhas. Initially, I had a straightforward idea of how the book should be written. I would primarily include the main events, such as the beginning of the Gurkha story, the main wars which the Gurkhas fought, and the countries they served in, and wrap up with details of their present status. For this task, I would give myself a year and a half: one year for the research and six months for the actual writing. I was quite confident of finishing the book by mid-2018.

Being a Gurkha myself, with the Gurung surname that belongs to the so-called martial races, would give enough authenticity to my work, I thought. But I was wrong. Whether it was my ignorance or complacency, I couldn't say for sure, but one thing was clear. By ignoring the most crucial factor in writing, I was about to make one of the gravest mistakes of my writing career. I was not planning to write the book for the readers but for myself. In short, I was too naïve and was considering the subject matter too lightly.

What I didn't realize then was the significance of my subject matter. I was short-sighted, if not foolish, which was evident the moment I started working on the book. The more I researched the subject, the more I wanted to know. Before too long, I was so into the subject matter that I hardly had time for anything else. I spent the whole of 2017 in my research by visiting more than half a dozen nations, talking with many people, reading almost three dozen books, watching numerous videos and documentaries, and reading as many articles as I could find on the internet. An institution that has lasted for more than 200 years and is still going strong as I write cannot be taken too lightly. Trying to depict it otherwise would have not only been unwise but would also be disgraceful for me as a writer.

Besides, I spent a whole month travelling from the east to the west of Nepal, covering more than 25 districts considered the heart of Gurkha recruiting, and met almost a hundred Gurkha veterans during the trip, especially those who had fought in WWII. We were extremely fortunate to find them still around and healthy enough to be able to share their stories. Being able to include their stories before they could have been lost was the greatest achievement of this visit.

However, there was one thing I already knew well before I started researching and that hasn't changed a bit, even now. All the books regarding the Gurkhas so far were mostly written from the Western point of view, mainly by writers with military backgrounds. No matter how much diversity they may have claimed, in the end, it was still one-sided. They mostly repeated the same two things again and again in all the books. One was the bravery of the Gurkhas, and the other was the self-aggrandizement of the parts the British officers had played in making the Gurkhas world-famous. Their romanticized portrayals sounded almost like a myth. Recently, there have been some new Gurkha books written by Nepali authors. But they lack the military dynamics, as well as international perspective, and are somewhat politically motivated.

The other side of the Gurkha story is unfortunately still not being told. Those who could have done so, didn't, and the Gurkhas couldn't write by themselves.

As a result, many stories, especially from WWI and WWII, were buried with them, leaving a large vacuum on their side of the story. But how did they do it? At what cost? And in the name of pride and honour, how many lives were lost? And was everything worth it? As humans lost their senses, it was humanity that took a severe beating.

It's the main reason why the Gurkhas are only known as the bravest soldiers to the world, while forgetting the fact that they are also humans like the rest of us. Just like the two sides of a coin, the Gurkha story also has two sides, and until that side of the story is told and heard, the story won't be complete. The Gurkha story is not only about bravery, but it's also a story of tragedy, which is what this book is all about: that other side of the story.

The other reason why I wanted to write this book was somewhat personal. My family, my village and the whole region where I belong are all about Gurkhas. Gurkhas are not only our way of life but also our destiny, and we live and breathe Gurkhas as a community. Our region, the Pokhara Valley and its surroundings, is considered one of the hotbeds of Gurkha recruiting in Western Nepal, and there is hardly a single household in those Gurung villages that have no connection with the Gurkhas. As an ex-Gurkha, a Gurung and an author, the responsibility was on me. I had not only to write a Gurkha book but also write a complete one, so none of my readers has to look further again. As I always write for a reason, being able to write a Gurkha book for our people is undoubtedly one of the proudest moments of my career, and I sincerely hope I have done a decent job.

As I have promised, this is a book of our complete Gurkha history, albeit in brief. By reading this book, you will know what our grandfathers did for us, our people and our country, and we must never forget their sacrifices. Writing their stories is the least we can do for them. If not, it will not only be disrespectful to them but also a disgrace on our part. It's not just us, but our future generations must know about the Gurkha legacy and cherish it.

Most importantly, this book is to, for, and by the Gurkhas. I do hope that our community will read and learn to value it. If the future generations of Gurkhas want to know about or understand what their grandfathers have done for their future, this is the right book. Jai Gurkhas!

CHAPTER 2

MY TIME IN THE BRIGADE AS A GURKHA SOLDIER

'I fought in Burma during WWII but couldn't remember where it was. I witnessed the Hindu-Muslim riots in 1947-48, and I fought in Sikkim, Ladakh, Manipur and Assam during my army career. I think I have fifteen war medals altogether. One was from the Jammu and Kashmir crisis, and the rest, sorry, I cannot recall.'

Hon. Capt. Gore Gurung (93), 5/4th GR, from Chhetrapur, Chitwan, joined the army in 1944 and retired in 1976. He won 15 war medals.

The village of Lwang/Ghalel and Machhapuchhre (Mount Fishtail) to the north, the hilly jungle range of Pothana to the west, the long and wide slope of Nau Danda (Nine Hills) to the south, and the knoll of Achham Danda (Achham Hill) followed by the vast, lush Suikhet Valley to the east: there lies the beautiful Gurung village of Dhampus in the middle. Pokhari or Danda Gaun is situated atop the hill. The Gurung families who lived there were descendants of a single couple and were all farmers. My great-grandfather had seven sons, and the offspring of his seven sons occupied almost the entire village. All the households living in the village were close relatives. A few houses of Kamis and Damais lived in the village too.

Due to the lack of family planning, the size of families was slightly larger in those days. Big numbers in the family also helped in the field. Besides, each household had a pair of oxen for fieldwork, a couple of buffaloes for milk and compost, and some chickens. A few families had a small herd of sheep and goats. All in all, life was straightforward.

My grandfather had seven sons and two daughters. Due to lack of suitable land for building new houses for his sons' new families, four sons had to move out of the village and lived in a separate area called Rajesawra, which was located within a half-hour walking distance from the main village. The family of your humble author was one of them. The four families had our own separate and straightforward life there, and we only went back to the main village during festivals and special events. In those days, only boys of the families were sent to school, and almost all the girls stayed at home and helped in the fields. However, every member of the family, including boys, had to pitch in and complete our share of family chores before heading to school. Once we returned from school, everyone was required to share the workload again, and we all worked until dinner. It was a hard-working generation.

Dhampus only had a middle school at that time. Once we completed middle school, we had two options to choose from for high school. One was Bhenabaari, and the other was Nau Danda High School. I went to

Bhenabaari High School, as it was the nearest one to my home. The school was at least an hour's walk away, but the hardest part was not the distance. Since the school was situated on the flat land surrounded by the Mardi and Eidi rivers, I had to walk down the hills in the morning and walk up the same route after school in the evening. As we all know, walking down the mountain with a full stomach is as hard as walking up a hill with an empty stomach and I was on the wrong side on both occasions. The common practice of having pocket money had not started yet, and poor village lads like us couldn't afford to treat ourselves with afternoon tea daily.

The nearest town was Pokhara, which was a few hours away from our place if one walked, and the villagers used to go down to buy sugar, tea, salt, kerosene, clothes, shoes, sandals and many more things. One could complete the trip in a day and still have time to visit the cinema hall for a new movie before heading back to the village.

Kaski, Syangja, Lamjung and Gorkha are considered the hotbed of Gurungs within Nepal. My village, Dhampus, includes the nearby Gurung villages of Lwang/Ghalel, Hengjakot, Ribhan, Lahchok, Ghachok, Paudur, Saabet, Tangchok, Vichuk, Ghandruk, Dangsing, and so on. They are places where the deep-rooted traditions of the Gurkhas had a big influence on people's lives. There was hardly a single house that had no connection with the Gurkhas. Becoming a Gurkha was always the main priority of the village youths and the arriving of the *Gallawala* was one of the most anticipated events of the year. (The *Gallawala* is the recruiting officer visiting villages in Nepal to select new recruits).

The British Army was always the first choice. Those who had lost hope of joining the British military would go for the Indian Army, and the Gurungs, especially from our areas, almost never went for the Nepal Army. I still remembered a saying from one of my village elders, who made a remark about potential matchmaking. 'Unless he becomes a *Malayako Lahure* [British Gurkha], he won't be able to marry that girl, even if he can offer gold equal to his bodyweight.' Growing up in such a society had its consequences. Each young man from my village grew up with one dream: each of us wanted to be a British Gurkha. I was no different.

I had another big reason. My father wasn't a Gurkha, and I was the first son of the family, thus the onus was on me to make it right. I was seventeen when I finally became a Gurkha in early 1980, one of the youngest ones from my village, and I made my family and community proud. I couldn't say for sure whether I was happy or proud on that day, but I was very relieved. Not because I had finally become a Gurkha but for a silly childish reason. I was part of a trio in high school – two of the friends were class seniors – and they were graduating a year before me. Had I not been selected for the British Gurkhas, I would have to spend the next year without them, and that was almost unimaginable for me. My life at the school would have been horrible without them, hence a massive sigh of relief for me. The only person who wasn't happy about me becoming a Gurkha was my headmaster and he called us 'stupid Gurungs' in sheer outrage. I happened to be quite good at school, and he genuinely thought I had a good future back in Nepal.

After spending a few days in Kathmandu, we took a night flight to Hong Kong. But the Nepal Airlines flight only took us as far as Bangkok, where we got on a Cathay Pacific flight. The first introduction to the modern world came in the shape of a face towel, which was yellowish, nicely rolled and packed in a plastic bag, and as country boys and first-time air travellers, we didn't know what to do with the thing. We looked at the *guruji* (the NCO guiding the recruits) for a clue. We watched and learned from him and saved ourselves from further embarrassment. That incident took place almost forty years ago, but I still remember it as if it were yesterday and will probably never forget it. The next memorable event was my first night-time view of Hong Kong seen from the window of a plane descending to the Kai Tak International Airport. Despite arriving in the middle of the night, the whole city was illuminated by millions of neon lights and lit up like it was daytime.

Upon our arrival in Hong Kong, we were herded into a military bus and taken to a supply depot where new kit was issued and, later on, we were driven to the training camp. By the time we arrived at the barracks, got assigned to our respective beds, put our kit away and readied for bed, it was already very late. It seemed as if we had just closed our eyes when we were suddenly awakened by a barrage of shrill barking noises. Before we could realize it, the basic training of the recruits had begun.

The Training Depot Brigade of Gurkhas (TDBG) was stationed at Shek Kong, near Kam Tin, in the New Territories of Hong Kong. Due to the unprecedented influx of Illegal Immigrants (IIs) from China in the late seventies, more recruits were enlisted in the Brigade of Gurkhas during that period, and instead of one intake, three intakes of recruits came to the TDBG in 1979-80. As a result, even the basic recruits' training course was shortened to seven months from the usual nine. Due to a lack of facilities, some of the recruits had to be accommodated in round-shaped tin huts (known as Nissen huts), and I was one of them. Some of the recruits had trained with the battalion stationed in Brunei.

The next hurdle to overcome was the weird smell of the central cookhouse; it had a stench. We couldn't locate the source of that strange smell, and it took at least a week or so before we got used to it.

The recruit training was tough and mostly consisted of fitness training, drill parades, weapons handling, shooting, jungle warfare, sports, swimming and educational classes, which were reasonable and largely as expected. The primary purpose of recruit training was to transform a raw and carefree civilian into a disciplined military man, and that was, understandably, not easy. A recruit's life was always busy and under pressure. Everything was done according to a preset timetable, and there was hardly any time for anything else. The daily routine was packed, and recruits were busy running from six in the morning to eleven in the evening. The level of hardship of the recruit's life also depended on the *gurujis* you had. Those *gurujis* who were more ambitious and looking for a promotion had set a very high standard for themselves and would go to unbelievable lengths to prove their point. The rivalry was fierce, expectations were high, and whenever the final result didn't match their hopes, the poor recruits were always the ones at the receiving end. Those recruits under the most ambitious commanders were the ones who suffered the most.

My section commander was a hard-nosed, proud and cursing *Limbu* from 7th GR, a sergeant instead of a corporal, and we never saw him smile. We were genuinely scared of him and never dared cross his path. But behind his back, we used to say he was either drinking or had quarrelled with his wife. My section 2IC (Second-in-Command) was a *Lamjunghe Gurung* from 1/2th GR, also a corporal instead of a lance corporal, and was pretty ambitious too. The traditions of recruit training hadn't changed in years. In the name of toughening up and instilling discipline in soldiers, anything was acceptable, and the doses of humiliation were a daily meal. Each recruit had a nickname, the worst imaginable, and cursing, beatings and humiliation was a daily routine. The insults were not limited to the recruits themselves, but also their whole families, and it was always sisters who got the most.

The worst punishment I can still remember today was the one that was mostly meted out after a poor performance at the shooting range. If the section wasn't doing well, the immediate punishment was to crawl across the entire shooting range in the summer heat. If the result still didn't improve by the end of the day, all the members of the section were barred from having dinner and had to go through the infamous 'Naala Parade.' It meant making a bridge over a gutter in a press-up position that lasted for as long as the *guruji* wanted. He would have a belt or a rifle's sling prepared at hand, and he would thrash whoever touched the ground, and the punishment would last for hours. To avoid further embarrassment, the weaker ones had to work hard and seek out help from the stronger ones.

As far as I was concerned, the recruit training was undoubtedly the hardest period of my life, and it felt like a long nightmare that would never end. However, by September of 1980, it was finally over, and we headed to our respective regiments. I went to 6th GR for only one reason – most of my relatives from the village were in 6th GR, which was stationed at Burma Lines, Queen's Hill barracks, near Fan Ling. We had four senior officers (captains) from my village in 6th GR alone. Although I was too young to understand the significance of nepotism, favouritism, and cronyism then, I genuinely thought my future was secure in 6th GR. I didn't know my old folks were just too simple and busy saving their own hides. Our intake was the biggest the regiment had received in recent years, and we were known as 'Bahu Dal' throughout the battalion, which had a double meaning. First, it meant 'multi-parties' and referred to the recent events back in Nepal when the whole nation was swept up in the new political aspirations of 1980. The second meaning was an unflattering one, and it suggested we were like a loud, unruly and bratty bunch.

On the first day we arrived at our barracks, we were sent to the China-Hong Kong border in the evening. The primary purpose why we were brought there in the first place (the prevention of illegal immigrants coming from mainland China to Hong Kong) was already starting to pay off within seven months, and without us having even the slightest clue about the bigger picture.

The three infantry battalions stationed in Hong Kong would take turns, and we were deployed at the borders every three to four months for about a month each time. Places such as Sha Tau Kok, Ta Kwu Ling, Pak Fu Shan, Man Kam To, Lok Ma Chau, Lo Wu, Mai Po, Castle Peak and Sai Kung at the northern parts of Hong Kong adjoining China were where most of our time was spent. When we were not guarding the borders, we were busy training in other rural parts of the New Territories for military drills. We visited places like Plover Cove, Tai Lam, San Tin, San Wai, Queen's Hill and Lantau Island on a regular basis. We were so familiar with the countryside that we knew every track and route of these places and never lost our way. As we hardly visited the central city areas, our knowledge of the city was somewhat limited.

The border duty team was mostly made up of four members. Sometimes we had a canine team from the Hong Kong Chinese dog unit joining us for the night, and the number of IIs caught in a single night was almost a hundred for the battalion. The most extended border tour was for nearly a month, deployed on a remote hilltop on the Sai Kung Peninsula. The four of us were equipped with a military radio. All the necessary supplies were air-dropped by the army helicopter.

When Lady Diana Spencer married Prince Charles in July 1981, we were in the middle of a five-nation training exercise in the jungle near Brisbane, Australia. It was my first overseas trip other than Hong Kong, and our company was taking part as the representative of the Brigade of Gurkhas. But I remember the event for another reason. While we Gurkhas were all in an alert position inside the trenches, the British officers were having a celebration of their own in the middle of the battle exercise. A table covered with a white tablecloth was set up in the jungle, a champagne bottle and glasses were somehow smuggled in, and they celebrated the Royal Wedding with cheers in the middle of the forest that night.

When the Falklands War started in 1982, our battalion was put on 48-hour standby, and we were not allowed to go outside without permission. It was a tense and difficult period for us all, but luckily, it passed without us having to go to war.

By late 1982, our battalion moved to Brunei, and I returned to Nepal for my first extended leave after three and a half years. The joy, excitement, and anticipation of seeing my family after such a long period was overwhelming. The feelings were surreal, and I could hardly put them into words. When I finally arrived home, it was almost dark, but the whole house lit up with joy and our happiness had no limits. Once the formality of meeting and eating was done, we shared the joy of gifts to my family, and we spent the whole evening talking. That was undoubtedly one of the best moments of my life, and I will cherish it for ever. I still remember those moments even today and wish they could be repeated.

Village life didn't attract me any more. I moved to Pokhara with one of my relatives and learned typing and driving. In comparison to today's prices, land in Pokhara was quite cheap then, and we even bought a piece of our own. After the first extended leave, I joined my battalion in Brunei and did my JLC (junior leadership course) for promotion. JLC is the basic course intended for the development of soldiers to NCOs and I did quite well. Once I got promoted to lance corporal, I got a chance to go to the UK for a one-year tour as a junior NCO of the Gurkha Demonstration Company at Sandhurst (the British Army's officer training college). By that time, my battalion had already moved to Hong Kong and was stationed at Gallipoli Lines, San Wai, near Fan Ling. Right after I returned from the UK, I went to Nepal on my second extended leave.

On my second extended leave, I got married, and we bought a small house in Bagar, Pokhara, from the money I had earned in the UK. By the end of my second leave, my life was about to change for good. Our first daughter was already on the way at this point, my battalion had already moved to the UK for a two-year tour, and I had to make a decision.

I had already written quite a lot by then, in Nepali of course. I mostly wrote songs, short stories, poems, and even a short novel. All writers crave for their name to appear on a book cover and I was no different. One of my friends introduced me to a printer in Pokhara. He was one of the locals and after agreeing on the price, cover design, numbers of copies and delivery for my first book, I paid him and the printed books were to be delivered before my departure. That didn't happen so I had to leave for duty before seeing the first copy of my book. The book was called *Bihaani Ra Sangjh* which means 'The Sunrise and the Sunset'.

When the books finally arrived, we were shocked and realized the unwarranted delay was intentional. The cover was plain white paper instead of a coloured image, the title and the author's name were written in bold blue ink, and the books were in odd shapes. They looked like hymn books printed in a hurry and at low cost. My dream of being a writer was shattered even before I could spread my wings.

After that unfortunate incident, I completely stopped writing for the next twenty-five years and started writing again only after I turned fifty.

Of the five infantry battalions that the Brigade of Gurkhas had by then, only three battalions remained in Hong Kong at a time, and the other two were stationed in the UK and Brunei. They used to take turns replacing each other every two years. The tour of both the UK and Brunei was much preferred over Hong Kong for one obvious reason – the pay was better! Due to the high value of the pound, the tour of the UK was the best one, and nobody liked to miss that chance. Still, regiments had to send their allotment of members to the units like the TDBG, and extra perks like permission for family to join or acting ranks (a lance corporal was made an acting corporal, a corporal an acting sergeant, etc.) were given to appease them.

I volunteered to become one of them without any perks, only because I chose to be with my family instead of going for money and promotion. Since I had already qualified for family permission, I received nothing extra as an incentive. Both my son and daughter were born in the Shek

Kong Camp. I joined my battalion at Cassino Lines, Ngau Tam Mei, only after they had returned from the UK two years later.

In two years, a lot had changed in my battalion, and I found myself in a pretty awkward position. I was almost the odd man out. There was no closeness or brotherly love among the soldiers as we had before. Everyone and everything looked unfamiliar, and I immediately felt like I just didn't fit in. The most significant change was that all the officers and senior NCOs above the rank of sergeant were to be transferred to other companies within the regiment. Previously, they had remained with the original companies throughout their career. I wouldn't say it greatly affected the conformity and well-being of the operational capability, but it certainly disturbed the trust, care and unity among the soldiers.

Most importantly, it compromised the significance of brotherhood and camaraderie, which play such an essential role in the army. Luckily, we were in peacetime. Had it been in war, the damage would have been enormous.

I didn't know at that time that it was a rehearsal before the big show. After all, they were the British who had ruled the world before, and they didn't do things without a reason. They were preparing for the big rundown later on, before 1997.

My army career was almost over by then. I had no interest whatsoever in military textbooks and did just enough to keep myself out of trouble every day. All the senior NCOs and officers of my company were strangers, and all of my old *gurujis* were already transferred to other companies. Understandably, my new commanders didn't give a monkey about me, and nor did I try to change their perception. The next few months were the worst of my army career. I felt like a stranger in my battalion and somehow toiled on until my third extended leave was due, which was soon.

I left my family back in Nepal before joining the battalion again after six months and spent the next few lacklustre months doing odd jobs in the army. Luckily for me, I had completed some courses in first aid training, education and Chinese language skills, and they came in handy in my later days in the army. I got to arrange some afternoon classes for the company's soldiers on those subjects. They were just some fill-in classes when the company had nothing more important to do.

The old promotion policy of the battalion had already been broken by now. In the old system, seniority was based on the year you joined the battalion, and the competition was held strictly among the *numbaries* (same intake) only. As a result, no one from the junior intakes could overtake the senior intakes in promotion, and that unspoken policy remained intact until they were to become a Gurkha Officer. But according to the new system, anyone could be promoted to higher ranks in the name of merit and modernity. In reality, it hurt those who still had hopes and aspirations for a brighter career. When the line of seniority was undermined, the whole concept of subordination that runs the entire institution was shaken, and that cannot be a good sign for the army. But, at least in my humble view, the policymakers seemed to have ignored or neglected that crucial factor of soldiering by then.

After all the so-called high-fliers had already jumped over me, I was finally made a corporal and sent to the TDBG again as an education instructor. Our job was to arrange classes in basic maths, English, map reading and general knowledge to the recruits, and that was the last stint of my army career.

As far as a promotion was concerned, many factors were considered, such as discipline, politeness, leadership, good grades in military courses, and being good at shooting, sports, running and entertaining skills (dancing, singing and playing music). Some superstars were talented at almost anything they participated in, while others were good in specific fields. Nepotism, favouritism as well as cronyism also flourished, and the main players were not only the senior Gurkha officers but also the British officers. Getting promotions through the acts of ingratiating and buttering up was pretty common, and even a rumour or two of buying promotions with gold were also whispered about among the rank and file.

The Nepal Cup Final (an inter-regimental football competition) and Khud Race (climbing up and down hills, also inter-battalion contests) were the two most popular events with the Brigade, and both events were awaited with much anticipation. The Nepal Cup Final was mostly held at TDBG. Spectators from all the regiments gathered there in large numbers, and the event was celebrated with a lot of joy, excitement and pride. The favourite footballers, as well as the Khud Race runners, were famous within the battalion, and their popularity helped enhance their army career. Those good shooters, especially in the army rifle competition, were also the ones who got fast-tracked with promotions, and many of them were eventually promoted to Gurkha officer.

According to J.P. Cross sahib (the British officer most revered amongst Gurkhas, a writer, historian and well-wisher of Nepal who lives in Pokhara), the Gurkhas from western Nepal were like dogs and their eastern counterparts like cats, and I am pretty sure he must have had his reasons for saying so. In my humble point of view though, the easterners were loud, expressive and show-offs, whereas the westerners were rather quiet, restrained and went to work without too much noise. At the same time, the easterners were more daring, and if necessary, a senior Gurkha officer wouldn't hesitate to speak his mind in front of a British officer. In contrast, Gurkha officers from the west were somewhat submissive and wouldn't dare speak out against the British officers. The eastern battalions were also way ahead of their western counterparts in promotions, and 6th GR was the slowest and the most conservative among the western battalions. In one typical case, a high-flier from the eastern battalion was promoted to Gurkha officer while his counterparts in the western battalion were still sergeants or below.

The examples I have given here were, of course, only from the infantry battalions. The corps units such as Queen's Gurkha Engineers (QGE), Queen's Gurkha Signals (QGS) and the Gurkha Transport Regiment (GTR) had their own sets of rules and regulations. As far as discipline and formality were concerned, they were a lot more flexible and less stringent in comparison to other infantry battalions within the Brigade. Just like any other workplace, on the lighter side, the Gurkhas also had a list of our own common words that could only be understood by members. For instance: 'Jhinge' (opportunist), 'Moluwa' (bootlicker), 'Ghudathokuwa' (hopeless at sports), and 'Paanimaruwa' (cowards) were the most popular ones and heard almost on a daily basis. Most of the senior officers (British and Gurkhas) also had nicknames such as 'Aaludam' (potato dish),

'*Sighane*' (watery nose) and '*Bakra*' (goat) sahibs and were called those names by the soldiers.

As the rundown of 1997 approached, life at the Brigade of Gurkhas became tougher. Stricter and more difficult training policies were applied, and everyone could feel the pressure. The motive behind that new policy was to weed out the weak ones from the force and keep the best ones only. One of the hardest training policies I remember was one that required troops to carry out a long march on a regular basis with sandbags or bricks in their pouches. There was hardly anyone who hadn't sustained rashes, peeled skins and boils all over their bodies. Those weak and frail, who lagged behind, were marked for the final rundown and, understandably, the new policy was extremely harsh.

There were many such tough situations in my army life. Physically, my poorly built body didn't fare well. My curious mind, noble heart and honest character also didn't fit well to the job. Thanks to my humble upbringing, I knew the value of money well before I was physically mature, and I always stayed away from drinking and unnecessary expenditures. Because of that, I had fewer friends. Despite the odd situations in army life, I always followed my principles and didn't compromise my beliefs for personal gain. My straightforwardness and my habit of speaking the truth also put me in many difficult situations, but I never regretted it. By the time I returned from my second extended leave, I knew I wasn't cut out for the army job and decided to hang around only until I qualified for a pension. I didn't have a body that could run like a horse, my education was like a half-cocked rifle, and I wasn't good at all in leading people. I was also profoundly afflicted from the inside by the general perception which stigmatized the Gurkhas as mercenaries. I hadn't studied the actual history of the Gurkhas then and didn't know much about them. The common saying, 'Despite being a citizen of one country, the Gurkha fights and dies for another country' kept on poking at my heart like a thorn, but I had no possibility of removing the thorn. I had no choice but to follow my heart.

While my peers worked their butts off competing for promotions, I spent my time reading books, magazines and newspapers. After serving the crown for thirteen years, I finally qualified for a pension and returned to Nepal by early 1993 as a civilian. As you can imagine, many good and bad things happened during my time in the British Army, but three main incidents immensely affected my perception of army life.

The first incident occurred in Australia, when we were on a month-long overseas exercise, and it had nothing to do with the army training. The practice was already over, we did our best as usual, and the whole company was treated to a nice dinner outside the camp before we returned to Hong Kong. The place was nice and tidy, somewhere in the middle of Brisbane. Once we were all seated and food was duly served, something unusual happened that prompted an unprecedented reaction from our Company Commander. We Gurkhas, being as loyal and obedient as usual, waited eagerly for the Company Commander's permission to start and didn't begin our dinner until the senior officer gave the nod. But our Company Commander, a major and a hard-nosed, no-nonsense Scotsman, thought the other way, and the display of our unconditional obedience irritated him. He somehow felt embarrassed and then snapped, 'Why don't you just use your bloody hands as usual and eat?' He shouted out in sheer frustration, speaking in Gorkhali which sounded very rude. We were all shocked.

I was too young to grasp the full impact of the situation then. I was also too junior to be able to make any difference in the case anyway. We looked to our seniors, saw them start eating after a while, and so we started too. After we had returned to the barracks, I saw our seniors talking about the incident, and they sounded humiliated and angry. One of the seniors even suggested confronting the Company Commander and roughing him up if necessary. Understandably, the debate was more like the old saying of 'talk among the mice on who was to put the bell around the cat's neck', and everything was forgotten by the next morning.

The second incident happened when I was in the UK. We were in a training camp in Brecon with officer cadets from Sandhurst, their instructors and support teams from various units. After a long and tiring day and our dinner, we headed back to our room in a small group of three to four people. We were stopped by a call from a senior British NCO who happened to be standing at a food counter, resting his huge frame on the table and eating potato fries with his right hand. As we stopped and turned towards him, he looked at us with a sneer. What happened next was unexpected. 'You Gurkhas, cheap as chips, ha!' He would pick up a chip, show it to us and eat it while insulting us. He was one of the instructors from Sandhurst Academy, and no matter how enraged we were, we could do nothing but swallow our pride and walk away. It has been thirty years since that incident, but I can still see his smirking face even today, and I will probably never be able to forget that.

The third incident happened in our regiment and was rather sad and unfortunate. This event shook not only our battalion but also the whole Brigade of Gurkhas. One of our men killed a Gurkha officer using a kukri in utter rage. Our battalion was deployed at the border then. The hostility between the two men is said to have started because of the officer's dislike of the man. So much so that the officer began a witch-hunt against the poor guy and found fault in everything. Whatever this man did, the officer was never happy and started using humiliation as a tool to break him down. Since they both came from the same company, there was no hiding, and the officer was said to have been hell-bent on ruining the man's career. The officer succeeded in making the man's life a living nightmare, and he finally cracked. The outcome was a horrible death for the officer and a prison term for the man. This evaluation was, of course, the general understanding of the event based on what we heard. What triggered such a chain of events that eventually ruined both lives and their respective families was beyond our grasp. The unfortunate incident did so much to shock the whole battalion that we never talked about it again. As far as I can remember, it was the first as well as the very last such incident that ever happened in the Brigade of Gurkhas, and I sincerely pray that it will never happen again.

It took years before I could realize the effect these events had on me. Although they were separate and occurred in different periods of time, they all had the same effect on me and were somehow connected. Ultimately, they helped shape my view of the army and made my decision easier. I wasn't cut out for the military, the regiment wasn't the right place for me, and I had to move on. As expected, the final axe came down in early 1993. Shek Kong was the camp where I joined and also left the

Brigade of Gurkhas. My time in the Brigade thus came to an end and I flew back to Nepal with my young family.

On completion of my resettlement course in Kathmandu, I came back to Hong Kong as a civilian and found a job in an international company working in China. My family joined me in Hong Kong after two years, and we have been here since then. I worked for the next twenty years in China, and witnessed its opening up, as it began to thrive as a modern and developed country.

My first career was in the army, my second career was in business, and my third and last career has just started as a writer. Life itself is a surprise. Not in my wildest dreams would I have thought that I would be where I am today. But wherever I am and whatever I am doing would not have been possible had it not been for the British Army. Despite my reservations about the military, I was never ungrateful, and will never be. My army life was not a long or glorious one, but it was indeed a blessing, and I learned a lot from it. It has been more than twenty-five years since I left the army, but the military is still affecting my life. I am writing a Gurkha book, for god's sake. Isn't that already enough?

CHAPTER 3

WHO ARE THE 'GURKHAS' THEN?

'I got into a kukri fight with a group of IIs at the Hong Kong border, got slightly injured and got a mention in despatches. Luckily, I also survived an IRA bomb blast while in the UK.'

Maj. (Retd) Dal Bahadur Rai, 7th GR, from Dharan, East Nepal served in Borneo, Hong Kong and the UK, with 27 years of distinguished service in the British Army.

The word 'Gurkha' might strike fear among their enemies but there is no official definition of the word itself that is widely accepted by all, at least in the literary world. It's a corrupted version of a variety of words used by the British to describe a particular group of people from the Himalayan nation of Nepal who have been serving the British Crown from 1815 to the present day. The British have been officially using this spelling since 1891.

When the John Company, or the British East India Company as it was more formally known, was rapidly expanding in India in the mid-eighteenth century, a daring, visionary and ambitious king of a state named Gorkha from the mid-western part of Nepal was on the move too, conquering other small princely states around him. His name was Prithvi Narayan Shah, and he was the founding father of modern Nepal. He had already assembled a formidable, well-drilled and fearsome force of his own, which originated in the kingdom of Gorkha, and was known as the 'Gorkhali Force'.

The John Company and the Gorkhali Force were the two leading powers vying for supremacy in the region at this time, and they would inevitably lock horns sooner or later. They eventually did in the early nineteenth century in the Anglo-Gorkha War of 1814-1816 (also known as the Anglo-Nepalese War), and the 200-year legacy of the Gurkhas had begun.

In its early days, there was little agreement on the spelling of regimental titles which led to some variations between them, and the word 'Gurkha' was no exception. Initially, it was spelled 'Gurka' followed by 'Goorkah', 'Goorka' and 'Goorkha' and, finally, 'Gurkha' was officially adopted by the British. Despite the official changes, the 2nd Goorkha Rifles kept the old spelling of 'Goorkha' until it disbanded in 1994.

After India's independence in 1947, the Indian Army adopted the official spelling 'Gorkha' for all the regiments in its service, and it was to conform later to the spelling widely used in Nepal and its army. British officers commonly used the colloquial term 'Gurk' for the Gurkhas.

'Johnny Gurkhas' was another commonly used name for addressing the Gurkhas, mostly by British civilians. Whether it was said with respect or disrespect, it depended on the individual. Although it might have been meant with admiration, at least in some cases it was still tinged with the British feeling of superiority and thus deemed a derogatory term.

If you go to Nepal today and ask around for the Gurkhas, you will be pretty disappointed at not finding many. Despite all the fuss outside Nepal, not to mention the excellent name Gurkhas have attained around the world, the word 'Gurkha' is still foreign to the people of Nepal. You won't be able to find any particular groups of people or communities calling themselves Gurkhas. The word 'Gurkha' was created for the convenience of outsiders and the right word for them in Nepal is *'Lahure'*. It's a corrupted version of the word 'Lahore' which is in the Punjab state of present-day Pakistan, where the famous Maharaja Ranjit Singh of Punjab used to rule before the British annexed it, and for the men from surrounding states including Nepal who served in his famous Khalsa army. Capt. Balbhadra Kunwor, who is respected as one of the brave martyrs of Nepal and rose to fame leading the Nepali forces in the Battle of Nalapani in 1814, was one of them. Men serving in a foreign army were called *'Lahure'*, those who served in the Indian Army were called *'Indiako Lahure'* and those who served under the British were called *'Malayako Lahure'*. Those names have remained unchanged since then.

Last but not least, as one of my friends said, 'All the Gurkhas are Nepalese, but not all the Nepalese are Gurkhas', and this raises a significant point. Due to the British policy of so-called martial races, only certain castes or tribes of men (Gurung and Magar from West Nepal and Rai and Limbu from East Nepal) can be Gurkhas. The policy was strictly enforced during recruiting in the early days. Men from other castes or tribes were forced to lie and change their surname to any of the four mentioned if they were to become a Gurkha. This strict policy has gradually loosened with time and men with different surnames are also accepted nowadays although the four tribes still make up the majority in the force.

After 200 years of continuous service, the Gurkhas have become such a phenomenon within those regions of Nepal that there is hardly a single household where they have no relationship with the Gurkhas, and every family has one or more members who served as a Gurkha – grandfathers, fathers and uncles, brothers and cousins, or grandmothers, mothers, aunties and sisters. Knowingly or unknowingly, the Gurkhas became a way of life for many, and there was no escaping. A rather potent force from outside had not only changed their fate but also their identity, and yet, the irony of the whole episode is that nobody ever bothered to tell them, let alone write about the Gurkhas' long and distinguished history. And that itself is a dark and unfortunate story.

CHAPTER 4

THE BEGINNING OF THE 200-YEAR LEGACY

'I should have won the VC for killing eleven enemies in an ambush but I only got the MC. Oh, by the way, I also have an MBE for killing forty-two enemies with my troops in Malaya.'

Maj. (Retd) Indrajit Limbu (92), 10th GR, a veteran of WWII, Malayan Emergency and Borneo Confrontation, from Dharan, East Nepal, won the MC and MBE in his 38 years of extended service.

By the start of the nineteenth century, the Gorkhali Army had already established a stable country for themselves, and its borders extended to Kangra in the west and Teesta River in the east. The Gorkhali Army and the British East India Company were the two main forces in the region; the others were the state of Maratha and Punjab. They were to cross each other's paths soon; a confrontation between the two driving forces was unavoidable.

The Gorkhali Army was built based on the Jagir System of Land Grants. Instead of fixed salary, the military commanders and soldiers were paid through land taxes. More new lands had to be conquered to keep the strong army happy and motivated. On the other hand, the British East India Company was suspicious of the growing force of the Gorkhali Army. They wanted to control it and keep open the lucrative trade route to Tibet for themselves.

The first-ever battle between the two powers occurred in 1767. To assist the Newari king, Jaya Prakash Mall, and help him resist the invading Gorkha king, the Company sent a strong force of 2,400 men under the command of Capt. Kinloch. The Gorkhali Army ambushed Kinloch and the British at Pauwaghadi, Sindhuli. According to Nepali historians, the Gorkhali Army with the strong support of the villagers, who were equipped with primitive bows and arrows, bunches of stinging nettles and active hornet nests, attacked the enemy with such velocity of surprise and determination that the enemy panicked and lost direction. Almost a thousand were killed, and the rest fled from the battleground. The fleeing force also had to face extreme heat conditions, and only a thousand out of 2,400 men are said to have survived. The unfortunate event was known as the 'Kinloch Expedition'.

The Gorkha forces of about 1,400 men defended the fort and were led by Agamsing Thapa, Bangsu Gurung, Birbhadra Upadhyaya and Bansaraj Panday, and suffered about 400 casualties. The remnants of the original fort can still be seen today as the local authority has been trying to revive the fort as a tourist attraction with historical value and putting the site under its protection. Signs of improvements were seen during our visit, but more is still needed to be done if this site is to achieve its potential and people nearby could benefit a great deal.

After the failed Kinloch expedition, the Company's ambition of bringing Nepal under its influence remained unfulfilled. Once the Newari king of Kathmandu Valley was defeated, the Gorkha king applied a policy of avoiding the Company, and the relationship between Nepal and the Company didn't improve at all.

By 1788, the relationship between Nepal and Tibet deteriorated, and the ongoing dispute between the two led to a war. When a Chinese army of 70,000 men arrived to help Tibet, sometimes coming within 50 kilometres of the Kathmandu Valley, Nepal had no choice but to seek help from the Company. As a result, under the treaty of 1792, Capt. Kirkpatrick came to Nepal as a mediator between Nepal and Tibet. By the time he arrived in Kathmandu, the war between Nepal and Tibet was already over, and he is said to have done nothing at all for the course of the war. Instead, he spent the whole time studying and making strategic plans in relations with Nepal, Tibet and China for the Company's future ventures, and subsequently went back to India.

By exploiting the internal disagreements within the ruling parties of the Nepal Durbar (the ruling elite), the Company eventually arranged a treaty between the two sides in 1801, which allowed the establishment of the British Residency in Kathmandu. After negotiation with the exiled Raja Ran Bahadur Shah in Benares, who was residing there as a guest of the Company, Capt. Knox was sent to Kathmandu in 1802 as the 1st British Resident of Nepal. But he returned to India after 14 months as the post became unworkable due to a lack of cooperation from Nepal's side, and the treaty was formally dissolved in 1804.

The cause of the Anglo-Nepalese war (1814-16) was said to be the greed the Gorkhas had for the fertile lands of the Company's plains to the south. After annexing Sikkim to the east, the Gorkhas found little attraction in Bhutan. Tibet to the north also did not offer much incentive, the mighty Chinese army was never far away, and the numerically stronger Sikhs held them at the western front. The only venture they could have was in the south, and the ill-defined borderlines between the Gorkhas and the Company offered many chances for misadventure. However, the matters that eventually led to the actual declaration of war were said to be many and petty. It was the Gorkhali Army's attack on a police station and the killing of police officers in the Indian side of Butwal that made Lord Moira, then Governor-General of Bengal, declare war on Nepal on 1 November 1814.

The campaign resources of the Company consisted of four divisions and a small holding force with an army of 50,000 men and 100 (artillery) guns. The Company's strategy was to use two divisions for attacking the main Gurkha Army in the west. A third division was to capture Palpa and cut the enemy's main line of control, and the fourth was to seize Kathmandu.

General D. Ochterlony's division with 7,112 regulars, 4,463 irregulars and 22 guns was to assemble at Karnal and Ludhiana, and their primary objective was to expel the Gurkha army from their position between the Sutlej and Yamuna at the western front.

General R. Gillespie's division with 10,422 regulars, 6,668 irregulars and 20 guns was to assemble at Saharanpur and his main task was to proceed via Dehradun to the assistance of General Ochterlony by ferrying through the Ganga and the passes of Yamuna.

General J. S. Wood's division with 4,698 regulars, 900 irregulars and 17 guns was to assemble at Gorakhpur, the first objective being the line of Batoli-Seoraj, the second Palpa-Riri, and having cut the main Gurkha line of control to the west, they were to advance towards Gorkha to assist General Marley.

General B. Marley's division with 13,424 men and 47 guns was to assemble in the area of Sarun-Dinapore and then, as the primary attack finally advanced, on to Kathmandu via Hetauda and Makawanpur.

Capt. Latter and his Rangpore battalion were to encourage the Sikkim Army, without getting embroiled, in the east so that the Gurkhas would be unable to call in reinforcements from their eastern forces.

On the Gorkhali side, they were estimated to have about 14,000 men according to historians, and the mobilization of such a massive force with guns clearly showed how highly the Company had regarded or feared the fighting skills of the Gorkha Army.

The campaign didn't go as well as planned initially for the Company, due to the unfortunate fact that of the six British generals, one was killed, another was removed, and three were severely reprimanded. All in all, had it not been for General Ochterlony, the campaign would have been a total disaster, and only he somehow managed to salvage the campaign for the Company.

Among them, General Marley's actions or rather inactions were the most cowardly, disgraceful and damaging to the Company. In spite of repeated orders and encouragement, he spent the whole time of cold weather around Sugauli, never ventured far into the Terai, and avoided engagement of his division of 13,500 men with an enemy force no more significant than an isolated post. General G. Wood eventually replaced him by early 1815, and when Wood arrived at the Division Headquarters, he learned that Marley had left the post ten days before without even informing his staff.

General J.S. Wood, who faced Palpa, was another general adding dishonour to the Company's reputation. His actions were not only bizarre, ineffective and evasive, but also wasteful, and his defensive approaches to the whole campaign didn't help at all in the primary cause. One of Wood's guns captured by the Gorkhas still stood at the end of Batauli Bridge pointing mockingly towards India in early 1950.

General Gillespie's division was the first to gain some success in this otherwise detrimental campaign. The first serious battle took place at the Khalanga/Nalapani Fort, a hill five miles to the southeast of Dehradun, and the commander of this area was the famous Capt. Balbhadra Kunwor, who had a small force of 600 men with him. On the very first attack, General Gillespie was mortally wounded with 267 other casualties and Colonel Mawbey took command of the force before General G. Martindell arrived. The second assault a month later with heavy guns inflicted another 751 casualties on the Company. The Gorkhali force fought with such unprecedented bravery that the British eventually had to cut off their water supply to force them out. Despite being surrounded by high wooden stakes and the heavily armed enemy and under the veil of darkness, Capt. Balbhadra Kunwor escaped with 90 of his surviving men, and all the conquering forces could find the following morning were corpses of men, women and children. It was said to be one of the most horrible scenes of human cruelty, so much so that even the dominant forces couldn't stay there for long to enjoy their hard-fought victory and hastily retreated.

Despite all the losses, one good came out of this bitter battle, and that was the very first introduction of the brave Gorkhas to the British, in which the bravery of Capt. Balbhadra Kunwor and his men played such a huge role. The British were so impressed that they would eventually seek a long and enduring friendship between the two sides.

In respect of two brave commanders, two white obelisks for both Capt. Balbhadra Kunwor and General R. Gillespie were erected side by side on the hill, and people from the surrounding countries visit the place in significant numbers, even today.

After the war, Capt. Balbhadra Kunwor left the Gorkha Army and joined the renowned Sikh Army of Maharaja Ranjit Singh of Punjab. According to historians from Nepal, he was one of the trusted generals of Maharaja Ranjit Singh and was paid Rs 15 on a daily basis. He was eventually killed in the battle of Nowshera between the Sikh Khalsa Army of Maharaja Ranjit Singh and the Pashtun tribesmen of Afghanistan in 1823. In both forces, he fought with unparalleled bravery and determination. If anyone deserves to be remembered as the first brave man of the Gurkha legacy, it should be Capt. Balbhadra Kunwor. But alongside him, another brave old commander should be remembered as well.

The only successful division was the one led by General Ochterlony, whose advance was slow and cautious, but brought senior Gorkha General Amarsing Thapa to bay at Malaun. Many battles ensued between the two forces and despite being severely outnumbered in ranks and weapons, the Gorkha Army held on. After the Raja of Bilaspur surrendered, the rear of the Gorkha army was exposed, and their supply lines were cut off. With more reinforcements arriving from Delhi, the Company encircled them, and after the fall of Almora with supplies running out, the outlying Gorkha posts were captured by the Company.

Before the Gorkha Army was to give in, one final display of bravery occurred in Deuthal under the leadership of a seventy-three-year-old Gorkha commander named Bhakti Thapa, who led the attack. According to author J.P. Cross, he had a kukri in one hand and a shotgun in the other. He and his team of brave Gorkhas repeatedly attacked the British artillery directly from the front, and he was eventually killed. The Gorkhas were unsuccessful, but their bravery was demonstrated to the British again, and they had so much respect for his act of courage that they sent his body wrapped in an expensive shawl back to General Amarsing Thapa at Malaun Fort. His two wives went with him on his burning pyre while both sides (British and Gorkhas, who happened to be positioned so that they could see each other) stood in utter silence and watched with teary eyes.

The Gorkhali commander at JitGadi, Butwal, who scared the hell out of the British, was a twenty-five-year-old man named Ujjir Sing Thapa. When I visited the JitGadi fort in 2018, the whole area looked abandoned and overgrown with weeds. Children played football on the open field, a neglected statue stood at the side, and a small part of the fort was enclosed with a metal fence. A place of such historical significance had been left abandoned and it saddened me to the core.

According to the village elders, the two Gorkhali commanders Nathu and Prahlad Gurung from Ribhan, Kaski, also fought against the British in India. They still have a *Khura* (an ancient weapon used during the actual fighting) at the village, which they bring out only in Kalratri (the eighth day of Dashain, the major Nepali festival celebrating the triumph of good over evil, which is held each autumn) for the worshipping ritual and women are not allowed to see it because it is considered inauspicious.

Bhakti Thapa's display of bravery was said to be not only an emotional but also a defining moment of the war, and General Amarsing Thapa helplessly watched from his fort. Defeat, as unthinkable as it was at the beginning of the war, was imminent and the old general could do little more to avert the fate of his army. With a shortage of rations and a barrage of British guns pointing at him, native soldiers escaping from the British attacks left the general with few soldiers. A group of almost 1,600 men left the fort and went to mix with the British. The leading cause of the defeat for General Amarsing Thapa in the Anglo-Nepalese war was said to be not a lack of courage or fighting spirit, but the soldiers under his command. They were not real Gorkhas from Nepal, but locals from those states newly acquired by the advancing Gorkha Army. General Ochterlony used it to his advantage by bribing and coercing their leaders to change sides. On 10 May 1815, the British moved in with big guns and started shelling, and the old General Amarsing Thapa had no option but to surrender.

On 15 May 1815, they signed a treaty with some agreed terms. According to the agreement, the Gorkhas would evacuate all the forts from Jaithak to the west of the river Yamuna, all of the Gorkhas were allowed to take their belongings to Nepal, and General Amarsing Thapa, his relations and officers with their weapons and belongings were to go to Nepal in safety.

What was not put in the treaty was said to be a crucial point that both General Ochterlony and General Amarsing Thapa had secretly agreed upon. Amarsing Thapa agreed to allow the Gurkhas to join the British side but strictly on a volunteer basis. According to Nepali historians, a secret letter, which was sent to Amarsing Thapa by the Nepali king, was intercepted by the British. The treaty, known to all as the 'Sugauli Treaty of 1815', was then orchestrated by the British accordingly. The offer made by the British to the Gorkhas of two lakhs rupees per annum as a sweetener was somewhat unusual and stopped the following year.

Lieutenant F. Young (respected as the father of the Gurkhas) had already witnessed the courage, tenacity and fighting spirit of the Gorkhas while fighting against them as an adjutant of General Gillespie. He was so impressed by the bravery of the Gorkhas that he was determined to add these fearsome soldiers to the British side. According to author David Bolt, by the end of the first phase of the Anglo-Nepalese war, Lieutenant Young, Lieutenant R. Ross, William Fraser, Sir R. Colquhoun and General Ochterlony himself had already assembled 5,000 men of the irregulars, deserters and volunteers from the local areas, and the first three Gurkha battalions were raised in 1815. The non-Gorkhas were posted to local corps and pioneers within the British Indian forces.

The 1st Nasiri battalion (initially there were two but they were later amalgamated into one battalion) raised at Subathu, is now known as the 1st Gorkha Rifles of the Indian Army with six battalions and is still stationed at Subathu, India. The 2nd Sirmoor Battalion raised at Nahan was later known as 2nd King Edward VII's Own Goorkha Rifles. It followed the British after the partition of 1947, and disbanded in 1994. The 3rd Kumaon battalion raised at Almora is now known as the 3rd Gorkha Rifles of the Indian Army, with five battalions, and is stationed at Varanasi, Uttar Pradesh. However, those enlisted were not initially from the hills of Nepal itself, but locals, mostly Garhwalis and Kumaunis, and deployed in the borders between Nepal and India during the post-war period.

The first phase of the war lasted for eight months. The defeat of the Gorkhali Army was a severe blow to the Nepal Durbar, which owned most of the rich Terai lands demanded by the British. They were also most reluctant to receive the British Resident. The whole summer and monsoon of 1815 went by while different factions among the Nepal ruling classes debated whether to accept the agreement, until Guru Gajraj Misra, the Nepal Government Representative, finally signed the peace treaty on 28 November 1815.

The ratified treaty with the red seal of the Nepal Durbar should have been presented to the British by Christmas. But the Nepal side dithered again, and General Ochterlony was ordered to advance into the Kathmandu Valley by way of Makawanpur with 14,000 regulars supported by irregulars and 83 guns. In the first campaign, General Ochterlony had been slow and cautious, but in the second one, he is said to have become rather rash and even foolhardy. However, his advance was successful, and a vigorous assault was mounted against Makawanpur. Although severe losses were inflicted on the Gorkhas, they retained possession of the fort and General Ochterlony pulled back and laid siege while waiting for more troops to arrive. The Gorkha supplies dwindled and holding the fort became harder by the day. Behind Makawanpur, there was only the one fort at Chisapani between the British and the Kathmandu Valley and this severe threat to the Valley forced Kathmandu to its knees. There were also rumours that the British had arrived near the Bagmati River in huge numbers. Having no desire to keep his army in such a notoriously delicate area in winter for too long, General Ochterlony reiterated his previous terms and gave orders for an immediate withdrawal.

I had the privilege of visiting both Makawanpur and Chisapani forts in 2018, and some of the original guns used during the actual war are still kept there. According to the locals, both forts attract substantial numbers of visitors these days, and the local authorities have been trying to promote the forts as a tourist destination. The remnants of the fortifications can still be seen there, and they still have the original temple inside the fort now. Unsurprisingly, the head pujari of the temple also acted as the tour guide and seemed to take the new job rather seriously.

The second phase of the war ended in just thirty days. The Anglo-Nepalese War officially ended in March 1816. The Treaty of Sugauli was finally ratified, Nepal lost all the lands that it had conquered hitherto, including the fertile plains of Terai, and was reduced to ruling the hills. It had to become a nation under the British protectorate by accepting the British Resident, and it never recovered. General Amarsing Thapa of Nepal accepted that Gorkhas would be recruited to the British side, although it was not mentioned in the treaty. This not only took the sting out of the Gorkhali Army but also made the country a toothless tiger and crippled it for centuries.

It was indeed a master stroke by the shrewd fox called General Ochterlony. By depleting the youth and able men of the nation for generations, he ensured that Nepal would never be able to raise its head again against the British, let alone bite. And this pressing problem called the Gorkha nation that had persistently been creating problems for the British, like a hornet's nest, was eventually cleared once and for all. Moreover, they didn't even have to go through all the hassle of colonizing it and bearing the consequences. By ridding the country of its youths and workforce, the soul of the country was thus lost, and the Gorkha nation was never going to be the same again.

The tradition of travelling to foreign lands in search of a better life was nothing new to the men from the hillsides of Nepal. They had done so even before the Gurkha recruiting to the British-Indian Army started. Joining Maharaja Ranjit Singh's army in Lahore, Punjab, was already a well-known practice, and it was made even more popular by the likes of Capt. Balbhadra Kunwor and other famous commanders from the Gorkhali Army. The word 'Lahure', which is still commonly used in

Nepal to describe those men, was coined. However, it was the British who made this word more famous, and its effects are still felt throughout Nepal as profoundly now as they could have been then.

An institution that's still going strong after two hundred years cannot rely on sheer luck alone. It must have something innately special, and that's what the Gurkha legacy is all about. And you won't know it until you've heard it directly from them. The world has long been reading a single stereotyped story. It's about time the world hears the other side of the story, and this book will provide just that.

Just like all good things take time, the Gurkha legacy was no exception. The beginning was said to have been difficult. It took a lot of trials and tribulations, not to mention sacrifices, to make them good soldiers. And there has hardly been a single war in the last 200 years in which the Gurkhas didn't fight alongside the British. The Gurkhas have always been at the forefront of the battles they have fought. That their bravery was legendary needs no more explanation here. But it was also their virtues, such as commitment, loyalty, tenacity, adaptability, discipline, respect and honour in their duty, that made them so special.

CHAPTER 5

THE EARLY YEARS AS SOLDIERS OF THE MIGHTY BRITISH EMPIRE

'After finishing basic training at Saharanpur, I was on the ship for the next 14 days to Italy. I fought at Taranto, Cassino and saw many dead. Luckily, I survived without injury and returned home in 1947 with 1,000 ICR [Indian rupees], one set of clothes, a piece of white cloth, a Gurkha hat and a tent.'

Rifleman Man Bahadur Ghimire (99), 1/9th GR from Bhojpur, a WW2 veteran, currently living in a residential home in Dharan.

Initially, the Gurkhas enlisted as irregulars. Since they had no code for uniforms, they wore their own clothes. They were armed with the old Brown Bess (the British Army's standard muzzle-loading smoothbore flintlock musket) with long bayonets and carried their kukris. It was only in 1816 that the matter of dress was finally considered, and the corps was dressed in a dark green coat with tails looped up, black facing with high shoulder wings, white braid, white drill trousers and native shoes.

The strength of the battalion at that time was two British officers, one medical officer, and ten companies of rank and file of: one subedar (captain), four jemadars (lieutenants), eight havildars (sergeants), eight naiks (corporals), two buglers and 120 sepoys (soldiers/riflemen/privates; the corrupted version of the Hindi word sipahi for soldiers) each.

The very first battle the Gurkhas fought alongside the British was the third and last Maratha War of 1817-1819. The Sirmoor Battalion were deployed in a marginal role as part of the Company's campaign eliminating the Pindari horsemen who were allied with the Maratha Empire. By the end of 1818, the Sirmoor Battalion was reduced to eight from the original ten companies.

The first battle honour claimed by both the 1st and the 2nd Gurkhas was when they fought under Lord Combermere against the Jats, also known as the 'Siege of Bharatpur 1825-1826', and they were part of 27,000-strong forces. The trouble is said to have started through the usurpation of '*Gaddi*' (throne) by one Doorjan Sal, who imprisoned the rightful heir recognized by the British on the death of the Raja Runjit Singh of Bharatpur (not to be confused with the famous Maharaja Ranjit Singh of Punjab). The number of casualties during the fight was said to have been around 13,000 to the enemy while the British suffered 1,100 fatalities. It was during the siege of Bharatpur that mutual respect between the English and the Gurkhas increased.

In 1823, the Sirmoor Battalion took part in the suppression of dacoits in the areas of Doon, Koonja and Thano, which was eventually completed in 1828 after the Gurkhas captured the dacoit leader Kour and hanged him. Capt. F. Young, then commandant of the 2nd Sirmoor Battalion, led the campaign with 200 Gurkhas at his side. During the operation, one havildar, four sepoys were killed, and two subedars, two jemadars, one havildar, three naiks, and 25 sepoys were injured. Several were said to have died later of injuries sustained in the campaign.

The period of 1826-1842 was said to be rather peaceful and inactive. In 1842, the Sirmoor Battalion was sent to Bareilly to deal with the dissatisfaction of Mohammedans and it took three months for them to put down the rioting and eventually re-establish order. They did the same job at Kythal in 1843.

After the death of Maharaja Ranjit Singh of Punjab in 1839, the heir was a minor and his mother as the guardian were said to have virtually no influence. So the Sikhs, fighters by birth and faith, realized the opportunity and began to clamour for power. As they crossed from Punjab and attacked British positions, the Anglo-Sikh war of 1845-46 began. Both the 1st Nasiri and 2nd Sirmoor battalions of Gurkhas were consistently in action. The Sirmoor Battalion was among the troops that saved Ludhiana in 1845, and both battalions fought bravely at Aliwal and Sobraon. The Gurkha battalions were awarded not only two battle honours but also almost a dozen Orders of Merit. For the very first time, the commander-in-chief, General Sir Hugh Gough, openly praised the determined hardiness and bravery of the Gurkhas in his battle report. The East India Company with Lord Dalhousie eventually annexed Punjab in 1849, and later on the great Sikh Army joined the British as well.

The three Gurkha battalions were assigned to general services as a regular army by around 1850. A petition for having their families with the Gurkhas started in December 1856. Once the final permission came, permanent homes in Almora (3rd Kumaon Battalion), Dehradun (2nd Sirmoor Battalion), and Dharmasala (1st Nasiri Battalion) were built.

India was divided into three main presidencies by then: Madras, Bombay and Bengal. Out of 180,000 troops deployed across the vastness of Bengal, there were less than 1,500 Gurkhas in the region. The Sepoy Mutiny (also known as the Indian Mutiny) of 1857-58 flared up in the spring of 1857 in Meerut, triggered by a rather trivial issue that could have been avoided had the British been flexible and used common sense. The Gurkhas were to play a huge role in it. It all started from the issuing of new Enfield rifles by the Company to the native troops. To load the rifles, the sepoys had to bite off the ends of greased cartridges, and rumour had it that the cartridges were greased with the fat of cows and pigs, which outraged both Hindus and Muslims because of religious beliefs. The Hindus revere cows as sacred while the Muslims regard pigs as unclean.

Eighty-five soldiers were chained for refusing the order and became the focal point of the mutiny. Once their comrades freed them, the mutineers went on a rampage, killing many of their officers, and then set out for nearby Delhi, where others joined them. The mutiny spread all over northern India as a raging fire, and the Gurkhas were pulled in from all directions. The Sirmoor Battalion, under the command of Major Charles Reid, marched 48 kilometres a day in the scorching summer heat to reach Delhi. They were not only persistently harassed by the rebels along the way but also got fired upon by the 60th Rifles, a friendly force they had come to support during the siege of the house of Hindu Rao (a Maratha nobleman). Once the misunderstanding was cleared, the battalions found themselves at home and quite surprised as well as pleased to find that someone had already erected tents for the soldiers. Unfortunately, the irony of the whole episode was something more sinister. Some of the senior officers from the British side still didn't trust the Gurkhas and secretly ordered the Sirmoor Battalion to be deployed at the furthest side of the famous Delhi ridge, so they could be finished off by the British artillery in case they changed sides.

As they dug in, the siege was to last for another four months, and the admiration between the two regiments (Sirmoor and 60th Rifles) grew. But the campaign turned out to be too costly for the Sirmoor Battalion, and they were said to have stood their ground in 26 attacks, often from as many as 8,000 rebels at a time. The King of Delhi had offered 10 rupees for every Gurkha's head, and the Gurkhas were killed or wounded in significant numbers. By the end of the siege, the Sirmoor Battalion had lost 327 out of its 490 men, eight out of nine British officers were killed or wounded, and one was killed and four injured out of 15 Pipawalas (porters) in the troops. The battalion was awarded 25 Indian Orders of Merit.

Meanwhile, both the Nasiri and Kumaon battalions had fought their way to Delhi through many skirmishes and finally joined other forces of Punjabis, Dogras, Sikhs and Pathans who had come down to Delhi against the mutineers for the final storming. On 14 September 1857, the grand assault on the city commenced, and the main body of the Kumaon Regiment under the command of General John Nicholson drove the rebels through the streets of Delhi. With support from the artillery, the task was finally completed in front of the grand mosque, Jama Masjid, by 20 September 1857.

By request and recommendation of Major Reid, the sepoys of the Sirmoor Battalion were officially called Riflemen and the regiment was renamed to Rifle Regiment in 1858. Other Gurkha battalions didn't achieve this status before 1891.

To commemorate its services in the Sepoy Mutiny, a truncheon was presented to the 2nd Sirmoor Rifles by Queen Victoria in 1863. The truncheon, designed by Major Reid, was six feet high, made of bronze, and surmounted by three replicas of Gurkhas of the period supporting the imperial crown, with the inscription, 'Main Picqet Hindoo Rao's House, Delhi 1857'.

After the end of the Sepoy Mutiny, nobody doubted the bravery, commitment and loyalty of the Gurkhas. The Gurkhas had firmly established themselves as one of the best in the services.

The mutiny didn't end after Delhi was liberated; fighting, mostly in guerrilla warfare, continued across the region and the Nepali troops, led by the then prime minister, were to play a significant role in quelling the mutiny once and for all.

Prime Minister Jang Bahadur Rana was anti-British until his landmark visit to England in 1850, where he was received by Queen Victoria and the Duke of Wellington at Buckingham Palace. During his one-month stay in England, he went to Epsom for the races, to the opera, down a mine, and inspected military and naval establishments. After seeing the might of the British Empire, he not only changed his views towards the British but also became a strong supporter of the British in India and threw his weight behind them. His admiration of Queen Victoria was legendary and recounting stories of their so-called affair became a pastime among the Gurkha soldiers during resting hours.

Among other things, at PM Jang Bahadur's specific request, the Company committed to raising an extra Gurkha Battalion, and the 4th Gurkha Regiment, initially known as the Extra Gurkha Regiment, was established in 1857. Its first operational task was to hold the Kumaon Hills during the outbreak of the Sepoy Mutiny, and it is currently stationed at Subathu, Himachal Pradesh, as the 4th Gorkha Rifles of the Indian Army with five battalions.

Although Lord Canning, the then Governor-General of India, had turned down PM Jang Bahadur's initial offer of 6,000 soldiers from the Nepal Army, the deteriorating situation at Lucknow, which had been besieged by the mutineers since July 1857, forced him to change his mind. He eventually accepted the offer with great appreciation. A strong force of 3,000 soldiers led by General Dhir Shumsher came rushing down to Gorakhpur and drove out the mutineers from the nearby towns. After joining the British, they started clearing the mutineers out of Maduri, Chanda and other nearby towns. Upon the request of Lord Canning, PM Jang Bahadur Rana came down with 9,000 more and joined the fight clearing the cities of Azamgarh, Jaunpur and, finally, Lucknow.

The Sepoy Mutiny was finally defeated in the summer of 1858. As a reward for its support, Lord Canning agreed to return to Nepal the fertile plains of Terai between the Mahakali and Rapti Rivers, which it had lost in the Anglo-Nepalese War of 1814-16. What's more, the Nepali troops of around 14,000 men were said to have returned home with loads of valuables (3,000 wagon trains and more bullock carts) found or plundered during the campaign, and the government of PM Jang Bahadur Rana benefited greatly from the adventure.

According to scholar Asad Husain, Jang Bahadur also gave refuge to rebel leaders in Nepal while fighting the rebels in India: leaders such as Nana Saheb, Bala Rao, the Begum of Oudh and her son, and Birjis Qadar, who were Brahmins of royal descent, and on friendly terms with Nepalese leaders Jay Kishen Pure and Badri Nar Singh who had power and influence in the Nepal Durbar.

The end of the Sepoy Mutiny also brought the end of the East India Company once and for all. The Company was abolished in 1858, and the administration of India was duly handed over to the British government.

By late 1858, another Gurkha regiment was raised as the 25th Native Punjab Infantry, also known as the 'Hazara Goorkha Battalion'. It was renamed the 5th Gurkha Regiment in 1861. The regiment is currently based in Shillong, Meghalaya as the 5th Gorkha Rifles (Frontier Force) of the Indian Army and has six battalions.

Another six Gurkha regiments were to be raised by the early twentieth century, and they were involved in more actions in both the north-west and north-east frontiers of then troublesome India, including the Afghan War. Those nasty skirmishes not only provided an opportunity for adventure but also training their fighting skills and they prepared the Gurkhas for the big one, the First World War.

CHAPTER 6

THE KUKRIS (KHUKURIS)

'I fought in so many wars, worked so hard and still got nothing in return at the end. They even refused to give me a welfare pension.'

Rifleman Umar Singh Gurung (97), 1/1st GR, WWII veteran from Kohla Arubot, Siranchok, Gorkha, who fought in Iraq, Iran, Egypt and then in Burma for four years, and returned home in 1946 with a monthly pension of 5 rupees. He worked in Kolkata as a railway police officer for 11 months and came back home to become a farmer.

Although 'kukri' is a commonly used word internationally, 'khukuri' is in fact the right word to describe the great knife from Nepal. Since this book is written for international readers, I am left with no choice but to use the word 'kukri' in this book.

The kukri is not only the national weapon of Nepal but also a utility knife of the Nepalese people, and it holds a unique and significant place in their culture. The kukri represents Nepalese traditions, history and to some extent even spiritual beliefs. In some communities, it is also used to define a social role as well as serve as a symbol of wealth, social status and prestige. The men from various communities of Nepal love to carry one all the time.

Although the kukri has a long, distinguished and vital history in Nepal, it was introduced to the British during the Anglo-Gorkha War of 1814-16 and became world-famous later on during WWI and WWII. Wherever the Gurkhas fought, the kukri went with them, and there wasn't a single battle where the kukri had failed. Whether it was Europe, Mesopotamia or Africa, or the thick and inhospitable jungles of Burma, Malaya or Borneo, the Gurkhas fought with bravery and unparalleled courage, and they did so with their beloved and trusted weapon, the kukri. By the end of WWII, Gurkhas and kukris had become so connected that hearing of one without the other had become almost impossible. The deadly combination of the duo has been scaring the hell out of the enemy since then. Facing a determined Gurkha with his kukri in a hand-to-hand battle always has one foregone conclusion, and death was a quick and easy one for the enemy. There are hardly any forces who dare to challenge that, and the fact of that myth-like invincibility of the Gurkhas still holds as much water today as it did during WWI and WWII.

The Gurkhas are still the only force in this world that can win a war by its reputation alone, and the kukri is the main reason behind that invincibility. A Gurkha without a kukri is not only incomplete but also unthinkable and vice versa. In brief, it's almost unimaginable for a Gurkha to go to battle without a kukri. That hasn't and probably will never happen.

The history of the kukri is much older than Nepal itself. Kukris were already a choice of weapon for the Gorkhali warriors, and this is said to have started around the 7th century BC by the Kiratis. Some believe its history stretches back to the time of Alexander the Great's invasion of India and compare the kukri with the Macedonian version of the Kopis, the single-edged curved sword used by Alexander's cavalry that was interestingly about the same size as the kukri. The relevance of both stories shows the history of the kukri to be at least 2,500 years old.

When Prithvi Narayan Shah, the then king of the independent Kingdom of Gorkha and the founding father of Nepal, invaded the Kathmandu valley in 1767 and finally conquered it in 1768, his victory was credited to the kukri to some extent, and it has continued as the principal weapon of the Gorkha soldiers ever since. It was his forces, widely known as the Gorkhali Army, that eventually clashed with the British troops and the story of the Gurkhas and their kukris began.

The kukri of King Drabya Shah, King of Gorkha in 1627, said to be among the oldest ones, is placed at the National Museum of Nepal. The other famous kukri is the Fisher Kukri, used by Lt J.F.L. Fisher during the Sepoy Mutiny of 1857-58, and is displayed in the Gurkha Museum, Winchester, England. It was here during the Sepoy Mutiny where the loyalty of the Gurkhas was tested and proven. As a reward, the Gurkhas were made Riflemen and were renamed Gurkha Rifles. The kukri played a significant role in achieving that status.

The world has many famous knives such as the Bowie knife, Stiletto, Scimitar, Roman short sword, Samurai Katana, Machete and Filipino Bolo that have great historical significance. But the most famous of them all is the kukri. The kukri can strike so much fear into the enemy that it was one of the most famous propaganda tools used by the British during wars. It might sound like bluffing, but history doesn't lie. The British have utilised the Gurkhas and their kukris in various forms, but the method used against the Argentines before the Falklands War of 1982 says it all. A cleverly depicted photograph of a Gurkha sharpening his kukri was enough to instil tremendous fear in the enemy's mind. The rest was done by the kukri myth: a Gurkha must draw blood every time he unsheaths his kukri.

The myth is well-drilled propaganda, orchestrated by the British with a tinge of brilliant shrewdness, and intended to make the world a fool from it. During the process, the British established the Gurkha as something like an exquisite breed, a bloodthirsty beast that cannot satisfy itself without tasting blood, and the kukri was the only weapon to execute those evil motives. The myth might have come from such stories. It is an illusion that fools the whole world, and the poor Argentines were no exception. So much so that even the Colombian author and Nobel laureate Gabriel García Márquez was trapped and forced to express his anger with the Gurkhas in various papers. The only excuse he had back then was that there was no Internet for cross-checking.

The myth of the kukri is untrue. It's nothing but well-conceived propaganda by the British. The only exception I can suggest is this: there are some huge ceremonial kukris permanently placed in some of the old temples, where animals were and are sacrificed during some occasions as rituals, and those big kukris are to be used only during those special occasions. There are still such places, and routines do exist in present-day Nepal, and the British propaganda office might have stolen the idea from those events.

The kukri is not only a national weapon of Nepal but also the emblem of the Gurkhas. Whether they are serving in the Nepal Army, British Army, Indian Army, Singapore Gurkha Contingent, or anywhere else in the world, they all use the kukri as their central emblem and a Gurkha soldier without a kukri is just unimaginable. Badges, symbols, flags, signage and colours used by various armies of the Gurkha soldiers all have the kukri on them. Even the barracks, vehicles and other equipment used by the Gurkhas have kukri signs all over them, and these are so conspicuous that one could hardly miss a place where the Gurkhas reside.

In addition to its military meaning, the kukri also carries significant value in religion, and that's no surprise in a religious nation like Nepal. The Hindus strongly believe that the kukri's curved blade represents the Hindu Trinity (Brahma, creator; Vishnu, preserver; and Shiva, destroyer) of Gods. The notch in the edge is the representation of the character

'Om' (the core mantra of all mantras) denoting prosperity and fertility, and worshipped by the believers as one of the essential spiritual talismans of their faith. This belief has prompted an ancient and common practice in Nepal – a kukri is placed under the pillow to prevent bad dreams, and dispel evils at night.

All in all, the kukri is not only a sign of pride, courage and bravery but also a spiritually revered companion that protects the beholder in both war and peace.

It's widely believed, at least from the Western point of view, that a Gurkha grows up with a kukri at hand. He is given a kukri by his father the moment he can hold it, and he has been using it ever since. This saying is only half right; the other half must have come through the same old British propaganda machine, and mostly Western writers are to blame for spreading this half-cocked truth. Not all the communities from where the Gurkhas are recruited use kukris as their prime weapon. My population was a typical example. The old Kaski District of western Nepal is considered the main recruiting area of the Gurkhas. One of the so-called martial races of Gurung, just like me, mostly live here, and we didn't use the kukri as our standard tool when we were young. It was the sickle instead. However, we had at least one kukri in every household, and a house without a kukri is still very uncommon even in present times.

The kukri is a multi-purpose tool, used in battles and ceremonies, as a utility tool, and for adornment purposes. It can be found in many shapes, sizes and designs in Nepal. The main blade is made from a single piece of high-grade steel; the handle is made of hardwood, metal or animal's horn; and the sheath is made of high-quality wood and hides. The process of making the high-quality kukri takes at least a week, and highly skilled blacksmiths are involved. An average kukri is 14-16 inches in length. It comes with two small knives at the top of the casing: one is blunt (Chakmak) and the other is sharp (Karda). The blunt one is for starting a fire with the flint stone, and the sharp one is a general-purpose knife.

The notch on the blade has a clear purpose. It stops the blood from spilling over the handle and prevents the grip from becoming slippery during battle.

According to kukri expert and blogger, V.K. Kunwor, all the kukris supplied to the Gurkhas until 1951 were made in either Nepal or India. The kukris made in 1901-1999 had five different patterns officially approved by the Ministry of Defence (MoD), and they were marked as Mark (MK) followed by 1-5 numbers. MK-1 represented the years of 1901-1915 when they were in use, MK-2 was for 1915-1944, MK-3 for 1944-1960s, MK-4 for 1951, and MK-5 from the early 1960s to current times.

MK-4 kukris, also known as '51 WSC', were the only batch produced by the honourable British steelmaker, the Wilkinson Sword Company (WSC), in 1951. About 1,400 kukris were manufactured and distributed to the British Gurkhas in East Asia. It was the first and probably last British-made kukri that the Gurkhas used as the WSC never produced kukris again for the MoD due to high costs. Due to its high quality and uniqueness, it has become a sought-after item among today's trophy-seeking generations, and only about thirty such kukris are said to exist in the world today.

Also, the 8th Gurkha produced kukris of their own during WWII, and kukris marked with 2/8th, 1/8th, etc., were found later on. They also had a metal butt plate on the handle, enabling them to be a much stronger stabbing weapon than the other common kukris in use.

Despite having their own approved kukri supplies, the MoD also acquired kukris from other suppliers as well during wartime as some of the kukris used by the Gurkhas during WWII had no markings. During WWII, places like Darjeeling, Dehradun, Rawalpindi and Quetta in the northern parts of India and Pakistan had plenty of kukri makers, and they exist even today.

In the regular British Army, when I was still in service, we were issued two types of kukri. The first was the regular kukri that we always had to keep clean, sharp and ready to use, and we had to carry it whenever we underwent military training. The second was the ceremonial one, which was clean, shiny and tidy. All Gurkhas sport a kukri during ceremonial parades. The first one had a khaki-camouflaged cover while the latter had a shiny black coat. Although the kukris were a militarily issued item and provided by the regimental fund in bulk, we still had to pay for them, and keeping the set of kukris in good order was one of the many responsibilities of a Gurkha soldier. A regular kukri inspection was carried out by the NCOs.

As the saying goes, there is no respect for soldiers in peacetime, and such was the case for the kukri in our time: kukris were mostly used for cutting grass at army barracks. Since the British were noted for cleanliness, Saturday mornings were fatigue days, and the main task of the fatigue day was to cut the crap out of the grass around the barracks until the ground became shaven red. 'The same kukris that made our forefathers world-famous are only good for cutting grass in their grandchildren's days,' we used to joke, but we didn't mean any disrespect to anyone.

The kukri is aptly known as 'the Gurkhas' fighting knife'. It played a critical role in making the Gurkhas' name world-famous, and it's almost impossible to talk about the Gurkhas without mentioning the kukri. The word 'Gurkha' is a synonym of the word 'kukri' and the legacy of the Gurkhas is incomplete without the legacy of the kukri. They started together at the very beginning, fought together in the most significant battles of their career, and they will undoubtedly remain together as long as the Gurkha legacy continues. As the old saying goes, nothing is certain except death and taxes, but I can be pretty sure that this partnership will go on for a long time and only fools will bet against it.

In modern-day warfare, it's quite understandable that people have reservations about a knife, and I don't blame them. It is the same reason why kukris are mostly limited to ceremonial parades and special dances in both the British and Indian Armies nowadays, and these still draw substantial numbers of people as spectators. But wars cannot be won by bullets and bombs alone. You need foot soldiers to clear the ground at the end, and hand-to-hand battles are still necessary to win the final war. And this is where the Gurkhas and the kukri reign supreme. The deadly duo still has no rivals.

CHAPTER 7

THE MAKING OF THE GURKHA BRIGADE

*He joined the army in Dehradun and won an MM (military medal)
for killing 17 of the enemy. However, he was so sick and bedridden
during our visit he couldn't even remember the dates of his enlistment
and retirement for our record.*

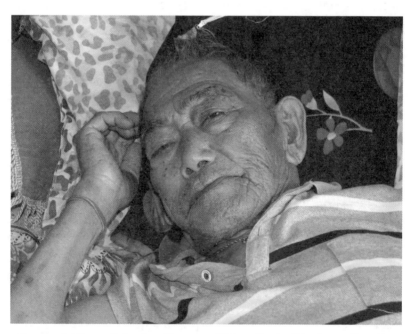

Corporal Tham Bahadur Gurung (89), 1/2nd GR, from Gumda,
Gorkha. According to the paper shown to us, he was one of the welfare
pension recipients.

By 1861 we had the 1st, 2nd, 3rd, 4th, and 5th Gurkha Regiments already raised. To bring them in line with the standard practices of the regular British Army, all Gurkha regiments were given the title of Gurkha Rifles in 1891 except the 2nd Sirmoor Regiment, which had already obtained that status in 1858 right after the Sepoy Mutiny. Although other regiments (to become the 6th, 8th, 9th & 10th) existed well before the end of the nineteenth century, they were of non-Gurkha origin and didn't take the Gurkha title until the first years of the twentieth century.

For instance, the 6th Gurkha Regiment was raised at Chaubiaganj, Cuttack, in 1817 as the 'Cuttack Legion' by Capt. S. Fraser. It evolved into an Assam Battalion, then a Bengal Regiment, and had a distinguished history of its own before it was finally made the 6th Gurkha Rifles in 1903. It was transferred to the British Army in 1947 and disbanded in 1994.

The 7th Gurkha Regiment was raised at Thayetmyo, Burma, in 1902 by Major E. Vansittart as the 8th Gurkha Rifles. It became the 2nd battalion of the 10th Gurkha Rifles in 1903 before becoming the 7th Gurkha Rifles in 1907. It was one of the regiments transferred to the British Army after 1947 and disbanded in 1994.

The 8th Gurkha Regiment started in 1824 as the 16th or Sylhet Local Battalion and went through many transformations before finally achieving the status of the 8th Gurkha Rifles by 1907. It was retained by the Indian Army after 1947 and is currently stationed at Shillong, Meghalaya, with six battalions.

The 9th Gurkha Regiment, also known as the *Khas/Thakuri* Battalion, was raised in 1817 as the 63rd Regiment at Fatehgarh Levy, then part of Bengal Native Infantry, and was incorporated as Gurkhas from 1861. Although it was awarded the status of the 9th Gurkha Rifles in 1901, it still had to wait for some time before officially being considered to be a part of the regular army, hence the irregularity in the numbering between the Gurkha regiments. It's a particular regiment mostly made up of Khas and Thakuri clans from Nepal. It was retained by the Indian Army after 1947, and is currently headquartered at Varanasi, Uttar Pradesh, with five battalions.

The 10th Gurkha Regiment was raised in 1890 by Lt Col C.R. MacGregor from the Kubo Valley Police Battalion and originally designated the 10th (Burma) Regiment of the Madras Infantry. It was awarded the status of the 10th Gurkha Rifles by 1901, transferred to the British side after 1947 and finally disbanded in 1994.

Once the government of India was taken over by the Crown, some irregularities appeared with the titles of officers and senior officers from the Gurkha regiments, who were called Viceroy's Commissioned Officers (VCOs). A council of five senior Gurkha officers was formed to deal with non-military arbitration and other Gurkha matters, a pandit was appointed for religious issues, and the English-speaking clerks were recruited mainly from non-Gurkha tribes, such as the Newars or the Indian-born Gurkhas.

In 1860, the 5th Gurkha had to defend the Palesina Camp from an attack by 3,000 men of Mahsud Pathans. A fist fight ensued, resulting in heavy casualties on both sides before the enemy was driven off. It was the 4th Gurkha which was in the forefront of the famous storming of Conical Hill during the Ambeyla Expedition of the Northwest Frontier in 1863. In 1868, the 1st, 2nd, 4th and 5th Gurkhas were deployed again on the frontier in a punitive expedition against the Black Mountain tribes in Hazara. On the other side, the Northeast Frontier of India in 1871-2, the 2nd and 4th Gurkhas fought Chins and Lushais in the dense forest of Assam where Major Macintyre won the Victoria Cross and Rifleman Indrajit Thapa received the Indian Order of Merit, Third Class.

The 6th Gurkha, still named as the 42nd Regiment at that point, remained at the Northeast Frontier for 77 years while the 5th Gurkha is said to have stayed at the Northwest Frontier for a staggering 90 years and was the only regiment officially designated as the Frontier Force.

The first overseas trip for the Gurkhas came in 1876 when the 1st Gurkhas were sent to Malaya as part of an Indian contingent when the British Resident in Perak was murdered. By the time they arrived, the rising was already put down, but the detachment was soon involved in fighting with the Malays, earning a Victoria Cross for a British officer, and the Order of Merit (the eligible bravery award for Gurkhas then) for two Gurkhas.

The 2nd Gurkhas became the first of the Gurkha Brigade in Europe when they went to Malta in April 1878 during the Russo-Turkish War as part of the 7,000 native soldiers from India. The regiment went under the command of Major Battye and had a strength of five British officers, 14 Gurkha officers and 637 rank and files for the trip.

The second Afghan War of 1878-80 was to begin soon, caused by the growing political rivalry between Britain and Russia and all five Gurkha regiments were involved. When the Russian Mission was established in Kabul, the team at the British Mission was confronted by the amassing of the Amir's forces, and they were obliged to retire. Once a formal demand for an apology was ignored, the British had no choice but to prepare for war. In the early winter of 1879, the 5th Gurkhas, alongside the Seaforth Highlanders under the command of Lord F. Roberts, started fighting through the heavily defended Kurram Valley. It was at the taking of the famous Peiwar Kotal in a dawn attack that Capt. John Cook won the VC, and during subsequent fighting the Gurkhas won a total of seven Orders of Merit.

On 19th April 1880, whilst on their way from Kandahar to Kabul, the 3rd Gurkhas were ambushed by a militant group of Afghans with cavalry. They stood firm under the attack, adopting a traditional defensive square which repulsed the assault and the Gurkhas won the day. Later that year a force of 10,000 fighting men and 8,000 auxiliaries including the 2nd, 4th and 5th Gurkhas took part in Lord Roberts' famous race to relieve Kandahar and covered 320 miles through enemy country in just twenty-three days. During the ensuing Battle of Kandahar, one daring man from the 2nd Gurkhas made a name for himself when he sprang onto one gun and loudly proclaimed his regiment's ownership by promptly pushing his cap down the muzzle.

Lord Roberts was said to have a soft spot for those fighting men from the highlands of Scotland, the Sikhs and the Gurkhas. His choice of a Highlander and a Gurkha for the supporters of his coat of arms during the peerage ceremony clearly showed how he had been impressed by those two tribes of fighting men. It was at his request, as the commander-in-chief of India at the time, that a 2nd battalion of each Gurkha Regiment was raised in 1886, except the 3rd Gurkha Regiment. Since the 3rd Gurkhas were mostly made of Garhwalis and were not recognized as a fully Gurkha unit until 1891, its 2nd battalion was only raised after that recognition was finally obtained.

In 1885, after the persecution of British and Indian business employees in Myanmar (Burma) by King Thebaw, the 3rd Gurkhas and the Gurkhas of the Assam Light Infantry (the 10th Gurkhas) were among the forces sent to take Mandalay.

While the 2/1st Gurkhas were sent to fight against Tibetans in Sikkim in 1888, the 2/2nd and 2/4th were engaged in the 2nd Lushai Hills Expedition at the Northeast Frontier, and the 2/4th remained there to operate against the Chinese through 1891.

In March 1891, when the chief minister usurped the throne of Manipur, the Raja appealed to the British for help, and the commissioner of Assam arrived in person at Imphal, the fortified capital. The forces consisted of a lightly armed detachment of Gurkhas from the 42nd and 44th Native Infantry (later 6th and 8th Gurkhas), their British officers, together with men from the 43rd (later 7th and eventually 2/8th Gurkhas), numbering around 500 men. A clumsily handled diplomatic approach collapsed, and fighting broke out in which a British officer and a few Gurkhas were killed. An invitation to talk after the truce ended in tragedy: the commissioner and his secretary, the British Resident and four British officers were mobbed inside the gate and beheaded. In the confusion, the remaining British officers withdrew, leaving behind around 300 Gurkhas without orders or leaders. They fought on, and when their ammunition ran out, they went out with bayonet and kukri and about fifty Gurkhas survived as prisoners in the hands of Manipuri rebels.

An initial relief force consisting of a platoon led by Jemadar Birbal Nagarkoti with 35 men and 50 sepoys of the Madras Infantry, together under Lieutenant Charles Grant, rapidly took the initiative. Against great odds, they fought brilliantly and an initial victory was finally won at Thoubal. It won Lieutenant Grant the VC, and both Jemadars Birbal Nagarkoti and Manbir Thapa of the 2/4th Gurkhas won the Order of Merit. Three further relieving columns then joined them, and the surviving captives in Imphal were rescued. Two British officers (Major L. Boileau and Capt. G. Butcher) who fled were court-martialled for gross neglect of duty, and the incident is still remembered as 'Thoubal Day' on 6th April annually by the 8th Gurkha Rifles.

From 1891 to 1895, the Gurkhas saw action against Nagir and Hunza tribesmen in the extreme north of Kashmir. They conducted bitter hand-to-hand fighting at the Afghan-Waziristan border and defended the Malakand Pass.

By the end of the nineteenth century, according to many books, the hostility of the tribesmen from the Northwest Frontier to the British Raj increased. When Muslim Turkey defeated Christian Greece in the summer of 1897, the Muslim world took it as the signal for Jihad, a holy war, and a full-scale uprising along several hundred miles of the frontier ensued. A massive force of 70,000 troops was deployed along the frontier for the next eight months of 1897 and 1898, and as always, units from all five Gurkha regiments were the first ones to be mobilized. The 2nd Gurkha Rifles alongside their old friends the Gordon Highlanders found fame storming the famous Dargai Heights. The 5th Gurkhas made history during the Tirah campaign as both battalions supplied the first organized body of scouts ever used in order of battle in India. The other regiments fought with unflinching courage, determination and discipline. The Gurkhas were more than a match for the reckless courage of fanatics.

It was the 1st battalion of the 4th Gurkhas which joined the international force assembled to put down the Boxer Rebellion in China in 1901.

During the height of skirmishes on the Northwest Frontier, Capt. Younghusband led an expedition to Central Asia escorted by six Gurkha soldiers. His mission was to protect British interests among the Hunza tribesmen from the influence of the Russians. He met the Mir of Hunza as well as the bearish Russian Colonel Grombtchevski, and returned safely home.

According to British author Bob Crew, Colonel (by then) Younghusband led a force of Indians, Sikhs, British and Gurkhas on his Tibetan excursion in 1904 and the newly formed 8th Gurkha Rifles was part of the team. It was also the very first time the Gurkhas were given pack ponies and mules for an operation. The expedition was made easier by taking the Tibetan fortress at Gyantse, built at the top of a rock and held by 6,000 Tibetans, and they marched unopposed into Lhasa on 3rd August 1904. The Dalai Lama's palace of 1,000 rooms with the golden roof was a walk away for the advancing troops. Lieutenant John Grant won the VC, and Havildar Karbir Pun won the Indian Order of Merit. The treaty signed after the campaign required that a company of infantry should be stationed at Gyantse for the next fifty years, nominally as escorts for the British and, later, Indian trade agents.

In 1919, Younghusband became the president of the Royal Geographical Society and also founder-chairman of the Mount Everest committee of mountain climbers. He was not only a man of action but also a thinker and writer.

In the first years of the twentieth century, no major wars were fought, and the Gurkha Brigade concentrated on peacetime activities such as shooting competitions, field manoeuvres, sports, attendance at palaces, large-scale ceremonial parades and routine training. It was during that looming conflict – the First World War – when most of the world was to hear about the Gurkhas for the very first time, for a good reason.

CHAPTER 8

THE GURKHAS IN THE FIRST WORLD WAR, 1914-1918

'Life was tough during the war. I only got a bottle of water a day, and food was scarce. After the war, I left the army and worked in India as a guard for the next 33 years.'

Lance Corporal Damar Bahadur Thapa (98), 1/2nd GR, from Gumda, Gorkha, fought in Iran, Iraq and Egypt along side Lal Bahadur Thapa VC during WW2, and won eight war medals.

Following in the footsteps of Prime Minister Jang Bahadur Rana, the then PM Chandra Shumsher Rana visited England in 1908, and the friendship between the Nepal Durbar and the British took a new turn for the better. When the newly crowned King George V visited Nepal in 1911, Chandra Shumsher accompanied him to the Chitwan National Park, and a large shooting expedition was arranged to honour the new emperor during which 21 tigers, 10 rhinos and two bears were killed. It was said there was a genuine rapport between the British king and Rana, and that was to be seen on full display, at least from the Nepali side, at the start of the First World War. In support of his new friend in trouble, Maharaja Chandra Shumsher not only opened his heart and the national treasury but also put the whole country at Britain's disposal and changed the course of Nepal's history once and for all.

It was during that historic visit that George V decreed the eligibility of the Victoria Cross (VC) to all Gurkha soldiers serving under the British in the Indian Army. The highest reward for valour that a Gurkha soldier could receive until then was the Indian Order of Merit (IoM).

The First World War (WWI), also known as the Great War, was sparked by the assassination of Archduke Franz Ferdinand of the Austrian royal family and his wife at Sarajevo on 28 June 1914. Britain, France, Russia and their allies were on one side and they initially fought against German, Austrian and Italian forces. More nations were forced to take sides as the war progressed.

Before the start of WWI, the Gurkha Brigade had ten regiments, each with two battalions, creating a total strength of 26,000 men as a peacetime force. With the unprecedented support and blessing of PM Chandra Shumsher, the total headcount of the Brigade was instantly doubled. A little nation like Nepal with a population of five million sent almost 200,000 men to the war between 1914 and 1918. Strict orders were sent out to the villages asking all able men to join the war, and only the old, the underaged and unfit were excused. Also, 16,544 men from the Nepal Army, including forces from the PM's personal bodyguards, came down and guarded the empty garrisons in India so the regular troops could go to war. While the Nepal Army defended India's long and porous borders, non-combatant troops, such as porters, medical staff, drivers, cooks and others helped run the country in the absence of the defence force.

In theory, the Gurkhas in the regular Indian Army were already at the disposal of the British, but in practice, they couldn't be sent overseas without the permission of the rulers of Nepal, as a religious matter. Like Hindus, the Gurkhas were forbidden to cross the *'Kaalo Paani'* (or 'black water' as they used to call the ocean at that time) and if they did, they had to go through a special ritual of purification called *'Paani Patiya'*. Without the proper permission and ritual, they would lose their caste and never be allowed to return home again. *Paani Patiya* was a ritual of purification that lasted for a week. During the routine, one had to take one meal a day, drink *gahut* (cow's urine), take a daily bath, attend the regular pooja and also be segregated from all others for an entire week. On completion of the seven days' ritual, and having offered the *Gurudakshina* (ritual money) to the pandit, one was declared pure and allowed to return to their respective regiment. As a result, the Gurkhas simply could not have gone. PM Chandra Shumsher, who was willing to please his British friend, found a ready-made solution. He arranged immediately with the supreme religious authority of Nepal, the Raj Guru (the royal pandit), for dispensation to be granted automatically to all Gurkhas going overseas with the approval of the Nepalese government. Needless to say, the British breathed a massive sigh of relief.

All regiments, except the 4th and 10th Gurkhas, increased their strength by one more battalion during the war. The 3rd even raised a fourth. An entirely new regiment, the 11th Gurkhas, was established during the war with four battalions.

Having never ventured outside of the Indian subcontinent before, nothing in their history had prepared the Gurkhas for the conditions in which they had to fight. The modern war of Flanders in Europe with a full barrage of artillery was very new to them. The sudden chill of the European winter didn't help. The acceptance of massive casualties at once was difficult. Besides, they were not only under-equipped but also poorly dressed. They occupied trenches dug out previously by taller British soldiers, which became hazardous because they couldn't shoot over them. Many drowned in the heavy pouring rain.

Before they even got to Europe, seasickness was rampant for the men from the landlocked nation. The 2/8th Gurkha Rifles was the first one to arrive at the frontline at Festubert, south of Ypres on 29 October 1914, and experienced a grim introduction to life and death in war. Within 24 hours of their arrival, six out of ten British officers were killed and three more wounded. In early November 1914, the 2/2nd Gurkhas lost all of its British officers. By mid-November 1914, all the Gurkha battalions were heavily engaged, casualties were mounting, and the most hard-hit were the 1/4th Gurkhas. In the trenches of Givenchy alone, it lost about 230 men out of 650. It was also here that the Germans experienced the wrath of the famous kukri for the very first time and were tormented for the rest of the war.

By mid-December, 1914, the Gurkhas were involved in the offensive launched at Messines by General H. Smith-Dorrien, causing heavy losses, and almost half of the troops were killed, wounded or missing. The first two months of 1915 were rather inactive, but the cold was harsh, especially for the Gurkhas, and many suffered from frostbite.

According to many books, in the battle of Neuve Chapelle in the spring of 1915, six Gurkha battalions (1/1st, 2/2nd, 2/3rd, 1/4th, 2/8th and 1/9th) were involved, and the German front line was broken for the very first time in the war. Neuve Chapelle was the first significant trench battle to be fought after the forces of the Western Front settled down. Troops from the 2/2nd Gurkhas were sent for an early patrol, and the 2/3rd Gurkhas were the first to engage with the enemy. Havildar (Sergeant) Bahadur Thapa, who led his men into one house storming through a barricade, killed 16 Germans and seized two machine guns. Rifleman Gane Gurung, despite his small stature, made a lone attack into a building and came out with eight somewhat taller Germans marching in front of him as he was cheered by friendly troops, who happened to be crossing ahead of them at that moment. Both men were awarded the Indian Order of Merit.

Despite gallant efforts by all the participating Gurkha regiments, the battle of Neuve Chapelle was lost, and many had paid with their lives.

Due to poor judgement, mismanagement and indecision by the war commanders, the attack failed and the weary battalions, including the Gurkha regiments, were sent to fight elsewhere. The next operation for the Gurkhas was the battle of Festubert in May 1915. The casualties for the Gurkhas were heavy, and the 2/2nd Gurkha alone was to lose over a hundred men there. All six Gurkha regiments that participated in this disastrous battle won the battle honour of 'Festubert' or 'Aubers' and General Sir James Willcocks, who commanded the Indian forces in France, was to recognize the Gurkhas as the best of his troops.

The 2/8th Gurkha suffered so horribly that the whole battalion was practically wiped out at the battle of Loos and left an indelible mark on the soil of Flanders that prompted Colonel Morris to remark in a sombre note that the 8th Gurkhas indeed did their duty and found their Valhalla.

According to many books, the Gurkha motto of *'Kafar hunu bhanda mornu ramro'* (better to die than be a coward) was further enhanced by the excellent action of Rifleman Motilal Thapa, the 1/4th Gurkhas, at the second battle of Ypres. He and Capt. Hartwell were both seriously injured by a shell. One of his hands was shattered, and they found cover in a crater while waiting for rescue. When Capt. Hartwell regained consciousness after a long period, he found Motilal at his side with his good arm holding a cap over the officer's face to keep the sun out of his eyes. Obviously in terrible pain, he kept saying to himself, 'I must not cry out, I am a Gurkha.' He died from loss of blood, yet he thought about another human being.

Despite all the doom and gloom, one good came out of the operations in France; one Gurkha was to win the first-ever Victoria Cross (VC). In the battle of Loos in September 1915, Rifleman Kulbir Thapa of the 2/3rd Gurkha, himself wounded, found a severely injured soldier of the 2nd Leicestershire Regiment behind the enemy's trench line and remained with him for the whole day and night. On the following foggy morning, he seized the chance to transfer the wounded soldier over the German trench, then secured him in a shelter. He left him there and went back searching for more Germans, but instead he found two men from his regiment who were severely wounded. Thapa transported these Gurkhas, one at a time, to the 39th Garhwalis line, positioned at the British front line. In broad daylight, this badly wounded Gurkha once again returned to rescue the injured Leicester even under heavy fire and was later even cheered on by the German forces for his heroic actions.

The Gurkhas were renowned as brave and as tough as metal, but the first-ever VC won by a Gurkha was not for bravery but for compassion and altruism. But nobody seemed to care much about that fact. He was promoted to sergeant and went to Egypt to fight another battle where he was injured and sent home on a medical pension. He spent his life as a simple farmer until he died at the age of 68 in his village on 3 October 1956.

The Indian Army and the Gurkhas who served with them lost 21,000 officers and men in France. The whole operation was an ill-conceived campaign, a total waste of human lives. Many historians, as well as military experts, had questioned the deployment of Indian forces in Europe. All in all, it was a disaster for the Indian troops, and they were eventually withdrawn from France after thirteen months.

That this participation wasn't for the last time was the saddest part of the whole operation. The proud British didn't learn, and the same mistakes were repeated in both Gallipoli and Mesopotamia (Iraq) in later stages of the war. The Gurkhas were the ones along with the Australians and New Zealanders who paid the highest price with their lives, which were lost by the thousands.

The Gallipoli campaign was a disaster from the beginning. Almost half a million men, including the Gurkhas, eventually lost their lives in this misadventure of the British generals. The justification for taking the Dardanelles Strait was to invade Turkey and take her out of the war to open up a way for Britain's ally, Russia, to wade in. The original plan of using only the navy faltered when three ageing British battleships, after initial bombardments, sailed into an unmarked minefield and sank. The allies were forced into an immediate retreat.

General Sir Ian Hamilton, who commanded the British, New Zealand and Australian forces in the disastrous Dardanelles campaign, requested a brigade of Gurkhas. But only three battalions (1/5th, 1/6th and 2/10th), known as the 29th Indian Brigade, were provided. By the time the Allied forces were ready to take action, the German officers commanding the Turkish defence had already amassed 60,000 troops along the coastline. At the hill of Chunuk Bair alone, the dug-in enemy force inflicted 5,000 fatalities on the advancing Anzac troops and forced them to retreat. The 1/6th Gurkha was the first to arrive at Gallipoli. The Gurkhas were leading an assault on a Turkish high point, a steep 300-foot rock defended by machine guns. The advance by both Royal Marines and the 1st Dublin Fusiliers had already failed. They also had to cross a steep ravine that was directly in the enemy's line of fire. Despite all the difficulties, the bluff was taken with speed and daring, and the 1/6th Gurkha lost 18 men, and 42 were wounded. In recognition of the feat, General Hamilton, whose writing commented that 'each little Gurk might be worth his weight in gold', clearly showed his respect for the Gurkhas. He ordered the feature to be known as 'Gurkha Bluff' from then on.

At the battle of Krithia, the mission of the 1/6th Gurkha was to dislodge the enemy from the 700-foot vantage point known as Achi Baba. But even after attacks and counter-attacks raged on for days and weeks, they still failed, and more reinforcements were called in. The 1/5th and the 2/10th joined in by early summer of 1915. All three Gurkha battalions were now engaged, and the famous kukris were used in hand-to-hand battle with significant effect. Despite all efforts, the campaign failed and both sides lost thousands. The Turks are said to have lost 10,000 men in a week. The British casualties were around 7,000 on that operation alone. The Gurkhas, who were always at the front of the advancing Allied columns, were the hardest hit. So much so that they urgently needed reinforcements and were sent to the Isle of Imbros for a month to rest while waiting for additional troops to arrive.

With 20,000 reinforcements, including the return of the 29th Indian Gurkha Brigade, General Hamilton began the new offensive on 7 August 1915. But his grand effort was thwarted by the inspired new Turkish leader, Kemal Ataturk, and the skilful German officers. The Gurkhas, as always, led the advance while the 1/6th Gurkha was to attack the nearby peak. This operation of high importance went ahead with such haste that not even a single reconnaissance, which the Gurkhas were very good at, was carried out before the actual assault, a fact that still baffles many.

According to many books, including by author John Parker, the terrain was harsh and steep with sheer cliffs, and navigating through the darkness was tough. At the battle of Sari Bair the 1/6th Gurkha, under the leadership of Major Allanson, was to gain fame by reaching the top with some of the men from the 6th South Lancashire Regiment and attacking the retreating enemy. They held the crest for the next 15 minutes. General Baldwin's column of four battalions was to sweep along the whole ridge of the mountain as planned, but they lost their way and never arrived. Unfortunately, the British Royal Navy then shelled their own troops, who were mistaken for Turks, and they had to dash for cover. The Turkish commanders saw the British blunder, rallied their troops immediately and counter-attacked. It didn't take too long before sweet victory turned into bitter defeat. The Gurkhas and the whole operation collapsed under the rocks where they had to take refuge after that unfortunate retreat. This operation alone is said to have cost the British forces 12,000 men. Thousands more died from diseases caused by unburied bodies and flies.

General Hamilton was finally relieved by General Monro, and the order for the final evacuation was issued. The whole Gallipoli campaign is said to have cost the British 205,000 servicemen. The French suffered 47,000 casualties, and the Turks around 250,000-300,000. All three Gurkha battalions suffered heavy losses during the campaign, and a total of 1,500 Gurkhas were killed or wounded. The 2/10th Gurkha was hit the hardest. The 2/10th arrived in Gallipoli with 13 British officers, 17 Gurkha officers, and 734 rank and file soldiers. When they finally departed after six months, only one British officer and 79 Gurkhas and other ranks remained in the ill-fated battalion. 477 cases of frostbite alone were reported for the same battalion, of whom 10 died and 80 were crippled for life. The Gurkhas were not only the first to arrive but also the last to leave.

Ironically, the final evacuation happened to be the only thing that the British did correctly throughout the Gallipoli campaign. However, Sir Ian Hamilton's cherished conviction was that had he been given more Gurkhas in the Dardanelles, he would never have been held up by the Turks. Later on, the secretary of General Hamilton praised the exemplary display of bravery, tenacity and adaptation in the war by the Gurkhas, and they were to be remembered by all.

The Turks were a formidable enemy, and they were to clash with the Gurkhas in many theatres of war later on in the Middle East. The next battles were to start when Ottoman Turkish Mesopotamia (Iraq) was invaded by the British and French from Persia, Arabia and Syria. The two primary objectives of the Allies were to maintain control of Suez and to protect the Persian oilfields. It was also a holy war between Muslims and Christians, declared by the Turks on 14 November 1914, and all of the 14 Gurkha battalions fought in Mesopotamia at some point during the war.

According to author Ed Smith, the battle of Mesopotamia started from Basra. General Nixon was the commander of the Anglo-Indian troops under the direct control of the government of India, and General Townshend led the 9th Indian Division under which the Gurkha regiments served. As they advanced towards Baghdad, fighting several minor battles along the way, they ran out of drinkable water, and half of the 2/7th Gurkha was struck low by dysentery. On 24 July 1915, the Gurkhas were held up by the Turkish outpost at Nasiriyah and as they were about to lose the day, Naik (Corporal) Harkaraj Rai charged the Turkish trenches with a bloodcurdling shrill of 'Ayo Gorkhali' ('the Gurkhas are coming') and with a kukri in his hand killed thirteen of the enemy single-handedly. The remaining units charged after him with the same ferocity and the lost battles were won for the day. For his gallantry, Harkaraj was awarded the Indian Order of Merit and later became an honorary captain. The 2/7th Gurkha, formed at the start of WWI in 1914, won the regiment's first battle honour, and 'Nasiriyah Day' has been commemorated as a regimental holiday ever since.

After the disasters in both France and Gallipoli, the British were to have another one here as well, and it seemed to grow out of a feeling of complacency from the victory on their way to Baghdad. Despite General Townshend's disagreement and request for more troops, he was overruled by Lord Kitchener and General Nixon, and ordered to march towards Baghdad. Taking the Kut-el-Amara 321 kilometres from Baghdad was easy, they thought. The British took 1,300 prisoners and all of their guns, and a decisive battle loomed at Ctesiphon, the former capital of Mesopotamia. The Turks were not only well dug-in but also fully reinforced with a total number of 21,000 men and 52 guns against the British force of about 13,000 men. The assault started on the night of 21 November 1915. It had four columns, and 2/7th Gurkha was with a column under General Delamain. Their task was to make the final frontal attack on the vital point that entailed a crossing of 5,000 yards of open desert before attacking the objective. Everything went as planned until the advancing Gurkhas met the Turkish wire. A way in was cut through, but casualties mounted. The next morning there was a severe sandstorm, followed by a robust Turkish counter-attack on a low mound near the historic Arch of Ctesiphon, which was fiercely defended by 300 men from the 2/7th Gurkha and 100 soldiers from the 21st Punjab Regiment. The small detachment, exposed and attacked from all sides by a complete Turkish division, fought for the whole day and forced the Turks to give up in the evening. In recognition of their bravery, the place was named 'Gurkha Mound'.

After losing more than 4,600 men, General Townshend and his defeated troops had to retreat to Kut. The seven-and-a-half-day retreat was said to be one of the most difficult ones in the history of the British Army. By early December of 1915, the Turks cordoned off the British encampment at Kut and called on General Townshend to surrender. He refused in the hope that reinforcements would arrive, and the fighting continued. While they were holding Kut, a relieving force under General Aylmer VC was advancing up the Tigris, and the 1/2nd and the 1/9th Gurkha were among them. Unfortunately, bad weather hindered their speed, and the situation at the siege of Kut deteriorated. As the food started to run out, animals were killed, and the native Indians refused to eat horsemeat on religious grounds. On the other hand, the Gurkhas, like their British colleagues, ate horsemeat and survived.

General Aylmer's relief column got into battle at the Dujaila Redoubt in early March 1916. A fierce hand-to-hand struggle ensued between the Turks and the Gurkhas, and the Turks eventually triumphed due to their superior numbers aided by well-sighted posts. Another attempt to reach the besieged garrison was made in April 1916, led by General

Gorringe, and the 1/9th and the 1/8th Gurkhas were involved. To save the 10,000 men in Kut, General Gorringe lost 21,000 in vain, and General Townshend was forced to surrender unconditionally on 29 April 1916, an event that shocked the whole world.

The 2/7th Gurkhas went with the Turks as prisoners of war. The long marches across the desert were harsh, the prison camps were primitive, and many never returned. Unfortunately, the whole battalion of 2/7th Gurkhas was wiped out, and it had to be raised again. The fall of Kut saw General Sir S. Maude as the new commander of the British forces in Mesopotamia. A massive army of 166,000 men marched towards Baghdad by early 1917 and 110,000 Indian and Gurkha soldiers were among them. After many fierce battles, the British finally entered Baghdad on 11 March 1917, and the 1/2nd, 4/4th, 1/7th, 2/9th and 1/10th Gurkhas were among the leading forces. Baghdad was an unattractive city with dirty streets. The British troops were stricken by cholera, and General Maude was one of the victims.

The other Gurkha battalions which participated in the war in Mesopotamia were the 1/2nd, 1/4th, 2/4th, 2/5th, 2/6th, 1/7th, 1/8th, 2/9th and 1/10th. The campaign ended on 29 October 1918, with the Anglo-Indian forces, including the Gurkhas, having lost 4,335 officers and 93,344 other ranks, of which 30,000 were killed.

Six Gurkha regiments including the 4th battalion of the newly formed 11th Gurkhas fought on in other parts of the Middle East under General Sir E. Allenby. It was in the battle of El Kefr, Egypt, on 10 April 1918 where the 2nd VC for the Gurkhas was to be awarded, to Rifleman Karnabahadur Rana of the 2/3rd Gurkha Rifles. During the fight, the advancing company of 2/3rd Gurkhas came under severe pressure and was held up by an enemy machine gun that created havoc among the troops. Rifleman Karnabahadur Rana crept forward with a Lewis gunner to silence the enemy gun, and he took over the gun when the number one gunner was killed. Despite being exposed to enemy fire, he knocked out the enemy machine gun and kept on firing at the enemy bombers for the rest of the day in silence. His heroic act enabled the company to move forward. He received the VC medal directly from King George V in London in 1919, and he died at the age of 74 back in his village on 25 July 1973.

The war on the Palestine front was over on 31 October 1918 when the Turks surrendered, and the Gurkha brigade of the Indian Army was finally able to return home.

Despite the British official number of 6,168 Gurkhas killed in the Great War, the Gurkhas suffered around 20,000 casualties out of 200,000, and they were either killed, wounded or they went missing during the war. One in ten who had come down from the hills to serve the British never returned home as many of them perished in various unknown places. The Gurkhas were awarded almost 2,000 gallantry medals including two Victoria Crosses in the different theatres of war. Most importantly, the Gurkhas, whose fame was limited to the Indian subcontinent until then, were finally introduced to the world. The brave Gurkhas from the tiny Himalayan nation had finally arrived on the stage, and as we all know by now, the world was awestruck.

CHAPTER 9

THE GURKHAS IN THE SECOND WORLD WAR, 1939-1945

'The fighting was tough, many of his friends were killed, and he managed to survive only by hiding underneath the piles of dead bodies. He used to tell such stories to us before, but now he remembers almost nothing,' his granddaughter-in-law told us.

Rifleman Amrit Bahadur Thapa (96), 2nd GR, from Toksar, Gorkha, who fought in Burma during WWII. He was very weak, had lost his hearing and remembered little about his past.

After the end of World War I, one or two battalions of all the Gurkha regiments were involved in the Third Afghan War of 1919 while other Gurkha battalions were moved up to the Northwest Frontier to defeat a widespread Mahsud rising. Again, the PM, Chandra Shumsher, saw trouble brewing at the Northwest Frontier and advised the British not to disband the Gurkha Brigade anytime soon. As a result, the Gurkha Brigade was kept at its full wartime strength and was only dissolved in 1921, after the troubles were over. At that time, the 11th Gurkha Rifles, which was raised during the war in 1918 and disbanded by 1922, had become the shortest-lived regiment of the Gurkha Brigade. Thankfully, the 11th Gorkha Rifles was re-established again in 1948 after Indian independence, and was stationed at Varanasi, Uttar Pradesh, with five battalions as part of the Indian Army.

Although the next twenty years were quiet and no big wars were fought, the battles with the Pathans and other tribesmen along the long and fragile borders of the Northwest Frontier provided enough war practice and kept the Gurkha Brigade fit and ready. While not being in the actual fighting, they practised mostly in sports, large-scale ceremonial parades, inter-battalion competitions, warfare training, and performed relief operations in case of natural disasters. Nepal was severely hit by a devastating earthquake in 1934 and a number of historic structures were destroyed. The following year, the Quetta earthquake of 1935 struck, and the Gurkha Brigade played a significant role during the rescue operations. Nepal was still a closed, remote and underdeveloped nation. No foreigners were allowed to enter the country and the flow of information was closely monitored. Unaware of the situation outside Nepal, the peace-loving people of the country didn't know that a destructive storm in the name of World War II was about to turn their lives upside down.

It was 1939, and the Germans had paved the way for WWII. There was Hitler's army crossing all over Europe in the west, and the Japanese Imperial Army already marching through the vast Chinese territories and heading menacingly south, threatening British interests in Asia. The principal warmongers were the Axis powers (Germany, Italy and Japan), and the Allies (Britain, the United States, the Soviet Union and to a lesser extent China).

The Indian Army Gurkha Brigade was still at its peacetime strength of twenty battalions, two battalions for each regiment, and they had to quickly reach wartime strength. When the British finally approached Nepal, they found Judha Shumsher, the prime minister, more than willing to help. Unlike Chandra Shumsher before WWI, they didn't even have to convince him. All the British had to do was ask, and PM Judha Shumsher was ready to offer all the available resources of Nepal to the British. First and foremost, he provided eight battalions of the Nepal Army for the internal security of India when the British and Indian forces went to war. The British asked for new recruitment and often more battalions to increase the total number of Gurkha battalions to 30, but within a few months it was increased to 45 battalions. Author Byron Farwell suggested that a total of 50 battalions were raised, which would have included volunteers, non-combatant troops and non-military services such as stretcher-bearers, porters, drivers, security guards and so on. All those young and able men from the hills of Nepal descended to India at once. Ten new recruiting centres were established near the India-Nepal border. All the Gurkha officers, as well as soldiers on long leaves and recently retired, returned to their respective regiments. The Gurkha NCOs helped train the recruits, transforming them into battle-fit soldiers in a short time.

The Indian Army, including the Gurkha Brigade, wasn't mobilized until after the evacuation of the British Expeditionary Force from Dunkirk in May 1940. When the Indian forces were finally called on in 1941, two million individuals would eventually respond to the call within the next four years, and the tiny nation of Nepal alone contributed 250,000 of its men to the British cause. Also, 2,000 Dotiyals from the western district of Doti came down to raise two new porter battalions.

The first of many journeys for all the battalions from the ten Gurkha regiments started in the spring of 1941. It would take them to North Africa, Italy, Greece, Southeast Asia and the Middle East. During the course of the war, the Gurkhas were always at centre stage wherever the main actions were played out.

In May 1941, the 10th Indian Division, under which the 1/2nd, 2/7th and 2/10th Gurkhas served, was led by General Slim. They went to Persia and the mission of re-establishing order there was completed without a real fight. Two Gurkha battalions remained there and didn't see any action until they moved on to Italy in 1944. When I asked 98-year-old Lance Corporal Damar Bahadur Thapa of the 1/2nd GR from Gorkha, West Nepal, who fought as a radio operator, to describe a day at war in Persia, he said 'we mostly marched on vehicles and counter-attacked only when attacked by the enemy'; he remembers that the soldiers weren't fighting, as they were just being reactive. But he vividly recalls that 'life was tough during the war, we only got a bottle of water a day, and food was scarce.'

According to author E.D. Smith, author of the book *Valour: A History of the Gurkhas*, the British were driven back to Egypt by General Rommel's Afrika Korps and their Italian allies by 1941. But the port of Tobruk was still in British hands, and Rommel was to strike again in May 1942. Despite knowing Rommel's plan and with superiority in numbers, the British lacked experience in handling large armoured formations, and their small two-pounder guns were useless against German armour. In the Western Desert, the 2/4th Gurkha was the first one to face the German tanks. They fought bravely for the next 48 hours without food or sleep and finally were overpowered on 6 June 1942. The following units to fall were the 2/3rd and 2/8th Gurkhas, and many were taken as prisoners. On the fateful night of 21 June 1942, the 2/7th Gurkhas came under attack. They fought bravely until they were forced to surrender and become prisoners of war with 25,000 other Allied troops. For the second time in its history, the whole battalion of 2/7th Gurkha was wiped out. Permission to raise the 2/7th Gurkhas was given again, and they were to see action later in the Italian campaign during 1944.

After the fall of Tobruk, the next battle occurred at El Alamein, and 1,200 guns were fired until the final rout of the enemy. By then, the 1/2nd and 1/9th Gurkhas were serving under the 4th Indian Division, which was led by General Tucker. The Axis forces of General Rommel were in retreat, and the British were in hot pursuit. By the spring of 1943, Rommel was virtually surrounded in the rugged mountains of central Tunisia. The 1/2nd and 1/9th Gurkhas were to play a vital role in chasing the Afrika Korps of Rommel and his allies out of Africa. The objective of the 4th Indian Division was to take the Fatnassa height in a silent night assault, so the 8th Army could get behind Rommel's forces through the Matmata Mountains.

On the night of 5 April 1943, the 1/2nd and 1/9th Gurkhas climbed the slopes in utter silence. As they located the enemy machine guns, they cleared them with the kukri. Before too long, the Germans fled across the plateau and by the dawn of 6 April, all the critical features in the area were in the hands of British forces, which opened the way for the next brigade to pass through. It was during this battle that the recipient of the Order of British India, 1st class and the Star of Nepal, 4th class Subedar (Major) Lal Bahadur Thapa, then the second-in-command of D Company of the 1/2nd Gurkhas, won the VC for an outstanding display of leadership as well as bravery. The 1/2nd Gurkhas led by him used their faithful weapon, the kukri, to kill members of the garrison's remaining outposts. The machine-gun posts were dealt with in similar ways. With kukris in their hands, the objective was achieved, the hills were secured, and the advance of the whole British division was made possible.

The officers and men of the 1/9th Gurkhas had to endure a fierce counter-attack by German forces at the bare rocks of Djebel Garci for three days and nights. The WWII veteran Rifleman Megh Bahadur Khatri of the 1/9th GR from Myagdi, West Nepal, 100 years old at the time of our interview, was one of the Gurkhas who fought in that battle. Now frail, he could remember almost nothing about the war. But when I asked him about the German counter-attacks he broke into a song, probably from muscle memory, and crooned, '*Baacheta yai bato aunla, mareta baluwa sirani*' ('If I survive, I will return by the same way home, if I die, I will have the sands as my pillow'). It was the regimental song they used to sing as they marched to the battlefield, and he, without remembering, gave us a glimpse into the Gurkha mindset when at war. The three days in Tunisia were close-quarter fighting, and the Gurkhas fought with just a kukri and grenades. Shaken by the ferocity of the Gurkhas, the Germans broke ranks and fled.

Due to changes in the battle plan, the main thrust of the attack was shifted to the narrow coastal plain north of Enfidaville, while the Garci operation was abandoned. The final victory in Tunisia came on 12 May 1943 when the Axis forces formally surrendered. A staggering 220,000 prisoners were taken, and Africa was finally cleared of German and Italian troops. It was the 1/2nd Gurkhas who met General von Arnim, the commander-in-chief of all Axis forces in Africa. He was ready to surrender at his headquarters. The long, arduous and costly war in the Western Desert of North Africa was finally over, and the Gurkhas, as a part of the 8th Indian Division, were moved to Italy, where they were to join the American Fifth Army.

The 1/5th Gurkhas saw their first action at the village of Mozzagrogna, near the River Sangro in Italy. They also suffered tragically from an artillery barrage by their own forces and were forced to give up some parts of the village that they had won after fighting hard. Only after the 1/5th was reinforced did the allies manage to retake the Sangro area by 1 December 1943. The battle was costly, and the 1/5th lost three British, four Gurkha officers and 129 other ranks.

After the fiascos in France, Gallipoli and Mesopotamia during World War I, the first tragedy of the World War II to hit the Gurkha Brigade was on the Malay Peninsula, and the brigade was to lose two whole battalions to the invading Japanese forces. Unlike during WWI, the allies were fighting on two fronts in WWII, and the formidable enemies were rather brutal and determined this time around. After bombing Pearl Harbour, Hawaii, on 7 December 1941, the Japanese entered the war and moved through Asia with such speed that they suddenly appeared on the beaches of the Malay Peninsula and the first air raids were being made on Singapore just one day later. Three Gurkha battalions, the 2/1st, 2/2nd and 1/9th under the 11th Indian Division, were stationed in the area, and whenever they encountered the Japanese on equal terms, the Gurkhas managed to beat them off. However, without any air or naval support, they couldn't hold off the superior Japanese force and had to retreat. The retreating troops were caught by the Japanese at Slim River on 7 January 1942, and the confused and disarrayed forces were separated into too many groups.

On the same day, General Sir Archibald Wavell, the allied supreme commander of the Southwest Pacific, decided to abandon the mainland of Malaya and concentrate all the available resources on defending Singapore. The long and treacherous retreat for the British, Indian, Gurkha and Australian forces continued until the main causeway between the mainland and Singapore was blown up on 31 January 1942. Many who didn't make it to the other side of the bridge were either killed or captured, and most of the unlucky ones never returned.

According to many British authors, the notion of 'Fortress Singapore' was a false belief held mostly by the British hierarchy. It wasn't to stand, and Singapore fell at 4 p.m. precisely on 15 February 1942. A total of 138,000 British troops were killed, wounded or taken as prisoners, and two entire battalions, the 2/2nd and 1/9th Gurkhas, went with them. They were forcibly marched to work, ill-treated and not given enough food, and repeatedly tortured if the continuous hard labour didn't kill them. Almost 18,000 out of 45,000 Allied prisoners died in Japanese captivity, and many were from the two Gurkha battalions.

During captivity, the Gurkhas were subjected to extreme torture from their brutal and cruel captors, and many didn't survive. The Gurkhas were then isolated, forced to work in inhumane conditions without food or water, no blankets in the cold night and no shade in the hot day, repeatedly beaten by bamboo sticks and clubbed by rifle butts, and persistently treated in an unimaginably undignified manner. Among them was Subedar Major (Gurkha Major) Harising Borha of the 2/2nd Gurkhas, who, despite being blinded and suffering internal bleeding, refused to submit to the Japanese demands and addressed a letter of protest. The Gurkhas had sworn allegiance to the British king-emperor, and as PoWs, they were entitled to decent treatment under international law. It frustrated the Japanese captors and caused a series of brutal beatings, which eventually killed the brave man. He was awarded the posthumous Indian Order of Merit. Many Gurkhas remained as prisoners of the Japanese forces for the next three and a half years.

On 20 January 1942, the Japanese 15th Army invaded Burma (Myanmar) from Siam (Thailand). The British had two infantry divisions in Burma by then, and one of the longest, most difficult and painful retreats in the British Army's history began. Five Gurkha battalions (1/3rd, 1/4th, 2/5th, 1/7th and 3/7th serving under the 16th and 17th Indian divisions) were among the retreating force. The Japanese were hot on its heels, and many fierce skirmishes ensued. To cut off the Japanese attack, the bridge over the broad and fast-flowing Sittang River had to be blown up. As a result, many Gurkha battalions were left behind. The river was about 1,200 yards wide, and with strong tides and no boats, hundreds were swept away while desperately trying to cross the river, and were never seen again. By the time the force returned to India, they had already lost two-thirds of their men, and all five battalions had to be re-raised with recruits.

According to E.D. Smith, the next battle the Gurkhas had to fight was at Monte Cassino, Italy, while overrunning the famous monastery stronghold in February 1944. Units of the 1/2nd and 1/9th Gurkhas participated, and two companies from the 2/7th Gurkhas were attached as a backup. In March, the men from the 1/9th Gurkhas fought for 16 days on the lower slopes, clinging like bats through constant bombardment on the famous Hangman's Hill, where their valour was commemorated by the emblem of crossed kukris carved on a rock. Despite all efforts, the Allies failed, and the final battle of Cassino didn't occur until 11 May 1944. Rifleman Man Bahadur Ghimire of 1/9th GR from Dharan, East Nepal, now 99 years old, described those eleven days and nights of fighting as 'constant bombardment by the enemy and bombs exploding nearby most of the time'. He revealed that, 'one cold and snowy night, the bridge that we were guarding was blown up by an enemy shell and many Gurkhas, including three from my battalion, fell into the river and drowned'; he paused and then exclaimed 'I was lucky to have escaped unharmed.'

It was here that the 1/5th Gurkhas played an important part and a gallant act from Havildar Raimansing Gurung inspired the attacking force. He not only led a bayonet charge against heavy German fire but also blew up a German machine-gun post with a grenade in his dying moments, which forced the Germans to surrender. He was awarded the Indian Order of Merit. After a fierce tank battle at San Angelo, the Germans retreated, and the action at Cassino was finally over.

The Gurkha battalions serving under the three Indian divisions had won many battle honours by now, among them names like 'Auditore – the 1/2nd; Monte Della Gorgace, and II Castello – the 2/3rd; Monte Cedrone – the 2/4th; Rippa Ridge – the 1/5th; and Poggio del Grillo – the 2/7th'. Remarkably, those battle honours were won even before the decisive battle of the Gothic Line had started.

The next German defence lined up at the Gothic Line, north of Florence, where the 2/3rd, 2/4th, 2/6th, 2/8th and 2/10th Gurkhas were to join up with the 1/2nd, 1/9th and 2/7th Gurkhas and fight on. It was here at the Battle of San Marino where Rifleman Sher Bahadur Thapa, the 1/9th Gurkhas, marched through a continuous hail of bullets and saved the lives of his section commander and two wounded soldiers, before being fatally shot by a machine gun. In recognition of his unsurpassed devotion to rescue and save lives, he was awarded the VC and became immortal in Gurkha history.

On 10 November 1944, a company of the 1/5th Gurkhas was ordered to send a fighting patrol on to Monte San Bartolo, an objective for a future attack. It was the Gurkha ferocity, tenacity and determination which allowed for a successful mission. There were two scouts on this patrol team, and Rifleman Thaman Gurung was one of the two. They were spotted by the Germans when they reached the top of the hill. Realizing the danger, he leapt to his feet and started firing; thus, taking the enemy by surprise. After crossing the open skyline, he kept firing at the enemy with his Tommy gun until his ammunition ran out, threw two grenades and then picked up a Bren gun, some magazines and ran to the hilltop and started firing at the enemy while the rest of the patrol withdrew to a safe position. Only after he had emptied two magazines, and the remaining sections were well on the way to safety, was he killed. The remaining German troops surrendered later on. In recognition of his bravery, he was awarded the VC. Monte San Bartolo was captured three days later.

The 2/10th made a good name for themselves at the battle of Passano Ridge and Sillaro River. The 2/6th led the campaign of Marino River, entering Medicina in Kangaroo tanks and supported by the tanks of the 14th/20th Hussars. The last battle of the Italian front was fought after crossing Gaiana River where the 2/6th, 2/8th and 2/10th Gurkhas took heavy casualties. The war on that front was virtually over on 2 May 1945, when the German Army in Italy capitulated.

Before they could leave Europe and return home, the 4th Indian Division was sent to Salonika, Athens and Patras in Greece, to engage in fighting with the Communist ELAS (the Greek People's Liberation Army). Units of the 2/7th, 1/9th and 3/10th Gurkhas were involved. They fought some brief but decisive battles and sustained 22 casualties while 120 were wounded during the operation. At the end of December 1945, most of the Gurkhas who had deployed to Europe finally returned to their bases back in India. However, the 1/2nd were to serve a few more years in ten different countries before they could finally return home.

Back to the Eastern front. After the hasty and desperate retreat from Burma, no significant actions took place at the India-Burma borders. The 1st Chindit (a corrupted version of the Burmese word 'Chinthe' for 'winged pair of stone lions', mostly seen in front of Buddhist temples as guardians) expedition named Operation Longcloth, led by the famous General Orde Wingate, was launched and only one Gurkha unit, the newly formed 3/2nd Gurkhas, was involved. The Chindit operation was based on the notion of operating behind the enemy line, with all supplies being air-dropped, and harassing the enemy from the inside and behind their own defences.

The first Chindit operation was a total disaster, mistakes were made, and General Wingate even criticized the Gurkhas for being mentally unsuitable for the role. But the Gurkhas were to go on and prove him wrong in the next expedition. The experimental operation did cost the 3/2nd Gurkha dearly; a total of 446 men were lost during the first operation alone, of which only 150 subsequently returned.

Among many raging battles within Burma during the period of 24-27 May 1943, Havildar Gaje Ghale of the 2/5th Gurkhas was in charge of a platoon of young soldiers engaged in attacking a robust Japanese position at Chin Hills. He taught the unassuming soldiers the Gurkha template of conduct and character while at war. They saw that even when wounded in the arm, leg and chest, a Gurkha continues to lead assault after assault, with the only chant raging from their lips, '*Ayo Gorkhali*'. Spurred on by the unbeatable will of their leader, the platoon stormed and captured the position after a bitterly contested hand-to-hand battle.

On 5 March 1944, the 2nd Chindit expedition named Operation Thursday had six brigades, and four Gurkha battalions (the 3/4th, 3/6th, 3/9th and 4/9th) were involved. The selection of Gurkha battalions in this expedition was not made by General Wingate himself but by his column leaders, like M. Calvert and B. Ferguson, who had formed a higher opinion of the Gurkhas by then.

General Wingate wanted to insert a substantial force into the guts of the enemy with the ability to penetrate deeply. The Chindits had their own base near the airstrip and groups were sent to harass the Japanese on a regular basis. In March 1944, General Wingate was killed in a plane crash and was succeeded by General J. Lentaigne. The Commander of 77 Brigade, M. Calvert, had two Gurkha battalions (the 3/6th and 3/9th) under his command, and the first battle they saw was at Pagoda Hill where fierce fighting with kukris and bayonets occurred. The next big fight was at Mogaung. The 77 Brigade was to assist the Chinese forces under US General J. Stilwell, and it was here the 6th Gurkha Rifles was to bring great honour to its already distinguished regiment.

According to a first-hand conversation with Hon. Capt. Kul Bahadur Gurung of Pokhara, a 99-year-old WWII veteran, a Chindit and an MM winner who served in 2/6th, 3/6th and 5/5th Gurkhas, they took a Dakota plane loaded with goods, equipment and six mules in the strength of a section (8-10 men) at Silchar airport and were dropped on a makeshift airstrip at Broadway.

'After walking for four days, we arrived at our destination, a place named Maulo. After we dug in, my commander was killed when the Japanese attacked. Luckily, the Japanese were a small team, and they withdrew. Our main tasks were to destroy railroads, roads and bridges, and our camp came under Japanese attack while we were away from it. Even after continued fighting for seven days and nights at Maulo, the

Japanese couldn't break our defensive line. I single-handedly killed three enemies and burnt two trucks full of the enemy on the way back. Many of my troops were lost on the road but we found 90 of them. When we finally repulsed the Japanese attack and recovered the camp, we lost 200 men.' His tone was full of nostalgia.

'I was also a member of the troops that fought the famous Mogaung battle,' he continued. Despite his age, and the incident having taken place over seven decades earlier, his memory was as sharp as if it was yesterday and that surprised me.

'My whole section was wiped out by enemy machine guns and it took twenty days to capture the objective that was [supposed] to take only four days. It was here when Tul Bahadur Pun, who was also a member of my section in previous battles, won the VC at the battle of Red House. We moved on after Mogaung was handed over to the Chinese force commanded by the Americans and on the way out we saw a lot of dead bodies on the ground. Only 450 survived out of 1,100 men. The whole village was empty, and only 20 mules out of 160 remained. I genuinely believed that I should also have been awarded the VC, but luck was not on my side as I had no witnesses. But I harboured no hard feelings. We walked for four more days and arrived in a Chinese-built airstrip at a place called Oraju in Burma before flying back to Silchar by plane again. The war was over by then, so we returned to India.'

The battle at Mogaung started in early June 1944. They fought fiercely for the next sixteen days, and by the end of it, the 77 Brigade was reduced to 806 of the 2,000 men that had entered the war. Alongside three British battalions from the 14th Brigade, the 3/4th and 3/9th Gurkhas participated in capturing a Japanese stronghold known as Point 2,171 overlooking the Mogaung River. They fought fiercely even after their commander, Major J. Blaker, was killed and eventually managed to drive the Japanese off the hill. The 4/9th Gurkha was later deployed under the 'Morris Force', whose duty was to block the road from Bhamo and to directly support General Stilwell's advances. They were withdrawn by 17 July 1944 after they had completed their mission.

The Chindits' operations in Burma carried on throughout 1944, and they were eventually disbanded. The decisive battles of Arakan, Imphal and Kohima were about to enter the final phase, and the fate of the Japanese Imperial Army was soon to be decided. The Gurkhas were destined to play a huge role.

The Arakan campaign started in December 1943. British, Indian, Gurkha and West African soldiers were in the force, and the Gurkha battalions of the 4/1st, 3/4th, 4/5th, 3/6th, 4/8th and 3/9th were involved. The first offensive was fixed for 7 February 1944, but Japanese General Hanaya decided on surprise attacks under the code name 'Ha-Go'. The Japanese were expecting the British to run away as they had done in 1942, but he was wrong.

The Japanese Tanahashi Force swiftly surrounded the 7th Indian Division and overran its headquarters. General F. Messervy managed to escape with his staff and reached safety at Sinzweya. Later on, the headquarters was to be known as the 'Admin Box', and other troops who were temporarily lost or detached during the melee would later rejoin there, including two companies of the 4/8th Gurkha. Soldiers, mules, tanks, vehicles and guns were crammed together within the confined area, and were persistently pounded by enemy artillery, mortars and machine guns for the next eighteen days. Despite the heavy fighting, the British received regular supplies and necessities by air, which the Japanese didn't. Without food and supplies, the Japanese were trapped, and a handful of soldiers started to surrender. When General H. Briggs, the commander of the 5th Indian Division, went into the Box on the morning of 24 February 1944, more than 500 wounded were waiting for evacuation, and the ordeal was over. Among the relieving force was the 1/8th Gurkha under the command of 26th Division.

The 4/1st Gurkha endured a barrage of attacks by the Japanese for five days during 'Abel', when they were repeatedly pounded by 150mm guns positioned within 3,000 yards, which blocked all their supply routes. As a result, they had to live on half a mess-tin of lentils, rice and two chapattis (flatbreads) a day, but they held the hill until they were relieved by early March of 1944. The 'Abel' area was cleared within the next two days, and the 4/1st Gurkha lost six British and two Gurkha officers and 225 of the rank and file soldiers.

The 2nd Arakan campaign was finally over. It was undoubtedly one of the main turning points of the whole Burma campaign, and as the monsoon approached, large-scale operations in the Arakan came to a halt. By the time the monsoon was over, the outcome of the Imphal and Kohima campaigns, known as the 'U-Go' offensive to the Japanese, was to decide the course of the whole Burmese campaign, and both the Allies and the Japanese were fully prepared.

The Japanese generals were confident that they could capture the towns of Imphal and Kohima on the westward route to Bengal. General Mutaguchi, the fierce and ruthless commander of the Japanese 15th Army, had about 100,000 front-line troops and advanced towards Imphal at such a speed that it even surprised General W. Slim, the Supreme Allied Commander of Burma (later Field Marshal and Governor-General of Australia) and he had to react with quick reinforcements by air, rail and road.

Among many battles, the first one was at a place called Tuitum Ridge. Units from the 1/3rd, 1/4th and 1/10th participated and helped scatter the Japanese advance guards, killing half of them. During the first stage of withdrawal, the 1/10th performed as the rearguard and had to endure a relentless barrage of attacks from the Japanese for several days and nights. For their gallantry, General Cowan of the 17th Division granted the 1/10th the privilege of flying his divisional 'Black Cat' banner, with the regimental crest imposed on it, outside the Quarter Guard, a custom that the battalion continued until it was finally amalgamated.

After many battles, the 17th Indian Division reached Imphal by the first week of April 1944. It had sustained about 1,200 casualties and took three weeks. The 2/5th Gurkhas alone suffered 250 losses. Rifleman Sri Prasad Gurung, a 93-year-old veteran of the 2/5th GR from Pokhara, West Nepal, who fought in the battle of Conneti Picket, 52 miles from Kohima, was one of them.

'We had just a one-month training before going to the war,' he remembered. 'Not enough food and sleep, we had to go patrolling almost on a daily basis and survived on dry rations. I have already forgotten most of the things by now but we drank rum before the final attack. Victoria Cross winner Gaje Ghale was in our group too.'

Similarly, 98-year-old Buddha Singh Rana of 1/3rd GR from Lamjung, West Nepal, who also fought in the battle of Kohima as a no. 1 gunner before moving to Tedim, Burma, recalled, 'When my colonel died, I also got hit on my chin by the machine gun, got dizzy and fell down. The next time I woke up, I found myself in a hospital bed covered in bandages. After being transferred to various hospitals, my chin got repaired with the bone, meat and skin from other parts of my body, and I remained in the hospital until 1949 before coming home on a medical pension. Almost seventy years later, I still have some difficulties eating properly.'

'During World War Two in Burma, the Japanese were within hearing distance of us on two sides of the hills,' he said. 'We used to tease them, "You didn't have enough tadpoles and frogs in your country so you have come here. We will drink tea in Tokyo." And in return the Japanese used to shout back, "We will drink tea at your Namle Bazaar."' And he laughed.

Many battles were fought in defence of Shenam Ridge and that was a major factor in the successful defence of Imphal. Three battalions from the 10th Gurkhas alone suffered over 1,000 casualties. When the last Japanese roadblocks were cleared from the Imphal-Kohima Road on 21 June 1944, all three battalions of the 10th Gurkhas were awarded the battle honour 'Imphal' in recognition of their gallant efforts.

The next big battle took place at 'Scraggy Hill', and the 3/3rd, 3/5th and 3/10th Gurkhas under the 37th Gurkha Infantry Brigade took part.

The battle of Imphal and Kohima was fiercely fought and won around Bishenpur. Three brave Gurkhas won the VC here, and even a battalion from the Nepal National Army fought alongside the 3rd Assam Rifles in this epic battle.

On the morning of 12 June 1944 near Ningthaoukhong, Burma, the Japanese made an intense artillery barrage against the brigade, which lasted an hour. This heavy artillery fire knocked out several bunkers and caused heavy damage, and was immediately followed by a powerful enemy attack by five medium tanks. After fierce hand-to-hand fighting, the perimeter was penetrated by the enemy, and the Allied troops were pinned to the ground. B and D Companies of the 1/7th Gurkha launched an urgent counter-attack, which was initially successful, but were subsequently pushed back by the enemy tanks. There was one Gurkha, the only VC recipient in that battle, who was neither a Gurung nor from Nepal. He was an anomaly from Sikkim of Nepali origin, but he displayed pure Gurkha traits. Rifleman Ganju Lama of the 1/7th Gurkha, the no. 1 gunner, crawled forward with complete disregard for his safety and engaged the tanks single-handedly. He was awarded the VC for this gallantry, transferred to the newly re-established 11th Gurkha Indian Regiment and promoted to Subedar Major (Gurkha Major) before retiring with the rank of honorary captain in 1968. Moreover, he was the only Gurkha who won both the VC and MM in two separate actions within the space of just a few days.

When the Japanese attacked on 25-26 June 1944 at Bishenpur, India, Subedar Netra Bahadur Thapa of the 2/5th Gurkhas was in command of an isolated hill post called 'Mortar Bluff.' The small force, inspired by the leadership of Netra Bahadur Thapa, held their ground and fought the enemy which resulted in heavy casualties. He requested reinforcements which came in the darkness of night, and they held off the enemy until lousy luck – both machine guns of one section jammed – got in the way. He went on to attack the enemy armed with grenades and kukris, got hit by a bullet and was killed by a grenade shortly afterwards. His body was found the next day with the kukri still in his hand and dead Japanese with cleft skulls by his side. He was posthumously awarded the VC for his bravery. His wife collected the VC on his behalf in 1945 and handed it to his regiment at the same time.

After they lost the strategic hill positions of Mortar Bluff and Water Piquet the previous night, the 2/5th Gurkhas were ordered to recapture them on 26 June 1944. After those positions were pounded by artillery, the Gurkha regiment went on attack. But on reaching a false crest about 80 yards from their objective, the unit was pinned down by heavy machine gun fire and suffered many casualties. The 2/7th Gurkha marched under direct machine gun fire and kept firing, and charged the enemy position, killing three of the crew of four. The section surged forward across the hail of fire and routed the whole garrison of Mortar Bluff. Then, they came under ferocious fire from the nearby hill, but soon silenced that as well, and helped support the rest of the platoon, making the final assault at Water Piquet. The enemy, demoralized by this calm display of Gurkha courage and complete contempt for danger, now fled before the onslaught and Water Piquet too was captured.

Many Gurkha units fought in this great battle of Imphal and Kohima: the 4/1st, 4/2nd, 1/4th, 2/5th, 4/5th, 1/7th, 3/8th and many more. The 1/4th Gurkhas fought bravely at the battle of Scrub Ridge, the 4/1st captured Basha Hill with great speed, and the struggle for Imphal and Kohima was finally over. The Japanese suffered the loss of 30,000 men officially, but many more died or were killed in the aftermath. Operation 'U-Go' was finally over after they started withdrawing to the east of the Chindwin River on 2 July 1944.

The Japanese were on the run, with the Allied force hot on their heels, and the time to cross the Irrawaddy River had come. General Slim's 14th Army planned two frontal attacks, one aimed at Mandalay and another at Myitkyina, and almost all the Gurkha regiments were involved. In the battle of Mandalay, the 4/4th, 1/6th and 4/6th battalions took part, while at the battle of Myitkyina, units from the 1/1st, 3/1st, 4/2nd, 3/8th and 4/10th Gurkhas participated. The fighting on both fronts was fierce, casualties for both sides were high, and the objectives were finally captured by late March 1945. The race for Rangoon (Yangon), the capital of Burma, was now on, and General Slim was determined to win it before the monsoon arrived by mid-May.

Before the war in Burma was to end, the Gurkhas won two more VCs, and the VC count for the Gurkhas reached a staggering ten in World War II. On 5 March 1945, a company of the 3/2nd Gurkhas attacked an enemy position known as Snowdon East, and were pinned down by heavy enemy fire, including machine gun, grenades and mortar. At the same time, more casualties in the company were sustained from snipers, and they were stopped from advancing. The only Gurkha to have won the Nepal government 'Nepal Tara' honour along with the VC in recognition of his bravery was Rifleman Bhanu Bhakta Gurung. Being unable to fire lying on the ground, he stood up, fully exposed, and killed the enemy sniper. He cleared four enemy foxholes, attacked a machine gun position and silenced them with his grenades and kukri. But this decorated war hero died without a pension at the age of 86 in Nepal.

In some cases of extreme injuries, the soldiers did manage to retire with a mere medical board pension. At Taungdaw, on the west bank of the Irrawaddy River on the night of 12-13 May 1945, Rifleman Lachhiman Gurung of the 4/8th Gurkhas was manning the most forward post of his platoon. His section was attacked in the middle of the night by at least 200 Japanese troops. Before the attack, one grenade fell in his trench. He picked it up and hurled it back. Another followed, and he threw it back again. The third grenade exploded in his hand, blowing his fingers off, shattering his right hand, and severely wounding him on the face, body and leg. Two of his severely injured compatriots lay helpless at the bottom of the trench, and the enemy, shouting and screaming, attempted to rush to the position in great numbers. Rifleman Lachhiman Gurung, regardless of his wounds, loaded and fired his rifle with his left arm, and somehow managed to repulse the avalanche of attacks. The attacks continued for the next four hours, but he didn't leave his trench. A total of 87 enemies dead were counted in the area; 31 lay in front of his trench alone. In recognition of his bravery, he was awarded the VC and later on went on medical board pension.

The final assault at Rangoon started with an airborne attack on Elephant Point, and was carried out by the combined parachute battalions. Among them were two Gurkha parachute battalions, the 153rd (mostly volunteers from other Gurkha units) and 154th (previously the 3/7th Gurkhas, which was transformed into a parachute battalion in 1943), and redesignated as the 2nd and 3rd Gurkha battalions of the Indian Parachute Regiment in November 1945. Sadly, they were almost wiped out during the war, both from the deadly fighting with the Japanese, as well as being wrongly hit by American aircraft, and were subsequently disbanded.

The city of Rangoon was finally captured by the Allied forces on 6 May 1945. The Japanese left after occupying Rangoon for three years and two months, and the Japanese Imperial Army was finally defeated in Burma on 25 July.

World War II was finally over on 2 September 1945. The tiny nation of Nepal provided 250,280 men and served the British Crown in its most challenging period. It suffered around 32,640 casualties (7,544 killed,

1,441 missing or presumed dead, and 23,655 wounded) in all theatres of war. The actual numbers of casualties are said to have been considerably higher. The Gurkhas were awarded 2,734 bravery awards, including the 10 VCs, during WWII and they established themselves as the bravest of the brave.

According to the *London Gazette* of 7 April 1944, Honorary Capt. Birta Sing Gurung, who hailed from Dansing village in Kaski, West Nepal, and belonged to the 1/3rd GR, was the only recipient of the Order of the Patriotic War, 1st Class Russian Red Star among the Gurkhas. The other recipient was Major (Temporary Lt Col) Dennis Charles Tarrant Swan from the Corps of Royal Engineers (who headed the sappers and miners of the 1st Burma Infantry Division from November 1941 to the end of the campaign). According to the Gurkha Museum in the UK, the following account was provided in an interview in the 1980s: 'In 1941-42, Japanese forces seized Kangla Tumbi Hill in Burma, threatening the Kohima-Manipur ration supply. British and British Indian forces attempted to retake the hill from the Japanese army for four days without success. On the fifth day, Birta Sing Gurung (then a subedar) planned and led another attack, which succeeded in taking the hill. He was then awarded the Order of the Patriotic War, 1st Class Russian Red Star for this action.' It is believed that Russia provided two Orders of the Patriotic War, 1st Class Russian Red Star to be awarded to British forces operating in Burma in WWII, to be granted to heroes, but how the selection process occurred was not recorded in the museum's archive. Besides, Birta Sing Gurung was also said to have been awarded free travel on the Russian state airline for life, but this freebie was cancelled later on for an unknown reason.

To find the WWII veterans and share their stories with the world, I visited Nepal for a month in 2018, starting in the east. The veterans were over 95 years of age, and the oldest one I met was 100 years old. Now, after the sun had set on their years of standing in the line of fire, they were mostly just grateful to have returned home alive.

'I hid underneath the piles of dead bodies and survived in Burma,' remains a lasting memory for 96-year-old veteran Amrit Bahadur Thapa.

'My husband came home with only one rupee and fifty paisa with him,' says the 80-year-old widow of veteran Khar Kumari Pun as she recalls her husband's return from the war.

Financial wealth wasn't their foremost concern, explains Bahadur Rai, a 99-year-old veteran: 'Although I received no pension or gratuity, I still find myself lucky, as I returned home without any serious injuries or loss of a limb.' For him, social security was a far-off thought, as he was just thankful to be alive. Because as 100-year-old veteran Tahal Sing Rana simply states, 'If you are not sure of your own life, we had no time to think about anything else.'

Some had vague while others held vivid memories of the war, but a common sentiment that remained was that of abandonment. 'They took us to the war, we fought and sacrificed for them, but at the end, they abandoned us,' muses 98-year-old veteran Buddha Singh Rana.

'We fought for them, we won so many bravery medals, and we should have better pension and welfare. But we don't. It's not fair,' is the sense of injustice still carried by 93-year-old veteran Dil Bahadur Thapa.

The Gurkhas had fought and been on the winning side in two great wars. Their reputation reached the farthest and the most remote corners of the world. But the world was changing, and the mighty British Raj was dwindling too. Most importantly, the subcontinent of India was on the verge of independence. The partition of India was a testing time for the Gurkha Brigade, and challenges even greater than the world wars were in the offing.

CHAPTER 10

THE PARTITION OF THE GURKHA BRIGADE IN 1947

'During a fight with the Japanese, I got my finger sliced off by a sword, I had to walk for days and nights without any food or water, and I still remember the socks I wore were full of lice.'

Lance Corporal Nar Bahadur Gurung (95), 4/6th GR, from Serra, Lamjung, fought in Burma and returned home right after the war. He is a farmer and lives on a welfare pension.

After the Allied forces dropped atom bombs on Hiroshima and Nagasaki on 6 August and 9 August 1945, Japan officially surrendered on 15 August. Hitler's Nazi forces had already capitulated in Europe, and World War II finally came to an end. Despite the end of the war, hostilities continued in other parts of Asia, and the Indian Gurkha Brigade played significant roles in handling them. The sudden capitulation of mighty Japan also shocked the whole of Asia. The Gurkha Brigade had to handle large numbers of prisoners and provide security for those prisoners' camps as well around Asia.

In French Indo-China (today's Vietnam, Laos and Cambodia) five Gurkha battalions were deployed under the 20th Indian Division and fought against the Viet Minh of the communist leader Ho Chi Minh. The first ever kukri battle took place at Long Kien, south of Saigon on 18 November 1945. The 1/1st Gurkhas were involved, and their mission was to rescue the French hostages held there by the Viet Minh. During the battle, the Gurkhas had to fight hard, charging with the kukri, and completed the mission on the same day. Although no hostages were recovered, about 80 Viet Minh were said to have been killed during the operation. The last big battle between the British and Viet Minh occurred in early January 1946, when the Viet Minh of about 900 men attacked the British camp at Bien Hoa, and the fighting continued throughout the night. After they lost around 100 men, who were mostly killed by British machine gun fire, and the British side suffered no casualties, the fighting was over by the morning. The Viet Minh were said to have avoided large-scale attacks after that. After seven months of intervention in Vietnam, the British Indian troops, including the Gurkhas, finally left on 26 March 1946. The British Indian forces suffered 40 casualties against 600 Viet Minh killed and left the French in full control of Indo-China as they departed.

The next battle the Gurkhas saw in the Far East was in Java, the Dutch colony, and four Gurkha units under the 23rd Indian Division were involved. The problem arose from the fact that the Japanese had handed over their arms and overall command to Indonesian nationalists in some places, who took Dutch nationals and other prisoners of war as hostages. When the 3/10th Gurkhas tried to land on Semarang on 19 October 1945, they were stopped from landing, and they had to fight on their way to the camps until they were able to regain full control by the evening.

The 23rd Indian Division served in different parts of Indonesia for nearly a year. The incidents were mostly tense, and sometimes insulting, and it was known as the 'Java Nightmare' among the troops. By 1946, Southeast Asia had become reasonably stable and the Gurkhas returned to India.

Elsewhere, the 2/5th Gurkhas went to Japan in May 1946 as part of the British Commonwealth Occupation Force while the 4/1st Gurkhas, under the 7th Indian Infantry Division, were deployed to Thailand from September 1945 and moved to Malaya in 1946 before returning to India. As Malaya, Singapore and Borneo were still British colonies, most of the Gurkha regiments operated there post-WWII, and they were to become the leading British bases after India's independence.

Upon the conclusion of World War II, the Indian Gurkha Brigade returned home one by one, including the prisoners of war, and the harsh reality of trimming the brigade down to its peacetime strength of 20 battalions (two battalions for every ten regiments) loomed again. Those who had returned after spending a difficult time as prisoners of war faced an extremely harsh situation. They were not only both mentally and physically broken, but had also been isolated from their regiments for way too long, and the sense of camaraderie was all but lost. Moreover, they found it extremely hard to work under junior commanders who were promoted during the midst of the war in the field, thus many decided to go home. Almost 60 per cent from the wartime strength were to be sent back without any form of pension. Most of them were wounded or crippled from the war, and all the roads leading to the hills of Nepal were filled with broken soldiers.

Even worse, the countdown for the British to leave India had already started, and the day of the final departure was fast approaching. Rumours flew around as the dark cloud of uncertainty hovered over the future of the Gurkha Brigade, and the British did almost nothing (intentionally or due to inefficiency or insensitivity, it is hard to say) on their part to counter them. The Herculean task of creating the independent nations of India and Pakistan kept the British busy. As a result, the end of the British Army in India and the division of the Gurkha regiments were unavoidable. Before the partition, the Gurkhas were destined to play another significant role in the history of British India, and they fulfilled their duty wholeheartedly as they had done since the beginning.

The Hindus and the Muslims were literally at each other's throats, slaughtering each other without mercy as if they were sacrificial animals, and the bitter hatred between the two had reached such a boiling point that the whole of India was burning. On one fateful night of 7 March 1947 alone, 293 people were massacred in Punjab and troops were sent to Amritsar. Before too long, the Gurkha units were running into trouble on all fronts, and they acted as a peace force between Hindus and Muslims. After the announcement of India's independence on 15 August 1947, millions of Muslims departed for the newly formed country of Pakistan, while the Hindus came the opposite way into India, and the Gurkhas played a significant role in facilitating them as a neutral institution. Under the guidance and protection of the disciplined forces like the Gurkhas, several trains left for both destinations and many lives were thus saved. Within the four-month period post-independence, tens of millions of people were mobilized, and according to one of the Gurkha veterans who had seen the infighting first-hand, the violence between Hindus and Muslims was said to have caused almost 80,000 deaths. Had it not been for the good works of the Gurkhas, including the Nepal Army, the losses could have been much more significant, and both Hindus and Muslims stranded on the wrong side of the border would have never made it safely to the other side. It was, undoubtedly, one of the ugliest incidents in history. One Gurkha veteran said it was even worse than the Second World War.

According to the book *British India's Relations With the Kingdom of Nepal* by Asad Husain, Pandit Nehru wasn't in favour of allowing the Gurkhas to follow the British as they could be used against allies of India in the future. However, the British still needed the Gurkhas to protect their other interests in Asia and wanted to keep some Gurkha regiments for themselves. The future of the Andaman and Nicobar Islands was still not decided, and both Burma and Pakistan had claimed sovereignty over the islands. The icebreaker of the deal was the Gurkhas, and the islands were eventually handed to India in exchange for India's acceptance of some of the Gurkhas joining the British.

No announcement on the future of the Gurkhas was made until the last minute. When it was finally made, it struck a severe blow to the admiration and trust between the Gurkhas and the British. Out of 10 Gurkha regiments, only four (the 2nd, 6th, 7th and 10th) would serve under the British while the remaining six (the 1st, 3rd, 4th, 5th, 8th and 9th) were to be transferred to the Indian Army. The reasons behind the final decision were said to have been logistic convenience, and everything else was flagrantly ignored. Bureaucrats from the War Office in London wanted to have two regiments each from the western and eastern parts of Nepal. The 2nd Gurkha Rifles as King's Regiment was the first choice, and the 6th Gurkha was chosen as they happened to be in Burma at that moment. The 7th and 10th Gurkha Rifles were obvious choices as they were the only two distinguished regiments, already known as the regiments of Rais and Limbus, from the east of Nepal and were stationed in Burma as well.

The Gurkhas from those four selected regiments were given three options: stay in India with a transfer to other Gurkha units, follow the British and move to a new place, or go for an early discharge. The Gurkhas were heartbroken and furious, and so were their British officers, who could do nothing to change the situation. For the very first time, the Gurkhas felt betrayed, and some of them were so angry that when their colonel turned up to wish them farewell, they spat at him and shouted pro-Indian and anti-British slogans. A staggering 95 per cent of the Gurkhas were said to have chosen to stay with the Indian Army for various reasons. In expectation of becoming full commissioned officers, the Gurkha officers, also known as VCOs (Viceroy's Commissioned Officers) by then, wanted to remain in India and gave the same advice to those soldiers serving under them. India also provided a sense of stability against moving to a new and unfamiliar place. The four regiments were to follow the British and move to Malaya/Singapore. Emotions ran high, there was a feeling of uncertainty, it was a stressful situation; so much so that even the 2nd Gurkhas had to be persuaded by their colonel to remain with the British. Only 53 men from the whole 2/7th Gurkhas opted for the British side, and many were said to have cried, as they felt abandoned by the British.

After Burma got its independence in 1948, the four Gurkha regiments which followed the British, and which were still very much under-strength, finally moved to Malaya/Singapore and were renamed the Brigade of Gurkhas. Those six Gurkha regiments chosen to remain in India are playing a crucial role even today as an integral part of the Indian Army (including the re-raised 11th Gorkha Rifles, who have established themselves as one of the elite forces).

The Gurkhas serving under the British in both India and Britain were and are covered by the tripartite agreement signed by the British, India and Nepal. As pointed out by historians, it was a bipartite agreement signed between the British and the Indians, and Nepal was subsequently added in a rather shady situation. Since this treaty was to play a critical role in the future of the Brigade of Gurkhas, it finds mention in the later chapters of the book. As the Brigade of Gurkhas moved to a new and unfamiliar place, new challenges and opportunities waited for them. They never failed to give their best. Despite having to start from scratch, virtues such as adaptability, hard work and perseverance came in handy, and they eventually prevailed.

The next battlegrounds for the Gurkhas were the thick jungles of Southeast Asia. The enemies they fought there were not only trained and determined but also elusive, and the Gurkhas had to learn new skills if they were to defeat the enemy in the unforgiving terrain.

CHAPTER 11

The Gurkhas in Burma/Myanmar

'Honesty is the best policy with simple living and high thinking. – It was not only his motto but also a way of life and thus he set an example for all of us.' – Patrick Sharma (son)

Col Tankadhoj Nepal (1928-2014), the highest-ranking officer in the Burmese Army of Nepali origin, a national award-winner, and a well-respected figure by all the Gurkha communities within Myanmar.

According to the elders living in Myanmar, the Gurkhas initially arrived in three phases. The first group was brought in by the British East India Company from 1824 to 1848 through Heindar Mine in the Tenasserim region as miners and subsequently spread out to Namattu Mine, Shan State, and Mawchi Mine, Kayah State. The second group arrived from India and Nepal through Kachin and the Chin Hill regions. The third group came with the British Army in or after 1852, as soldiers, security guards, miners, farmers, gardeners and herders. They mostly lived in the hill areas and have been living in Myanmar for six generations.

The colonization of Burma by the British was completed in 1885-86 and the country was presented to Queen Victoria as a New Year's gift by then Governor Lord Dufferin and his generals. The name of the country was changed to Myanmar from Burma and that of its old capital city to Yangon from Rangoon in 1989.

As described in the previous chapter, Burma was a main battlefield in World War II, and the Gurkhas played a huge role in defeating the Japanese there and turning the tide of the war against them.

After Burma's independence in 1948, the No. 4 Burma Regiment (Gurkhas) was formed on the request of General Aung San, and all members were Gurkhas. After independence, Myanmar got itself tangled up with civil conflicts, and the Gurkhas were said to have played a significant role in saving the nation from a total breakdown. There is a long, rich and meaningful history between the Gurkhas and the Burmese people, and they have a sense of mutual liking, respect and understanding. After all, the Gurkhas saved the Burmese on many occasions: besides World War II and the chaotic years of internal insurgencies, they prevented it from virtually being rolled over by the Kuomintang (the KMT, China's nationalist army). It is said to be the main reason why the Gurkha communities are welcomed and respected by the Burmese people.

The Buddha-loving nation of Myanmar also respects the Gurkhas for hailing from the same country where Lord Buddha was born. The majority of people in Myanmar are Buddhist.

In World War II, tens of thousands of British Empire troops were killed, missing or unaccounted for in Burma. Thousands of Gurkhas were among the dead. All of those killed or lost are honoured at the Taukkyan War Cemetery in Yangon. A total of 27,000 brave souls (including Gurkhas in the thousands) are peacefully at rest there. I had the honour of visiting the place while researching this book. The memorial site is the biggest of its kind in the whole of Asia, and is built and managed by the Commonwealth War Graves Commission (CWGC), a non-governmental organization based in the UK.

Initially, almost 80 per cent of Burmese Gurkhas were either in the army, or in the mining or agricultural industries. Nowadays, they have entered many fields, such as business, education and medicine. They are also doing well in the field of literature, excelling in both Myanmarese and Gorkhali languages and winning awards and accolades along the way. Most importantly, to preserve Nepali traditions, customs and languages, they are working extremely hard. Among the population of 150,000 (which is said to have reached 300,000 at its peak, but many have migrated to Thailand, Malaysia and Singapore), Gurkha communities have built about 260 schools and 250 temples throughout the nation, which are solely funded by the Gurkha/Nepali communities within Myanmar.

The community has produced some prominent members of its own, like Suk Bahadur Rai, the winner of the Aung San Thuriya medal (the highest military award in Myanmar); Lieutenant Colonel Laxman Rai; Major 'Zeya Kyaw Htin' Bhagiman Subba; Major Suk Bahadur Thapa (captain of the Burma national football team); Police Colonel Miss Ohnmar Rimmy; E. Nyein Thazin (taekwondo multi-award winner); and Professor Attar Sing Chhetri.

Also among them is Colonel Tankadhoj Nepal, the winner of several national awards, born on 6 March 1928 at Myitkyina, who was the highest-ranking officer in the Myanmar Army from the Gurkha communities. He joined the Burmese National Army in 1951 as an officer cadet. During his long and distinguished army career, he served at the Chinese border, fought all kinds of rebels and insurgents in the tumultuous period of 1952-1960, and earned many awards, including a .38 Webley pistol from the president on Independence Day. Then, he was involved in the

Sino-Myanmar border demarcation mission, also known as the Ba Ba Operation and received the 'Zeya Kyaw Htin' (one of the highest awards in Myanmar) and a gold medal in 1962. After his regiment helped wipe the Burmese communists out of Peghu Yoma and the Shan State, he was promoted to lieutenant colonel and was made the commanding officer of the battalion in 1971. Before being promoted to a full colonel and transferred to the School of Combat Forces as the commandant in 1978, he served as the General Staff Officer Grade 1 (GSO 1) at the Northern Command of Myitkyina, and finally retired at the age of sixty in 1987. In his retirement, he served as an adviser to the Trade Ministry, wrote many books and articles, and devoted his time to volunteer work in support of the well-being of the Gurkha communities in Myanmar. He passed away peacefully on 5 March 2014. He is survived by his family (three sons and a daughter) and is still revered by all the Gurkha communities of Myanmar.

The legacy of the 4th Gurkha Regiment in the Myanmar Army is alive. They are now known as the 4th Regiment, and the Gurkhas are still serving as officers and in other ranks. To unite the Gurkha communities and preserve their good name in Myanmar, a noble endeavour named All Myanmar Gurkha Central Board is taking shape. It was initiated by retired Gurkhas, social workers, intellectuals and business individuals. As a new NGO, it intends to be the first organization that represents all the Gurkhas in Myanmar and will help preserve the Gurkha traditions for many generations to come.

Despite living abroad for generations, the Myanmar Gurkha community seems to be one of the most caring, passionate and vibrant among the Nepali diasporas around the globe. Their love, concern and understanding of Nepal has no limits. Most importantly, they are undoubtedly the proudest among the Gurkhas, and it was my honour to get to know them. Meantime, may the good name of Gurkha live the longest and shine the brightest among other stars in this beautiful place called Myanmar.

CHAPTER 12

THE GURKHAS IN MALAYSIA

'It was in Tidim, Burma, in 1944. I was hit on the chin by a machine gun burst, got dizzy, fell down and only woke up when fully bandaged that evening in the hospital. I had to go through many operations to repair my broken chin, stay in the hospital for the next five years and finally came home on a medical pension in 1949.'

Rifleman Buddhiman Joshi (98), 1/3rd GR, from Dui Piple, Lamjung, fought in Kohima, Basha Hill and Burma.

After the partition of India, four Gurkha regiments (the 2nd, 6th, 7th and 10th with two battalions each) followed the British and moved to Malaya and Singapore. Due to heavy losses in World War II and the fact many had opted to stay back in India, all the Gurkha regiments were very much under-strength and more had to be recruited from Nepal in a short period. As they first landed in Malaya in April 1948, each battalion had only 300 men on average with new officers, a handful of new NCOs, no specialists, no clerks and no books, and they were thrust into an entirely new system and environment. In a new and unfamiliar place, with little or no knowledge of English or Malay, and no time for any familiarization courses, the introduction of the Johnny Gurkhas into the British Army was anything but ideal. What's more, a new and determined enemy led by Chin Peng and his communist forces were waiting for them.

They didn't even have a permanent base. The troops (including their families) were camped in tents, and the temporary bases had to be moved regularly as the regiments moved with the calls of duty. Initially, the 2nd Gurkhas were based in Singapore. One or two battalions at a time took turns moving to Hong Kong and back, and the remaining units were spread over various parts of Malaya. Sometimes, if the whole battalion was not required, one to three companies were deployed under the command of the leading battalion as detachments, and the total strength of the troops were adjusted according to the size and importance of the operations. In some cases, the Gurkhas were so in demand that even the recruits were sent out to guard vital points and sometimes without the experience of firing their weapons on a range. In that case, they were ordered to use either kukris or bayonets in case of an emergency.

In order to protect those British interests of the early 1950s in Southeast Asia (Malaya and Singapore, and Sarawak, Sabah and Brunei in Borneo), the first battle the Gurkhas had to fight was the 'Malayan Emergency'. It was a long, nasty and costly guerrilla war that lasted from 1948 until 1960. The battles were fought between the Commonwealth armed forces led by the British and the Malayan National Liberation Army (MNLA), the military arm of the Malayan Communist Party (MCP). The conflict was intentionally called the Malayan Emergency for insurance reasons; the British insurers Lloyd's wouldn't have covered the losses of rubber plantations and tin-mining industries if it had been termed a war. The Communists called it the 'Anti-British National Liberation War'.

It all started on 16 June 1948 at Elphil Estate, near Sungai Siput town, Perak, when three Chinese men killed three British plantation workers. It prompted the British to bring emergency measures into law, first in Perak on 18 June and then nationwide in July. Under the newly implemented rules, the MCP and other leftist parties were outlawed, and police were given the power to arrest them and their collaborators. The MCP, led by Chin Peng, went into hiding, formed the MNLA in January 1949, and waged a guerrilla war against the British from the safety of the thick jungles of Malaya.

Ironically, Chin Peng was a former British ally, who was not only trained by the British but also helped form a crack force known as the 'Malayan People's Anti-Japanese Army' during World War II, and he was even awarded an MBE (Member of the Most Excellent Order of the British Empire) for his contribution. His force was officially disbanded in December 1945, and there were economic incentives to return all of its weapons to the British. But almost 5,000 men rejected the British offer, went underground and came out fighting as the MNLA of MCP under Chin Peng.

The tactics used by the MNLA were guerrilla warfare: sabotaging installations, harassing rubber plantations and destroying government infrastructure and transportation. Their supporters were mainly from the ethnic Chinese communities, known as 'squatters', and the authorities had already started calling them 'communist terrorists' (CTs).

A well-known element of the Briggs Plan (named for General Sir Harold Briggs, the British Army's director of operations), was the forced relocation of some 500,000 rural Malayans, including 400,000 Chinese from the squatter communities, into guarded camps called 'new villages.' Initially, the British had 13 infantry battalions, including seven partly formed Gurkhas, three British battalions, two Royal Malay regiments, and a British Royal Artillery regiment. As those forces were not enough, the British brought in more soldiers from outside and deployed the Special Air Service (SAS) as a specialized reconnaissance, raiding and counter-insurgency unit.

After the assassination of Sir Henry Gurney (the British High Commissioner) on 6 October 1951, Sir Gerald Templer replaced him, and he was duly credited for turning the campaign in Britain's favour. It was under his supervision that the new policy known as the Hearts and Minds Campaign began, and the army provided medical and food aid to the Malays and other indigenous tribes while the guerrillas were driven deeper into the jungle and denied resources. The conflict was said to have involved a maximum of 40,000 British and other Commonwealth troops against about 8,000 communist guerrillas.

Describing the politics behind the campaign is beyond the scope of this book. The primary purpose of this book is to follow the Gurkhas, and I am just trying to briefly set the scene, so that readers can relate better to the Gurkha story.

Fighting an invisible enemy in the thick jungles of Malaya was not an easy job. But the Gurkhas, being not only brave, loyal and professional, but also adaptable and tenacious, read the situation well and learnt fast. The invaluable lessons learnt during World War II in the Burmese jungle came in handy and, slowly but firmly, they gained the upper hand over their elusive enemy. Operational successes followed. The Gurkhas were always on the move, clearing more ground, and chasing the enemy out. But the achievements started to happen when large-scale operations were abandoned in favour of small-sized operations, mostly involving a platoon or a section after a carefully planned reconnaissance was carried out. It was a testing time for the Brigade of Gurkhas. On the one hand, it was fighting a resilient enemy, and on the other, the brigade was trying to establish itself at the same time. Each Gurkha battalion of the Brigade of Gurkhas used to get two months' rest while spending the remainder of the year in the jungle.

Navigating the inhospitable jungles of Malaya was tough. On top of that, they had to carry rations, ammunition and equipment for a week or so and be ready for an encounter at any time. During the emergency, the

Gurkhas must have carried out hundreds of such successful operations but including all of them here is not possible.

In June 1953, a platoon of the 1/10th Gurkhas under Lieutenant (QGO) Dhojbir Limbu was sent out to investigate an ambush by a team of CTs at a rubber plantation, and the platoon kept following the enemy's tracks until the game of cat and mouse came to an end. By 8 July, the Gurkha platoon had used up their rations. The Gurkha officer had to do something before he lost the enemy's tracks, so he divided his platoon into two groups. Before long, his group found an enemy camp and they instantly attacked. Despite being under fire from the enemy's machine guns and grenades, the Gurkhas entered the field and killed two terrorists before the remainder fled. One of the dead terrorists had a price tag of $75,000 on his head, as he happened to be the political commissar of the MNLA.

Another notable incident was the 17 November 1955 killing of communist leader Goh Sia, who had a reward of $35,000 on his head. It was carried out by a team of six men from the 1/7th Gurkhas. After keeping a vigil for three days and nights under the hot sun and damp cold without cooking, Goh Sia suddenly appeared in front of them. A rifleman, with a swift and accurate shot, killed the communist leader to the relief of the locals.

Amid the fighting with the communist guerrillas, the Brigade of Gurkhas was also busy establishing new regiments and corps while preparing itself as a specialist and self-reliant force. The birth of the three most prominent regiments in the brigade: The Queen's Gurkha Engineers (QGE), the Queen's Gurkha Signals (QGS) and the Gurkha Transport Regiment (GTR) took place in the same period. The exploits, achievements and future of those newly formed regiments and corps will be explained in more detail in later chapters.

Another early success achieved by the Brigade was the complete eradication of the leading Chinese Pahang gang who had been responsible for the killing of two European railway officials at Kuala Krau, among other attacks. The leader of the group, Chin Nam, with a price tag of $10,000 on his head, was among the 15 killed and 30 wounded. The

1/6th Gurkhas led the operation and the B & C companies of the 1/10th Gurkhas were also involved.

It might sound insensitive, but it was like a normal day for the Brigade. Just as in a game of basketball, football or any other sport, each Gurkha battalion had a score chart hanging at a prominent place within the battalion where all could see it. It was not an ordinary score chart at all. No sir! It was a chart showing the numbers of bandits killed during the ongoing Malayan Emergency and somehow created competition within each battalion as well as within the Brigade itself. In defence of the hard-pressed soldiers, I would say that if you have to perform these duties almost on a daily basis, you tend to get used to them, and whatever effects they had before, for good or bad, won't apply any more.

The 1/10th Gurkhas killed another legendary terrorist leader, Manap Jepun, under 'Operation Habitual' in Kuantan. There must have been dozens of such operations carried out by each regiment. They had equal shares of good or bad days and played significant roles in defeating the enemy. As far as the Gurkhas were concerned, the Malayan Emergency ended in 1960 when the communist leader Chin Peng fled to Thailand. With the independence of Malaya on 31 August 1957, the insurgency lost its rationale too, and the Malayan government declared the end of the state of emergency on 31 July 1960.

The twelve years of fighting took a considerable toll on both military and civilian lives. Tens of thousands were killed, wounded, unaccounted for, or displaced. The Brigade of Gurkhas itself suffered 204 fatalities during the emergency. Graves honouring the fallen ones are built in places like Seremban, Tai Ping and Ipoh, and memorials are held every year. Your humble author had the honour of attending one such event at Ipoh on 10 June 2017. This is organized by the Warriors' Association Malaysia (WIRA) each year, and attended by various dignitaries from the involved nations.

After Malayan independence, Tungku Abdul Rahman, the then prime minister, proposed the formation of a Federation of Malaysia in 1961. It was to unite Malaya, Singapore and the three British territories in Borneo. This was initially accepted by all, but later both Brunei and Singapore dropped out. The new Federation of Malaysia was officially formed on 31 August 1963. The Sultan of Brunei had no interest in being part of a constitutional monarchy while Singapore opted out as their Chinese majority didn't fit well with the Muslim Malays. As a result, Singapore left the federation and became an independent nation on 9 August 1965.

Many historians and experts believe that had the Gurkhas not been on the ground in the dark days of the emergency, the communists would have won and Malaysia could have become a completely different country.

The shrinking British Empire in Southeast Asia would put the Brigade into forward gear again, and they would eventually end up in that backyard of China called Hong Kong. Before that, however, they still had one more fight to win, and Indonesia had already been working on that front. The Borneo Confrontation was about to begin, and troops from both sides were soon to lock horns in a lengthy and costly battle along the stretched and inhospitable borders on Borneo.

For the Brigade of Gurkhas, the 1950s were a time of trial and error, and the Brigade had to go through a long and painful process of growing up and learning along the way.

The Government of Malaysia introduced the 'Pingat Jasa Malaysia Medal' in 2005 and awarded it to British and Commonwealth veterans who served in the conflict in Malaya between August 1957 and August 1966. All the Gurkhas who served under the Brigade of Gurkhas during that period should be qualified for the medal, and they should make an inquiry to the Malaysian Government if they haven't yet received it through the Nepalese Embassy in Kuala Lumpur.

CHAPTER 13

THE HISTORY OF OTHER GURKHA REGIMENTS

'In Manikap in 1971, I fell into a trap while counter-attacking, and got battered by both enemy and friendly forces. Only four managed to get out. I got into a minefield again and lost a leg when one of the mines exploded. I even tried to finish myself off but gathered enough strength to nurse my wound and finally got out of the minefield by crawling while I bled. I felt dizzy and sleepy but kept on moving, crossed a river and was finally rescued by Indian troops. I cried for a month over my leg and finally came home with an artificial one. My only complaint is that I should have been given at least a bravery medal but I got nothing.'

Corporal Ram Bahadur Gharti/Chhetri (80), 3/9th GR, from Damauli, Tanahun, fought in the 1962 Sino-India War and the 1965 and 1971 Pakistan-India Wars.

In its early days in Malaya, the Brigade of Gurkhas was precariously under-strength and the two recruiting depots still in India were fully utilized. As they fought in the ongoing battle against the relentless communist guerrillas, the restructuring of the newly formed Brigade went into full swing, and many new regiments and corps were born as a result. In May 1948, both battalions of the 7th Gurkha Rifles were ordered to convert into an artillery role. They were tentatively called the '101 and 102 Field Regiments, Royal Artillery', and went through rigorous training as gunners. Thanks to the worsening emergency and representations from Field Marshal Slim, they were reverted to infantry battalions again in 1949.

The other regiments, corps or companies that were formed and some that were disbanded during that period of emergency were the following:

The Queen's Gurkha Engineers (QGE)

It was in September 1948 at Kluang, Malaya, that the first batch of Gurkhas was sent to the Corps of Royal Engineers to form a Gurkha Training Squadron there. In 1949 a single squadron of Gurkha engineers was created and called the '67th Field Squadron RE (Royal Engineers)'; the 68th Field Squadron RE was formed in 1950, and the RHQ (Regiment Head Quarter) of 50 Field Regiment RE followed in 1951. The newly formed regiment became a part of the Brigade of Gurkhas on 28 September 1955, and was titled the 'Gurkha Engineers'. It was only on 21 April 1977 that it received the Queen's title and it has been called the Queen's Gurkha Engineers (QGE) since then.

The first ever operation that the squadron undertook as Sappers was 'Operation Borrowdale' in the Lake District of Pahang in July 1949. It was mainly waterborne with the Sappers playing a prominent role ferrying stores and men among the waterways in power-operated boats. Then, they were deployed over a large part of Johore, mostly finding enemy camps and destroying them. By September 1950, both 67 and 68 squadrons moved to Hong Kong and were widely credited with building those blue metal bridges (known as Bailey bridges) on Hong Kong roads. The Gurkha Engineers played essential roles in assisting troops in both the Malayan Emergency and Borneo Confrontation and contributed a great deal.

After moving to Hong Kong in 1971, the regiment was permanently based at Perowne Barracks, near Tuen Mun in the New Territories, and worked in various locations in Hong Kong and overseas as required by their duties as army engineers. A new squadron called the '69 Gurkha Field Squadron' was formed in 1981 at Kitchener Barracks in the UK and was deployed in the Falklands War in 1982. After the Gurkha Brigade permanently moved to the UK, the 70 Gurkha Field Support Squadron was established in 2000. Both 69 and 70 squadrons are stationed at Invicta Park Barracks now, as part of 36 Engineer Regiment, and are the only two surviving squadrons of the whole regiment. They have served in Iraq, Kosovo, Afghanistan, Africa and other parts of the world as the Support Field Squadrons of the British Army. In October 2019 it was announced that 67 squadron would be reformed in 2021, and 68 squadron in 2023.

The Queen's Gurkha Signals (QGS)

The concept of the Gurkha Signals was born in 1948, but it was only on paper at that time, and was known to the Brigade headquarters in Kuala Lumpur as 'X' Brigade Signal Squadron. It was supposed to consist of British Other Ranks (BORs), Gurkha Other Ranks (GORs) from existing units, and recruits. After having set up a small group of instructors (eight BORs and seven GORs) and two establishments (one for Gurkha Signal Training Wing and another for Independent Brigade Signal Squadron), the first batch of potential signalmen was set to arrive by 1 January 1949. But due to the burden of the worsening Malayan Emergency, the battalions couldn't meet the target date, and it had to be postponed until 1 May 1950.

The unit was finally moved to 64 Reception Camp in Kuala Lumpur, and the training for the first batch started on 1 August 1950. Out of 110 men who attended the course, only eight were rejected. The second batch had 188 ex-soldiers from India and 22 ex-boys from the Boys Company, and their basic training was given by the training wing of the 6th Gurkha Rifles before they could go for the signal tradesmen's training. On 20 December 1950, they moved to Pahang and were known as the 48th Gurkha Brigade Signal Squadron with its training wing. By 1952, it was called the '17th Gurkha Divisional Signal Regiment/Royal Signals Gurkha', with three new squadrons and a training wing. By then, they were already operating like a well-established regiment.

By providing necessary communication services to the Brigade's fighting forces, the Gurkha Signals played a crucial role in both the Malayan Emergency and Borneo Confrontation and established itself as an integral part of the Brigade. Once they moved to Hong Kong, they were stationed at Shek Kong Camp, Gun Club Hill Barracks and the Prince of Wales Building at Tamar (the Army's old HQ) and worked in the fields of communication for both military and government purposes. The Queen's title was awarded to the regiment on 20 April 1977 and its official title has been the Queen's Gurkha Signals (QGS) since then.

After the withdrawal from Hong Kong, the regiment moved to the UK and has been based there ever since. It has three squadrons: the 246 Squadron based in York, the 248 Squadron in Stafford and the 250 Squadron and Regimental Headquarter (RHQ) at Gamecock Barracks, Bramcote. Besides, it has troops in Nepal and in Brunei as detachments, and the regiment has served in Iraq, Afghanistan, Belize, the Falklands, Europe and many parts of the world as a supporting force of the British Army.

The Gurkha Transport Regiment (GTR)

This regiment was initially raised in Singapore on 1 July 1958 as the Gurkha Army Service Corps (GASC), a part of the Brigade of Gurkhas, and it was mostly formed with a mixture of both British and Gurkha officers and other ranks from the existing units. It was fully formed by 1962 with Regimental Headquarters (RHQ) based in Malaysia and had four fully trained companies (they were called companies like infantry battalions before they became squadrons) serving in the UK, Malaya, Singapore and Hong Kong.

The new regiment took part in operations during the Brunei Revolt of 1962 and Borneo Confrontation as the supporting force and officially became the Gurkha Transport Regiment (GTR) in 1965. After moving to Hong Kong in 1971, it provided transport support to the Hong Kong Garrison and operated the Garrison's armoured personnel carriers (APCs). It was the only regiment from the Brigade of Gurkhas that served in both the Gulf wars (1991 and 2003) by offering ambulance services and later in Cyprus under the United Nations force. In recognition of its service, the regiment was given the official title of the Queen's Own Gurkha Transport Regiment (QOGTR) in 1992.

After the regiment moved to the UK, it was redesignated the '10 Queen's Own Gurkha Logistic Regiment' (10 QOGLR) and has been stationed at Gale Barracks, Aldershot, ever since. The regiment has served in Iraq, Afghanistan, the Balkans, Sierra Leone, Kosovo, and other parts of the world in its long and distinguished career.

The Gurkha Independent Parachute Company

During World War II, two wartime parachute battalions were raised under General Slim, and deployed in the ongoing war in Burma. The 153rd Gurkha Parachute Battalion was formed in Delhi in October 1941 with volunteers from other Gurkha battalions and was part of the newly created 50th Indian Parachute Brigade. The 154th Gurkha Parachute Battalion was formed from the 3/7th Gurkha Rifles in August 1943 and served under the 50th Indian Parachute Brigade as well. It played a critical role in the battle of Sangshak between 19-24 March 1944 when the whole Parachute Brigade was overrun but managed to blunt the Japanese offensive against Imphal and Kohima. When the battalions returned from Burma after the war, only 300 out of 700 men survived, and both Gurkha parachute battalions were disbanded after World War II.

The idea was rekindled again in Malaya, and the Gurkha Independent Parachute Company was born on 1 January 1963 as part of the Brigade of Gurkhas. It is said to have had 128 men initially, volunteers from all eight existing battalions and corps of the Brigade, and their original role was to seize airfields for the Brigade forces during operations.

During the operations of the Borneo Confrontation, they were mostly divided into small groups and deployed in many places and roles. These included training and commanding the border scouts, acting as the fire brigade, operating in the position of Special Air Services (SAS), guarding and patrolling the Indonesian border and taking part in many cross-border operations.

After the end of the Borneo Confrontation in 1966, it was officially associated with the British Parachute Regiment and allowed to wear the maroon beret and badge of the regiment. It reverted to the organization of a conventional rifle company and acted as a demonstration company in 1968. When the Brigade of Gurkhas left Malaysia and Singapore and moved to Hong Kong in 1971, no role for an airborne unit existed, and the Gurkha Independent Parachute Company was disbanded.

The Gurkha Military Police

The Gurkha Military Police started as the '17 Gurkha Division Provost Company' on 1 June 1950 and originally consisted of six sections (four BORs and two GORs on each section) in Kuala Lumpur. It had a shaky start but gradually steadied itself despite the sceptical views of those who were in doubt of its capabilities.

In traffic control, the Gurkhas were an immense success. Their traffic signals were given with regimental precision with inborn patience, and they gained respect from both civil and military drivers. Both BORs and GORs patrolled the streets of Malaya together. The Gurkhas' bilingual skills in Malay and Indian tongues proved invaluable and established authority. The secret of success was said to be the trust, respect and comradeship between the BORs and GORs and being able to act as a team.

It was renamed the 'Gurkha Military Police' by 1957 and was disbanded by 1970, just before the Brigade of Gurkhas moved to Hong Kong.

The 5th Gurkha Dog Company

The 5th Gurkha Dog Company was established in January 1963 as part of the Gurkha Military Police and subsequently disbanded in September 1964.

The Boys Company

We need to throw light on the distinction between the 'Line Boys' and the 'Boys' to avoid any confusion. The Line Boys were the sons of serving Gurkha officers, and the Boys were boy soldiers serving in the 'Boys Company' of the Brigade of Gurkhas, who were mostly Line Boys.

Back in India, the young sons of serving Gurkha officers and soldiers used to follow their fathers and helped assist in carrying water, rations and ammunition during operations. It was such a common practice that they even followed their old men during wars and helped reload rifles and carried extra ammunition. Out of the 25 men who received the Order of Merit during the siege of Hindu Rao's house, in Delhi in 1857, 12 were Line Boys, while of the seven who were awarded the same Order of Merit at Aliwal in the 1st Sikh War, five were Line Boys again. In brief, all the Boy Soldiers were Line Boys but not all the Line Boys were Boys.

The Boys Company of the Brigade of Gurkhas was established in Sungei Patani, Kedah, Malaya, in early 1949 and stationed at Sungai Laya. The severely depleted and under-strength Brigade was in urgent need of new blood, and the formation of the Boys Company was one of the many new measures taken by the Brigade to solve that issue. Its main objectives were to produce tradesmen for the newly formed regiments of Engineers, Signals and Mechanicals while the others were to serve as clerks, technicians and education instructors within the Brigade. Most importantly, it was to produce good and educated future leaders for the Brigade, including Sandhurst commissioned officers (all commissioned officers of the British Army are trained at Sandhurst Military Academy). Those with strong family ties were earmarked for joining the infantry regiments on the completion of the recruit training courses.

The first batch of 1949 had 140 boys, aged 14-15, and the same numbers of boys were to come to the Company annually. The training was for three years, and by the first passing-out parade, the Company had 420 boys. In November 1949, a total of 82 boys attended the passing-out ceremony and half of them went to the infantry regiments while the other half went to the Engineers and the Signals in equal numbers. None of the boys completed the three-year-long training because they were already too old to be kept on as boys and were well up to the standards of the average recruit in both physique and education.

In addition to basic military training and education, the Boys platoons were mostly involved in sports, and competition was fierce. For administration and competition purposes, they were named after regimental battle honours such as Delhi, Cassino, Gurkha Bluff, Mogaung, Imphal, Tavoleto, Myitkyina and Shargat, and mostly competed in basketball, football and boxing. Later on, they even participated in the Nepal Cup, the inter-battalions football competition within the Brigade. The Boys managed to defeat a team or two.

By the late 1960s, more educated recruits to fill those specialist posts were already available back in Nepal, and the Boys Company had somehow become irrelevant. As a result, the Boys Company was closed in 1968, although the last few batches of boy soldiers were still recruited. Unlike those previous batches, they neither stayed at the army camp nor received any formal army training. Instead, they were sent back to school and allowed to join the army once they finished.

The potential boy soldiers had to go through various tests, especially in both written and oral English and maths, followed by interviews. Once they passed the tests, army numbers were issued, and the boys were sent back to the army schools to finish their studies. Major (Retd) Lalit Chandra Dewan MBE, who joined the Boys Company at sixteen, in 1969, was one of them. After the selection, he went back to St. John's School in Singapore (which was the most prominent secondary school of the British Army at the time) and then moved to Hong Kong in 1971 when the Brigade left Malaysia and Singapore. Upon completion of his studies at St. George's School at Kowloon Tong, he joined the 6th Gurkha Rifles as Rifleman in 1973, and he eventually retired in 2000 at the rank of Major, after a distinguished military career of 32 years (including boy service).

Just like Major Dewan, many boy soldiers succeeded in their army careers and became highly decorated officers within the Brigade. All of the Sandhurst-trained commissioned officers of Gurkha origin were boy soldiers and some of them even commanded a Gurkha battalion. Despite its brief existence, the Boys Company was very successful, and its effects were felt within the Brigade of Gurkhas for a long time. Yesterday's boy soldiers had become today's leaders of the Brigade and succeeded in leading their men by example.

CHAPTER 14

THE GURKHAS IN SINGAPORE

'When I finished my basic training, WWII was over. We went to Ladakh in 1962, but the war ended again before we saw any action. We were among the counter-attacking forces in Thamjodiya in the 1965 Pakistan war, but a Garhwal battalion was already occupying the enemy position, and friendly fire killed some of our men. In many cases, I am fortunate to be able to share my story with you.'

Hon. Capt. (Retd) Himan Singh Gurung (91), 3/4th GR, from Damauli, Tanahun, joined the army in 1944 and retired in 1972. He participated in both the 1965 and 1971 Pakistan-India wars.

Singapore had been one of the colonies of the British since they had landed there on 29 January 1819, led by Sir Stamford Raffles, who turned it into a port ready for trade by 1820. Singapore was the primary defensive base for the British in Asia during World War II. The British decided to fight the Japanese aggression from there with a false assumption. They were not only convinced that the base was impenetrable but also genuinely believed in defeating the Japanese from there. But under the assault of the Japanese, the Allied forces crumbled, and Singapore fell on 15 February 1942. It was one of the most significant surrenders in British history. Almost 80,000 Allied troops were taken as prisoners; amongst them were two Gurkha battalions, and many of them never returned home.

After the partition of the Indian Gurkha Brigade in 1947, four Gurkha regiments followed the British side and moved to Malaya and Singapore. One Gurkha regiment among the four, the 2nd Gurkha Rifles, was stationed at Slim Barracks, Portsdown Road, Singapore, and they remained there until 1971. They were replaced by the 5th Singapore Infantry Regiment (5 SIR), following which they finally moved to Hong Kong.

When the Sikh Contingent, based in Singapore, reverted to the Indian Army after India's independence in 1947, the Gurkha Contingent (GC) was formed on 9 April 1949 with just 149 men. Initially, it had two British officers, five Gurkha officers, and the usual proportions of NCOs and men to make up a company of four platoons. The Gurkha officers, as well as men, had to have previous military experience and initially the force was to be split: two-thirds Magar and Gurung, and one third Limbu and Rai. The formation of the GC was completed in May of 1949, and the first batch of 40 new families and assortments of children came with them as well.

It was initially based at Duxton Plain, guarded vital installations such as the Istana (the residence of the Governor, and later the President of Singapore) and prisons, and mostly functioned as a riot squad. Despite its humble beginnings, the GC was to play significant roles in keeping the peace and stability of Singapore and established itself as one of the irreplaceable institutions of the city-state. During those tumultuous periods of racial violence, the GC played a crucial role in safeguarding Singapore's interests. The GC as a neutral force turned out to be an asset that the nation couldn't do without.

The first task the GC was given was to send two platoons over to Johore in 1950. They were to assist the police there in their campaign against the communists in the jungle. The GC remained there until April of 1950, and during those operations, the Sergeant Major of the GC was killed in an ambush, and a PC (police constable) severely injured and paralysed when a falling tree hit him.

According to Singaporean authors Zakaria Zainal and Chong Zi Liang, the GC was deployed again during the case of young Maria Hertogh in 1950. After she had been raised as a Muslim for eight years, the court ruled to give the custody of young Maria to her biological Dutch Catholic parents, and rioting broke out between the Malay and European community. In 1955, the GC was dispatched again to neutralize the rioting caused by Hock Lee Bus workers demanding higher wages and better working conditions. The rioting was infiltrated by the pro-communist element within the union which exploited the dispute to force a confrontation with the government. The next call of duty brought the GC to the premises of Singapore Chinese Middle School in 1956. The Students' Union had staged a sit-in and camped at several schools, and the GC was called in to disperse them.

The GC was also a part of the Brigade committed to the Borneo Confrontation of 1962-1966: guerrilla warfare perpetrated by Indonesia in response to the proposed merger of the Federation of Malaya with Singapore, Sabah and Sarawak, and both sides were involved in deadly skirmishes along the border.

When 20,000 Muslims were celebrating the birthday of Prophet Mohammad at Pedang in 1964, major rioting broke out between the Muslims and the Chinese, and the GC with military reinforcements were sent again to maintain the peace.

The period of 1970-1990 was rather peaceful, with no major riots occurring, and the GC was mostly involved in guarding key installations, escorting VIPs and training local officers.

In the wake of 9/11, the GC was involved in Singapore's overseas security and humanitarian missions in East Timor, training recruits from the police academy and helping to complement the police force by guarding key installations throughout Singapore. In 2003, a team of 30 men from the GC was deployed in Iraq, and they trained about 1,500 Iraqi instructors and police officers for the next three months.

The GC was part of a massive search party of 700 police and military personnel in 2004. They were after three armed fugitives from a Pulau Tekong robbery and the GC apprehended two of the trio of armed robbers. In a similar case in 2008, the GC was deployed in a massive search for detained Jemmah Islamiyah leader Mas Selamat Kastari who had escaped from the Whitley Road Detention Centre. The next operation in which the GC participated was at the Little India Riot, when hundreds of South Asian workers went on a rampage killing one person, injuring 39 and burning an ambulance and two police cars.

The GC is one of the few Gurkha institutions that still exist outside the UK, and its commander and deputy commander are both British ex-Gurkha offficers. The current number of the GC is said to stand at around 2,000 active personnel. They serve as a particular unit under the flag of the Singapore Police Force and provide specialized training to elite police officers as well as military personnel. The new recruitment of the GC is still arranged through the British Army recruiting centres in Nepal, and they enlist around 35-80 men a year.

The GC consists of nine Gurkha Guards companies based at Mount Vernon Camp, including their families, and they mostly stay away from the public. As in many places where the Gurkhas were deployed, members of the GC are not entitled to take citizenship in Singapore, and they all have to return to Nepal upon the completion of their services. The children of the senior officers are allowed to study but not work, and they also have to leave Singapore before their 21st birthday. The GC are also not allowed to marry locals while they are still in service. As a result, the opportunities for a civilian Gurkha community to flourish in

Singapore are minimal. A small Nepali population of around 500 families (mostly students, businesspeople and skilled workers from surrounding nations like Malaysia, Thailand, Myanmar and Nepal) is currently living in Singapore, and they are said to have no connections with the GC.

The Gurkhas who have died fighting various enemies during World War II, the Malayan Emergency and the Borneo Confrontation are buried and commemorated at the Singapore Kranji War Cemetery located at 9 Woodlands Road, Kranji. The headstones for the fallen Gurkhas can be found on the right-hand slope from the topmost hill of the cemetery and that particular area is known as the Gurkha Garden. During the process of researching this book, your humble author was able to visit the place and spent the morning there remembering those fallen heroes.

CHAPTER 15

THE GURKHAS IN BRUNEI AND THE BORNEO CONFRONTATION

'Baacheta yai baato aunla mareta baluwa siraani! ('If I survive, I will return by the same way home; if I die, I will have the sands as my pillow.') We sang the regimental song, walked many days and nights without food, and ate cooked leather boots out of desperate hunger.'

Rifleman Megh Bahadur Khatri (100), 1/9th GR, from Pangtaar, Myagdi, fought in Europe, Iran and Iraq during WWII. As he cannot hear or speak any more and sleeps in the day and walks at night, his son narrated his story.

Indonesian president Sukarno was a powerful man. By the early 1960s, his dream of creating a powerful confederation of Malaysia, the Philippines and Indonesia called 'Maphilindo' gained momentum. It was an economic and political union between nations and was to include Sabah, Sarawak and Brunei as well. Indonesia, as the most significant country in land and population, would become the dominant partner of the federation. He also thought that Kalimantan (the Indonesian name for Borneo) rightfully belonged to Indonesia, and he was determined to recover the northern parts of the island which it didn't control. However, the British stood in the way, and he had to remove that thorn if he was to make his dream a reality.

Besides, those nations which were to form 'Maphilindo' were sovereign and independent in their own right. Even worse, some were still either British colonies or under British protection. The real battle was to take place on Borneo where the borders of the feuding sides met. Given their similar ethnicity to the Indonesians, President Sukarno felt confident that the Northern Borneo peoples would take his side, and he already had an ally in the Chinese there who were mostly communists, known to the British as the Chinese Clandestine Organization (CCO). The Indonesian agents had already infiltrated those areas, and they became active in acts of subversion.

There was a group of pro-Indonesian activists in Brunei led by Sheikh Azahari, who had been an Indonesian freedom fighter against the Dutch. The military arm of the rebels had a commander named Yassin Affendi. He started recruiting, arming and training a secret army around Brunei town and the nearby areas. They called themselves 'Tentora National Kalimantan Utara' (TNKU) or the 'North Kalimantan National Army' and plotted a rebellion against Brunei's sultan. The people of the oil-rich Sultanate of Brunei were widely impressed by the possibility of a Borneo Confederation. Their sultan, Sir Muda Omar Ali Saifuddien, would lead the new confederation.

To meet the newly found aspirations of the public, and pressure from the British and the Malaysian government, Brunei held its first-ever elections for the Legislative Council, and all sixteen seats were won by the new 'Partai Raayatt' (People's Party) led by Azahari. Sir Omar cleverly appointed another seventeen members from his support base and maintained overall control over the council. His provocative action created unprecedented anger among the public, and thus the TNKU was spurred to take action.

The Brunei revolt came on the night of 7-8 December 1962 with three main objectives. First, the TNKU were to seize the sultan and declare him head of the Borneo Confederation. Second, they wanted to capture as many weapons and ammunition as possible by seizing the main police stations. Finally, they wanted to take control of the oilfields in Seria and seize as many European hostages and equipment as possible so they could be used later on as bargaining tools with the British. The rebels succeeded in all three of the plans. But according to experts, they overlooked two things that eventually failed them. They forgot to inform their allies beforehand and left the airfields unattended.

According to author E.D. Smith, British reinforcements were quickly dispatched from Singapore over the next three days. They were deployed by air and sea, and two companies of the 1/2nd Gurkhas were the first to arrive. The rebels were confronted on four fronts: at the Shell depot of Miri by the 1st Royal Greenjackets, at Limbang by the 42nd commando Royal Marine, at Seria by the Queen's Highlanders, and on the coastal road of Seria by the 1/2nd Gurkha Rifles. In just eight days, the under-trained and under-armed rebels were thoroughly defeated although the clearing up took longer. Sheikh Azahari fled to Manila and the 1/2nd Gurkhas suffered two dead and almost a dozen wounded. The privilege of rescuing the sultan from the rebels fell to the 1/2nd Gurkhas, and the relieved sultan remained grateful to the Gurkhas for the rest of his life.

To escape retribution from the authorities, the TNKU split up into small groups and hid. Affendi, the commander, had a price of $15,000 on his head, and the search continued until he was finally captured on 18 May 1963 when his team of four men met a tough Gurkha rifleman called Naina Bahadur Rai, B Company of the 2/7th Gurkhas. The brave rifleman single-handedly killed two rebels and captured the remaining two, including Affendi, and he was awarded a Military Medal for his bravery. With this last action, the final remnants of the rebels were wiped out, and the Brunei revolt came to an end.

When the Federation of Malaysia – which combined Malaya, Singapore, Brunei and the British territories of Sabah and Sarawak in northern Borneo – was formed in 1963, Sukarno's dream of 'Maphilindo' vanished once and for all. Singapore and Brunei dropped out of the federation later. But Sukarno wasn't prepared to forget so quickly and initiated army-sponsored guerrilla warfare in Borneo. The first shot of the Borneo Confrontation was fired by the Indonesian side on 20 January 1963. A group of armed men crossed the border from the Indonesian part of Borneo into British-protected territories, and their mission was to destabilize the communities there.

By now the British had restored stability in Borneo and deterrence was established along the 1,000-mile border by bringing in more troops. The irregular Border Scouts were raised, SAS, Parachute and our very own Gurkha Parachute Company were brought in, and further reinforcement of Gurkha and British units were deployed. General W. Walker, as the Joint Force Commander, had established his headquarters on Labuan Island where a transit airfield was already in use, and controlled the whole operation from there. The Indonesians were said to have around 20,000 men deployed along the border while General Walker had to begin with just a single brigade composed of three battalions and fifteen helicopters in support.

The tactics applied by the Indonesians during the operation were straightforward. A group of soldiers (around 20-60) would carry out raids across the border and try to infiltrate and influence the communities living in the surrounding areas. Several varieties of tribesmen lived there. Initially, those tribesmen were wary of both sides and weren't helpful to the British. However, that was all to change after the incident at Long Jawai, Sarawak, in September 1963. It was a British forward post manned by four Gurkhas from the 1/2nd Gurkha Rifles, two from the local Police Field Force (PFF), and supported by 21 local border scouts and militiamen.

According to *The Gurkhas* by John Parker and *Valour: A History of the Gurkhas* by E.D. Smith, as the villagers were not helpful to the Gurkhas, the post had to be built in a school hut which was far from ideal. Unknown to the Gurkhas, they were not the only visitors there, and a full-scale raiding party of the Indonesian force was already in the village. A border scout returning from an errand to his home spotted them and informed the Gurkhas. Corporal Tej Bahadur Gurung grabbed a case of grenades and returned to the hill position, while his colleagues desperately tried to send a signal to headquarters, which was 70 miles away. Before too long, the school hut came under automatic and 60mm mortar fire, killing one Gurkha and one PFF, and the remaining troopers had a lucky escape.

The Gurkhas kept on firing from the hilltop for several hours. Most of the border scouts had already slipped away by now, and Tej Bahadur had just four men to call on. Outnumbered and outgunned, and with the enemy getting bolder, he had no option but to retreat. The nearest scout post was at Long Linau. With meagre rations and over steep terrain, they arrived there a few days later and were relieved to find that a border scout had already made it there before them and raised the alarm. Then, the weary team marched on to headquarters to give a full report on the attack. Tej Bahadur was awarded the Military Medal for his determination and wise leadership. Meanwhile, the Indonesians had plundered Long Jawai before moving to a new camp where they mercilessly killed the ten captive border scouts they had with them.

The indigenous people who lived in the border areas were the most affected. They were already aware of the acts of extreme intimidation used by the Indonesians, and the brutal killing of the border scouts at Long Jawai turned the tribesmen against them. It was the turning point of the whole operation. Information provided by the tribesmen on the raiding Indonesian troops was invaluable, and the results gradually started turning in Britain's favour.

The Borneo confrontation was like a game of cat and mouse, with the British side mostly applying defensive tactics. As the enemy remained invisible under the thick canopy of Borneo's jungle, fighting would only break out when either side crossed each other's path, often in the form of an ambush, which the well-disciplined Gurkhas were good at.

After fighting the gruelling war against the Japanese in Burma and the communist bandits in Malaysia, the Gurkhas had become experts in jungle warfare, and their prior experiences would become invaluable in Borneo. In addition to their adaptability, professionalism and attention to small details, the Gurkhas are also quick learners, and unlike their British counterparts, they were adept at language. Their knowledge of the local language made communication a lot easier, and it helped significantly in extracting valuable information from the locals.

The Gurkha units were deployed to the front line for a six-month tour. Their main tasks were handling the observation posts, patrolling and executing reconnaissance, communicating with the locals, searching for enemy raiders, setting up ambushes, collecting information and so on. The weary British had no intention (or budget) to escalate the operation and merely played a defensive role. Despite a lack of results, incursions by the Indonesian forces continued in Borneo, and the frustrated president Sukarno decided to raise the stakes. In 1964, he gave clearance for Indonesian regular units to be used openly for the cause and made the blunder of attacking the Malay Peninsula in the hope of reviving the communist movements there.

On 17 August 1964, a group of more than 100 Indonesian marines and paratroopers landed in Johore. They didn't receive the rapturous welcome from the locals as they had expected and instead were rounded up very quickly. Another team of nearly 200 paratroopers flew in with four aircraft. They were to drop at Labis, about a hundred miles north of Singapore and a former communist stronghold, and were hit by a severe storm on the way. Only two out of four aircraft managed to reach Labis, and the scattered paratroopers were rounded up by the Gurkhas as they landed.

A million copies of a statement by the captured Indonesian commander Sukitno were dropped over Indonesian territory by the RAF, and it warned the Indonesians that Malaysia wouldn't greet them as liberators. It also forced the British side to take offensive action. The Allied forces of Britain, Malaysia, Australia and New Zealand were called in, and the Gurkhas were as usual at the forefront. 'Operation Claret' was launched, and General Walker was given permission for counter-incursions, and allowed to operate and strike targets up to 5,000 yards within enemy territory. They were to target mostly Indonesian bases and supply routes and in the height of the confrontation in 1965, the British units were striking much deeper, sometimes up to 20,000 yards. Under many such operations, 'Operation Kingdom Come', for instance, the 2/2nd Gurkhas were involved and executed a series of ambushes at the Sentimo river within the enemy area.

In a similar operation, Capt. (QGO) Damar Bahadur Gurung of D Company, the 1/6th Gurkhas, won an MC for killing five and wounding four enemies. Corporal Bir Bahadur Gurung of the 1/2nd Gurkhas won an MM for saving the whole operation by exposing himself to the enemy machine gun before pinpointing the enemy position and eventually blowing them up.

All eight Gurkha infantry battalions were heavily involved in the operations, including the newly formed Gurkha Corps elements of Engineers, Signals, Transport and Paratroopers. By 1965, the Allied forces had around 18,000 men involved in the operation, and the Gurkhas still had a few more battles to be fought before the Borneo Confrontation would come to an end.

On 21 November 1965, C Company of the 2/10th Gurkhas, backed up by its reconnaissance and Assault Pioneer platoons, was sent out to neutralize the enemy presence in the Bau area. The entrenched enemy of around 30 men was found on top of the hill. As they prepared for the assault, the enemy spotted the Gurkhas and started firing. When the left assaulting platoon was held up by the enemy machine gun, Lance Corporal Ram Bahadur Limbu, supported by his two-person LMG gun team, charged forward and silenced the enemy with a grenade. As they charged forward, clearing more enemies, his two gunmen got hit by enemy fire, and after killing the adversaries, he returned to help his fallen comrades. While under heavy fire, he carried his two wounded friends one by one to a relatively safe area and went out again for the third time to retrieve the discarded LMG. The Gurkhas eventually destroyed the enemy at the hilltop. The fighting lasted about an hour and a half. The two men rescued by Ram Bahadur eventually died. The unit lost three men, while one was severely wounded in that battle, later known as the

'Battle of Bau'. The enemy lost 24. For their gallantry, Capt. K. Maunsell and Lt (QGO) Ranjit Rai both received the Military Cross, while Lance Corporal Ram Bahadur Limbu was awarded the Victoria Cross.

After a long and distinguished army career, Ram Bahadur Limbu retired as Capt. (GCO) in 1985 and served another seven years in the Gurkha Reserve Unit (GRU) in Brunei. He was the first Gurkha to receive the VC after WWII, and also the only surviving Gurkha recipient. He now lives in Kathmandu, back in Nepal. I had the privilege of meeting him at his residence in Kathmandu with our team in 2018. We had a brief conversation that made him recount his war experiences again, as he must have done many times before. Despite his age, and yet to nobody's surprise, he still had the same vigour, excitement and zeal.

The Borneo Confrontation was soon to end but there is still one more story to be told here, and it is known as the 'Sumbi Saga' throughout the Gurkha Brigade.

Sumbi was a communist guerrilla and jungle warfare expert, ironically trained by none other than the British, and he was said to have trained a substantial number of men on a daily basis. The British had to take this thorn out of their side, and he was listed as the number one on their 'Most Wanted List'. No points for guessing – the job of hunting him down went to the Gurkhas, and it was the 1/7th Gurkha Rifles that eventually apprehended him. More interestingly, it was a piece of tinfoil and a half-folded leaf that undid him.

According to *Gurkha Tales* by J.P. Cross, the story goes something like this. An ever-alert, disciplined and attentive-to-every-detail Gurkha found a shred of tinfoil and a half-folded leaf on the floor of Borneo's jungle. It was covered with piles of dead leaves. How he saw it, only God knows. The troops were alerted to the new finding. They followed the lead and the notorious terrorist leader was finally captured.

But the story doesn't end there either. According to *The Gurkhas* by John Parker, Sumbi was a tough nut to crack. He didn't say a word during interrogation, and the Gurkhas were called again as a last resort. A Gurkha officer, intelligent and fluent in the local language, was sent to the cell where Sumbi was kept, carrying a bottle of rum. His mission was to get Sumbi drunk, and by the wee hours of the next morning, the job was done. Sumbi had broken down and told everything. The British officer in charge of the case was awarded the MC.

President Sukarno's costly movement only benefited the communists in Indonesia. The communists even fought the Indonesian army and rioting broke out. Before it was too late, President Sukarno was pushed out of power and replaced by General Suharto. With a new establishment in Indonesia, hostilities ended and the Borneo Confrontation was officially ended on 11 August 1966 when a formal peace treaty between the involved nations was signed.

The total number of casualties suffered during the Confrontation by the Allied forces was 114 deaths and 181 wounded soldiers. The Brigade of Gurkhas won 29 Military Crosses (MC), four Distinguished Conduct Medals (DCM) and 31 Military Medals (MM), lost 43 men and 84 were injured. The only Victoria Cross (VC), as already described, won by the Gurkhas was awarded to Lance Corporal Ram Bahadur Limbu of the 2/10th Gurkhas in the Battle of Bau. With the end of the Borneo Confrontation, most of the major hostilities in Asia ended as well, and the Brigade of Gurkhas was to be hit by another kind of shock.

Once the Malayan Emergency and Borneo Confrontation were concluded, the Brigade of Gurkhas faced a dilemma of significant and painful redundancy, and the numbers of the Brigade were to be cut by half. Furthermore, the time for the Brigade to remain in Southeast Asia was also running out as a strong current of independence fever had swept over the lands.

The final axe came down in 1968. Each regiment was to retain only one battalion out of two, and half of the Gurkhas from the whole Brigade were sent home. Most of the newly formed corps didn't survive, except for QGE, QGS and GTR, and the final rundown was completed by 1970 before the Brigade moved to Hong Kong.

By then, all of the Gurkha regiments (6th, 7th and 10th) had one battalion each except the 2nd Gurkha which still had two battalions – the 1/2nd and 2/2nd. The ever-grateful Sultan of Brunei saved the 2nd battalion of the 2nd Gurkhas as a gift for saving his nation during the Brunei Revolt of 1962. One Gurkha infantry battalion, including some detachments from the QGE, QGS and GTR, were to be stationed in

Brunei as a defensive force. The remaining five infantry battalions have taken turns in defending Brunei since then. The duration of stay for each battalion was two years, based at Tuker Lines, Seria. All the costs of the retaining battalion were paid by the Brunei government, and not much has changed since then.

By the early 1970s, the government of Brunei faced important security issues from prison breaks and escaped prisoners, and desperately needed some trusted security guards. Needless to say, as far as trust and loyalty were concerned, the Gurkhas were always at the forefront, and the Gurkha Contingent was formed by enlisting large numbers of recently retired or laid-off Gurkhas from Hong Kong and Singapore. Although Gurkhas were already working in the 'Brunei Security Guards' before, their numbers were insignificant. On 25 February 1974, Mohansing Gurung, as Security Guard No. 15, became the first Gurkha to serve in the newly formed force and subsequently many thousands followed him.

Initially, the Gurkhas worked together with the Royal Brunei Malay Regiment and the Royal Brunei Police. Their main tasks were to maintain the security of essential buildings and installations of both governmental and private sectors. After being officially renamed the Gurkha Reserve Unit (GRU) in 1980, it has worked independently and provided security in various parts of the nation as a regular force. Ensuring the security of the royal family and the royal palaces is the GRU's main job, and it has never failed at this task.

At its peak, the GRU had more than 2,300 Gurkhas serving in two battalions. In the late eighties and nineties, applying to the GRU was the highest priority for all Gurkha retirees from Hong Kong. Stories of Gurkha officers carrying briefcases full of money on behalf of the Brunei sultan were everywhere, and the pay was good as well.

However, in 2009, the Gurkhas won a landmark victory giving them right of abode in the UK, and they have started to settle there since then. As a result, the GRU has become less attractive, and its numbers have dwindled. Besides, more opportunities for Gurkhas opened up in various other countries, including the Gulf nations. There are still Gurkhas currently serving in the GRU, but their number is less than 300, and they are mostly from the Indian Army ex-Gurkhas.

CHAPTER 16

THE GURKHAS IN HONG KONG

'It took us 29 days and 29 nights at sea to reach Japan. As a peacekeeping force, we mostly did ceremonial and guarding duties, and stayed two months in Hiroshima, two months in Ogaya, and three months in Tokyo before returning to India.'

Rifleman Prem Bahadur Gurung (92), 2/5th GR, from Phedikhola, Syangja, joined the army in 1942 as a boy, went to Japan and participated in the Hyderabad Campaign in India, and left the military in 1951. He later joined the Nepal Army and retired with a pension.

Hong Kong is a tiny administrative region of China. It is situated at the southern tip of Guangdong Province, at the estuary of the Pearl River Delta, and had a population in 2019 of 7.3 million. It geographically consists of three main parts: Hong Kong Island, Kowloon Peninsula and the New Territories. It is not only one of the top financial centres of the world, but also a shopping paradise and considered one of the wealthiest cities on earth. It mostly offers service industries for business and tourism; takes pride in being the main gateway to Greater China; and became the Hong Kong Special Administrative Region (HKSAR) of the People's Republic of China (PRC) on 1 July 1997. Along with Macau, Hong Kong is a part of China ruled under a unique political arrangement called 'One Country Two Systems' and is run as a slightly autonomous region with its own administration, currency, banking system, police force, disciplinary services and borders. It is renowned for its array of glittering skyscrapers as well as being one of the freest economies of the world.

Hong Kong was previously a collection of farming and fishing villages, and the British used it as a military base during the First Opium War of 1839-1842. After the British had defeated the Chinese during that war and signed the treaty of Nanking, Hong Kong Island was ceded in perpetuity to the British on 29 August 1842, and the similar cession of Kowloon Peninsula was completed under the Peking convention on 18 October 1860. The New Territories were leased on 1 July 1898 for 99 years, and Hong Kong reverted to China on 1 July 1997 after it became clear that it was not practically possible for the remainder of Hong Kong to function without the New Territories.

After India's independence in 1947, the Brigade of Gurkhas moved to Malaya and Singapore, and as we know by now, four Gurkha regiments followed them. Although the main base of the Brigade of Gurkhas was in Malaysia during this period, the British had gathered a substantial number of forces in Hong Kong. The reason for this was the raging Korean War of 1950-1953. The British were wary that the war would spill over into its colony and took necessary precautions before it was too late.

Before World War II, only the British regular forces, as well as two native Indian regiments, were deployed in Hong Kong, and no Gurkha regiments were ever sent there. What's more, the Gurkhas were busy and bogged down in both the Malayan Emergency and the Borneo Confrontation until the mid-1960s. The only respite the Gurkhas had during those never-ending fighting years was the two years' tour to Hong Kong. The first Gurkha battalion to be posted to Hong Kong was the 2/10th Gurkha Rifles on 17 March 1948. It returned in 1950.

According to veterans we met during our Nepal visit in 2018, some of the Gurkha battalions were sent to Hong Kong for a week or two on a leisure trip right after the end of WWII in 1945. They boarded the ship with their families that took 18 days and nights to reach Hong Kong and visited the principal markets of the city as they tried to unwind from the stress and fatigue of the war.

Although the Hong Kong tour for each battalion was set for two years, and one battalion was supposed to be stationed in Hong Kong at a time, the records I have found in the regimental logbooks show some irregularities, and sometimes there were even four battalions in Hong Kong all at the same time.

The 2/6th Gurkhas came in January 1949 and left in 1950. In addition to the infantry battalion, the newly formed 67 Gurkha Field Squadron of Royal Engineers (RE) was also moved to Hong Kong by September 1950 and helped in the construction of governmental and military installations. No records of infantry battalions being stationed in Hong Kong from 1950 to 1953 were found, and the 2/2nd Gurkhas moved into Hong Kong only in September 1953 and left in March 1956. The 2/7th Gurkhas arrived on November 1954 and left in March 1957. The 1/10th Gurkhas were in Hong Kong for only a year, from March 1956 to March 1957, while the 1/6th Gurkhas stayed from April 1957 to September 1959. The 2/10th Gurkhas came in 1960 and left in 1962, followed by the 2/2nd Gurkhas in 1963. The 1/2nd Gurkhas replaced them in 1965. It was in the tumultuous period of civil disobedience and riots in 1967-68 that four Gurkha battalions were deployed (1/7th and 1/10th were in action, 1/6th was in reserve and 2/7th was brought in from Malaysia).

After the 2/10th Gurkhas arrived in Hong Kong in 1948, they were initially stationed at Whitfield Barracks (today's Kowloon Park; the military barracks was handed over to the government in 1967). But by the summer, the battalion moved to a horse stables near the Beas River to make room at Whitfield for the reinforcing battalion – the 1st Royal Leicesters. The stables, situated in the New Territories and owned by the Hong Kong Jockey Club, were dirty but the cleaning up was delayed to a certain extent until the final 16 horses were removed. It was a pleasant sight as they could swim and bathe in the nearby river. Once the massive task of cleaning up started, gardens sprung up overnight, the NAAFI (Navy, Army and Air Force Institutes) Officers and Sergeant Messes were built, and everyone was sitting pretty well. The open areas of the New Territories provided good training grounds, including a firing range.

Once the Gurkhas settled in and felt at home, they were ordered to hand over the stables to a newly arriving battalion – the 1st Middlesex – and they moved to a tented camp near San Wai. The bad luck didn't stop there. Once the tented camp was up, it was hit by a severe typhoon, and they had to take refuge in other camps nearby. Thankfully, the small group of Gurkha families was safe back at Whitfield Barracks. It took several days of hard labour and persistence to re-establish the tented camp, but one good thing came out of the ordeal – respect for typhoons.

Just like back in Malaya, the brigade had no ready-made camps for the troops during their first stay in Hong Kong, and the Gurkha battalions had to make do with the tented camps in the open grounds of the New Territories. Living in the tented camp was terrible, especially in the rainy season and even the slightest rain would make the road almost impassable for vehicles. The daily routine mostly involved guarding frontier police stations, training recruits, army training, sports, maintenance of the camps, inter-battalion competition within the garrison and ceremonial parades. Among them, the Khud race at Queen's Hill was the toughest and most respected as the Gurkhas climbed up and down the hills in record time, and the race was a competition of sorts for the Gurkha battalions. The New Territories were still mostly a vast and empty farmland with few motor roads.

The influence of the communists in China was rising. One of the weekly routines of the Gurkha battalion was to send out a patrol carrying the Union Jack to the villages of the New Territories to remind the villagers who was in control and help dissipate communist influences.

When the 2/10th Gurkhas were to return to Malaya, their families were to stay behind in Hong Kong until the tented camp back in Malaya was up and ready, and it took six months before they could join the battalion again. The families of the 2/6th Gurkhas lived in a hutted camp in Kowloon which had once been a Japanese prisoner-of-war internment camp, and the small group of 65 families altogether were well looked after by a Miss Nunn of the WRVS (Women's Royal Voluntary Service) and a nurse.

During the fifties, the newly formed Gurkha Engineers worked tirelessly in Hong Kong and built as many roads, bridges, camps, water catchments and government and military installations as they could. It not only provided them the necessary training but also the actual sense of duties and responsibilities as an engineer regiment. The famous blue-painted 'Bailey Bridge' that could be seen all over Hong Kong at that time had somehow become the hallmark of their achievements. Besides, the engineers also trained in water-borne tactics using rafts, dinghies, rubber boats and motor-propelled vessels, and perfected their trades.

Since the headquarters of the Brigade of Gurkhas was still in Malaysia, the presence of the Gurkhas in Hong Kong was limited during the fifties and sixties, and it was only in the 1967 Hong Kong leftist riots when four Gurkha battalions were deployed there. The riots, initially starting with a minor labour dispute, turned into a full-blown civil disobedience and unrest movement, one that was fought between the pro-communists and their sympathizers and the British colonial government. The Hong Kong Police mostly dealt with the demonstrators, and the army garrison acted as a reserve force. They were subjected to taunts and harassment, with objects thrown at them and verbal abuse, and had to face the hostile community on more than one intimidating occasion. Curfews were imposed, clashes between the police and the demonstrators took place in various parts of Hong Kong, and the whole city was in turmoil.

The situation reached a boiling point on 8 July 1967, when hundreds of demonstrators from China (including Chinese militiamen) crossed the border at Sha Tau Kok and attacked the Hong Kong police. The attack killed five and injured 11 police officers, and the policemen were kept as captives. The 1/10th Gurkha Rifles with 500 front-line troops commanded by Lieutenant Colonel (later Major General) R. McAlister were called in to rescue the policemen, and by 5 a.m. all captives were evacuated, and the Sha Tau Kok village was reclaimed.

According to *Imperial Warriors* by Tony Gould, in another similar incident at the Man Kam To border crossing, the farmers who traded across the border fiercely objected to a barrier put up by the security forces. After talks failed, the villagers held the British team hostage. The team consisted of a British district officer, the commanding officer of the 1/10th Gurkhas (Lt Col R. McAlister again), and police superintendent Bill Paton. Under the command of Major B. Niven, a rescue force of three infantry platoons from the 1/10th Gurkha Rifles supported by a Saladin armoured vehicle was dispatched right away. When the troops arrived at the border, they were confronted by more bad news and discovered that some of the battalion's weapons had been removed and taken across the bridge by the Chinese. Thankfully, the other side only wanted a photo opportunity with the media for a propaganda victory, and the weapons were moved back to the Hong Kong side and handed over once that goal was achieved. A quick phone call was enough to release the hostages, and the tension was defused.

The incident prompted the British to close all the gates at the Hong Kong-China border, which ended up aggravating the situation. As the farmers could no longer work on their fields across the border, it angered them, and they attacked a platoon of the 1/6th Gurkha Rifles with sticks and stones. Since the Gurkhas were not allowed to shoot back, they were forced to take shelter in a police station. Reinforcements were sent out immediately and in order to not provoke the Chinese side, all the gates were instantly reopened.

In a similar incident, when a British officer was grabbed by an angry mob in the border area, a substantial force of Gurkhas was sent out to rescue him and had to fight their way barehanded. In the heat of the moment, some rubber bullets fired by the police detachment during the melee were mistaken for real ones, and the Chinese soldiers from the other side responded with a warning burst of automatic fire. Thankfully, it didn't lead to counter-firing from the other side, order was finally restored, and all heaved a sigh of relief.

Many historians considered the Sha Tau Kok incident as the turning point of the Hong Kong leftist riots, which continued through 1968, albeit on a small scale, and eventually died down.

The Brigade of Gurkhas moved into Hong Kong from Malaysia and Singapore in 1971 and remained stationed there for the next two and a half decades. It had five infantry battalions (1/2nd, 2/2nd, 6th, 7th and 10th Gurkha Rifles) and three corps units (Gurkha Engineers, Signals and Transport). The military camps were mostly situated in the New Territories. The other corps and companies, such as the Gurkha Parachute Company, Gurkha Military Police and the Boy Company, which were raised in Malaysia and Singapore, had all been disbanded by then. After the amalgamation of the Gurkha battalions, the numbers of Gurkhas in the Brigade were significantly lowered, and only about 8,000 out of the previous 14,000 troops moved into Hong Kong, the rest being demobbed.

Three infantry battalions were based at Burma Lines at Queen's Hill (near Fanling), Gallipoli Lines at San Wai, and Cassino Lines at Ngau Tam Mei, San Tin. The Gurkha Engineers were based at Perowne Barracks, Tuen Mun. Both Gurkha Signals and Gurkha Transports were located at Borneo Lines, Shek Kong with other detachments at Gun Club Hill Barracks in Kowloon and the Brigade Headquarters at the Prince of Wales Building in Tamar, Hong Kong Island. The Training Depot of the Brigade of Gurkhas (TDBG), Education Corps and the Brigade's Administrative Headquarters, including a detachment of the Royal Air Force (RAF), were also stationed in the Shek Kong barracks. Unlike the infantry battalions, the base camps for the corps units were permanent and they operated from there throughout their stay in Hong Kong.

There was also a separate British Military Hospital (BMH) at King's Park, Kowloon, for the servicemen and their families, including the Gurkhas, although it has since been demolished to make room for a new residential estate. Each battalion had family quarters, a medical centre and a primary school. For the higher education of the Gurkha children, the Brigade had one central high school called the Gurkha High School at Shek Kong camp. Students were ferried by bus on a daily basis from all the camps around Hong Kong. All the Gurkha children went to the Gurkha High School.

Only three out of five infantry battalions of the Brigade were stationed in Hong Kong at a time. The remaining two battalions were always outside Hong Kong (one in the UK and the other in Brunei), and the five battalions rotated every two years. The 1/2nd Gurkhas, as the Sultan of Brunei's favourite, was the first battalion to be stationed in Brunei while the 7th Gurkha Rifles went to the UK and were stationed at Church Crookham barracks. Although the 7th Gurkha Rifles was the first Gurkha unit to start and complete the two-year tour in the UK, they weren't the first Gurkha battalion to be stationed in the UK. That title went to the 1/6th Gurkha when they went to the UK in 1962 with 68 Gurkha Field Squadron, 247 Gurkha Signals and 30 Squadron of Gurkha Army Service Corps, including a small number of wives and children, and stayed at Tidworth Barracks, Wiltshire. A total of 1,700 Gurkhas went along and trained in England, Wales, Northern Ireland, and certain parts of Europe. Their stay in the UK was cut short, however, by the emergence of the Borneo Confrontation, and the new plan of deploying Gurkha units in the UK had to be postponed. The resumption of that old plan was only possible after 1971, and the 7th Gurkhas were the first ones to go to the UK as intended.

While on the UK tour in 1974-75, the 10th Gurkha Rifles were deployed in Cyprus alongside other elements of the British Army, and helped defuse the trouble caused by the coup led by the Green National Guard. The coup prompted an invasion by Turkish troops on the north coast and created an influx of refugees moving into the Greek side of the island. The Gurkhas had mainly two roles: first, to defend the territorial integrity of the British bases and protect British personnel and installations, and second, to assist the refugees, regardless of their nationality. Once the partitioning of the island between the Greek and Turkish Cypriots was agreed upon, the tension eased, and the 10th Gurkha Rifles returned to their home base in the UK.

The UK-based Gurkha battalion also had to carry out a six-month tour in Belize, the tiny British colony (until it gained its independence in 1981) in Central America, as a deterrent force to the hostile neighbour, Guatemala. The main tasks of the Gurkhas there were to maintain the integrity of the land border by patrolling on foot through the vast tracts of jungle, operate observation posts (OPs) along the border, and help train the small Belize Defence Force. The 6th Gurkha Rifles was the first Gurkha Unit to carry out those duties in Belize during its 1978-79 UK tour.

A small detachment from the corps units (QGE, QGS and GTR) was stationed in the UK, and a company made up from all Gurkha infantry battalions was attached to the Sandhurst Military Academy as a demonstration company. It was the very first time I had the chance to go to the UK and I spent a year there working in the demonstration company as a junior NCO.

The 1970s were a harsh and critical period for China. The Cultural Revolution crippled the whole nation, which desperately needed a new direction. Even worse, Chairman Mao was ailing and the power of the country was in the hands of the 'Gang of Four'. Poverty was rampant, people became hopeless, and the combined force of hunger and uncertainty forced people to seek an escape route. A tiny bright place across the border – Hong Kong – promised a way out. People can do unimaginable things in desperation and crossing a border marked by a small river was the most natural. As a result, the tiny place was inundated with an influx of new arrivals from the north, and preventive measures had to be taken quickly if the establishment was to stop it from spilling over. Before long, the Brigade of Gurkhas was busy again in protecting the border, and every available soldier from the Gurkha units was deployed along the border.

The infantry battalions guarded the border day and night. Gurkha Engineers helped build the barbed-wire fences along the border. Gurkha Signals helped provide the communications and radio systems, and the Gurkha Transport helped transport the men and supplies. By the end of the seventies, the illegal immigrants (IIs) issue had become so severe that an average of 400 IIs were captured each night, and the IIs' numbers reached a staggering 90,000 in 1979. The Brigade struggled, and to cope with the situation, more recruits were enrolled from Nepal. The brigade usually used to enlist recruits once a year, and they would start in the early part of the year, and after the completion of nine months' recruit training, they were sent out to their respective battalions as new soldiers right before the Dussehra, a major Hindu festival. At the height of the IIs crisis in 1979-80, however, the Brigade had to bring in three new intakes of recruits, and I was in one of the intakes.

According to Major (Retd) Dal Bahadur Rai of 7th Gurkhas, when he was leading a team of four on border duty at Man Kam To in 1975, a group of four or five IIs arrived, and one of them, who was the strongest one, hid in the bush. As Maj. Dal Bahadur tried to capture him, the II took a knife and stabbed him in the stomach, from which he sustained a slight cut. In his defence, he took out his kukri, which was quite a big one, and struck the II. His blow made a deep cut on the II's back and slightly cut his spine. Only then did he manage to apprehend the II and had to go through a three-hour interrogation from the Hong Kong Police. The II was rushed to hospital and survived, got a Hong Kong ID card, and a local newspaper covered the incident. In return, Maj. Dal Bahadur was congratulated by the II, and he also got a mention in army dispatches from the Brigade of Gurkhas.

A new Gurkha battalion was raised from the combination of extra men, NCOs, and officers from the other five Gurkha battalions in 1981 and the newly formed battalion, known as the 2/7th Gurkha Rifles, was stationed at Lei Yue Mun barracks on Hong Kong Island.

A real battle the Gurkhas faced in the modern era was the Falklands War (2 April-14 June 1982), and the 1/7th Gurkha Rifles, which was based in the UK at that time, took part. After the British islands near the southern tip of South America – which the Argentines called the 'Malvinas' and had been claiming for years – were occupied by Argentine forces, British forces were sent out from the UK and around the world to reclaim the Falklands.

However, as far as the Gurkhas were concerned, the real trouble was not the fighting but the 45-day sea voyage of 8,000 miles from the UK to the Falklands on the *Queen Elizabeth II (QE II),* the mother ship. It was also a war won by the Gurkhas' name alone through carefully orchestrated propaganda by the shrewd British.

After the 1/7th Gurkhas had arrived near the Falklands, they left the mother ship and were ferried by the ship *MV Norland* to Port San Carlos. On 2 June 1982, they moved to Goose Green and scoured the East Falkland hills in search of pockets of enemies said to be hiding there. On 9 June, they marched through rough terrain with heavy bags for almost seven kilometres and came under heavy enemy mortar fire. One Gurkha officer and three soldiers were hit and had to be evacuated. The showdown at Mount Tumbledown and Mount William was about to begin. On 13 June, the 1/7th Gurkhas were flown by helicopters to a point south of the Two Sisters feature, heavy bombardments pounded the enemy at midnight, and during the night of 13-14 June, they slowly but firmly moved towards the final assaulting position. After a long night of frustration and delay, the battalion was finally about to attack. But something incredible happened: white flags suddenly appeared over Port Stanley, the capital of the Falklands, and the war came to an end without fighting, at least for the 1/7th Gurkhas.

A fierce propaganda war had broken out before the actual fighting. Both sides did their utmost to strike a psychological victory over their enemy, and because of the Gurkhas, the British came out on top. I will write more on this subject in a later chapter.

On 9 August 1982, the 1/7th Gurkhas were greeted with a rapturous welcome by the locals in the town of Fleet, near Church Crookham barracks, and victory in the Falklands War further enhanced the Gurkhas' reputation.

Apart from the 1/7th Gurkhas, 69 Squadron, Gurkha Engineers served in the Falklands and carried out dangerous jobs of clearing the mines and other munitions on the ground. A Gurkha corporal, Budha Prasad Limbu, lost his life on 24 June 1982 to an accidental explosion while filling in a trench. He was the only Gurkha lost in the Falklands War.

Although the 1/7th Gurkhas were the only Gurkha infantry battalion participating in the Falklands War, the other units of the Brigade of Gurkhas in Hong Kong were also put on standby, and I still remember the tense moments when we were restricted from going out of the barracks in case of calls on duty.

In the early eighties the Brigade of Gurkhas was stretched to its limits. Besides handling the influxes of IIs from China, Hong Kong was also inundated by an unprecedented arrival of Vietnamese boat people, and the Gurkha Brigade had to deal with this new problem as well. Gurkha battalions were involved in building new refugee camps, assisting the police as well as other disciplined services in operating those camps, and providing security reinforcements whenever necessary. Even half of the runway of the Shek Kong military airstrip had to be closed and used as a temporary refugee camp.

After Chairman Mao's death in 1976, Deng Xiaoping outmanoeuvred Mao's chosen successor Hua Guofeng in 1978 and started a new open policy for China. The second-generation leader, also known as the paramount leader and the 'Architect', started with three new Special Economic Zones (SEZs) as a trial for this new policy. The southern coastal cities of Zhuhai, Shenzhen and Xiamen were selected initially, and more cities were to add to the success of the first so-called SEZs. His saying, 'It doesn't matter whether it's a white or a black cat, as long as it catches the mouse,' was not only made famous by the Chinese people but also wholeheartedly applied in practice. For the next three decades, all they did in China was make money. More than half a billion people rose out of poverty, a feat surely never achieved elsewhere, and it was why Deng Xiaoping was affectionately called 'Uncle Deng' and revered by the whole country.

As a result, the numbers of IIs arriving gradually died down by the mid-eighties. So did the arrival of Vietnamese boat people, and the recently raised battalion was deemed surplus. The 2/7th Gurkha was disbanded in 1986, and the remaining battalions absorbed the men and officers within the Brigade.

Regardless of heat, rain, storms, day and night, had the Gurkhas not been at the border, the deluge of IIs would have spilled all over Hong

Kong, and the city would be a completely different place today. Besides safeguarding Hong Kong's borders on land and sea, the Brigade of Gurkhas had other tasks. It included supporting the Hong Kong Police in case of riots and civil disobedience, working as reinforcement in relief and emergencies, and maintaining government and military installations. Most importantly, it had to be fully trained, fit and always battle-ready and kept at its visible presence as the primary defence force of Hong Kong. The Gurkhas were the main army of Hong Kong, supported by detachments of Royal Air Force and Royal Navy.

As a regular international force of the British Army, the Brigade of Gurkhas also needed to be prepared for different terrains and types of warfare when necessary. The Gurkhas were periodically involved in overseas exercises in countries such as Fiji, Malaysia, Australia, New Zealand, Papua New Guinea, Belize, Cyprus, and so on. In such activities, troops from various countries, especially those from Commonwealth and allied countries, used to combine forces and train together as a united force. Although all were friendly, the rivalry between the troops from different nations was quite fierce.

Moreover, a small detachment of a ceremonial guard squad was also sent to South Korea on a yearly basis, and the responsibility of providing the men was rotated within the Gurkha battalions in Hong Kong. I still have a faint memory of when it was our battalion's turn, and men from our very own company were sent to South Korea.

After the signing of the agreement between the Chinese and the British in 1984, the return of Hong Kong to China was put into motion. As the official date of the handover – 1 July 1997 – approached, a dark cloud hovered over the future of the Brigade of Gurkhas, and even the danger of the First Gulf War (2 August 1990-28 February 1991) destabilizing the world's peace couldn't clear that cloud. A very small detachment of Gurkhas (from QGS, GTR and Brigade's Pipes and Drums) from the Brigade went to the First Gulf War as ambulance drivers and members of a relief team and luckily sustained no injuries or deaths.

By early 1990, the future of the Brigade of Gurkhas was decided, and the first phase of redundancies started immediately. The five remaining Gurkha infantry battalions were to amalgamate into only two battalions, the corps units were to be reduced substantially as well, and by the time the final trimming of the Brigade was completed by 1994, only about 3,000 men were to remain from the previous total of about 8,000. They were moved to the UK before the 1997 Hong Kong handover and have continued as the new Brigade of Gurkhas since then.

The list of the units currently serving the British is: The 1st Royal Gurkha Regiment (1 RGR), the 2nd Royal Gurkha Regiment (2 RGR), the Queen's Gurkha Engineers, the Queen's Gurkha Signals, the 10 Queen's Own Gurkha Logistic Regiment RLC, Gurkha Staff and Personal Support Company, the Band of the Brigade of Gurkhas, the Gurkha Company Infantry Training Centre, the Gurkha Company (Sittang) Royal Military Academy Sandhurst, the Gurkha Company (Mandalay) Infantry Battle School Brecon, Brigade of Gurkhas Training Team and Gurkha Language Wing, Catterick.

The total number of Gurkhas serving in the British Army is said to have risen to 3,500 by now, and the possibility of drastic changes can be ruled out at least at the time of writing.

It has been more than twenty years since the Gurkhas left Hong Kong, but a small and vibrant Gurkha community is still alive in Hong Kong today. Once the rundown of the Brigade of Gurkhas had begun by early 1990, the Gurkhas started coming back to Hong Kong as civilians and found work as security guards and in construction firms. Unlike their grandfathers, they didn't want to go back to farming, and sought out opportunities in various nations around the globe. The driving force behind this new trend was the concern the Gurkhas had for the future of their children, and Hong Kong was an ideal and familiar place where they felt comfortable establishing their new homes. Before too long, there were over 50,000 Gurkhas and their families living in Hong Kong, and I and my young family were among them.

However, when the Gurkha justice campaign successfully won the right of abode for Gurkhas in the UK in 2009, many Gurkha families living in Hong Kong moved to the UK. As of 2020, there were about 20,000 Gurkhas still living in Hong Kong. However, they are mostly of the second or third generations of Gurkhas.

Starting off in the security, guarding and construction industries, the Gurkhas in Hong Kong have moved on to new and diversified fields, and many have established businesses. Restaurants, grocery shops, travel agencies, novelty shops, security firms, construction companies, human resources companies, and logistics and courier services are just a few sectors the Gurkhas are involved in. Although Gurkha families are scattered around various districts in Hong Kong, Jordan and Yuen Long are the two places where most Gurkhas reside at the moment, and it is not hard to find Gurkha-owned shops and businesses in those areas. Construction is the industry where most Gurkhas work, and due to the hard and risky nature of the work, it pays well. Gurkha women mostly work in hotels, services and hospitality industries.

Despite all the difficulties, the new generation is catching up and getting breaks in various industries such as IT, education, medicine, entertainment, insurance and banking as professionals. The new generation is not only highly educated but also tech-savvy and already working at management levels. For instance, Niraj Gurung joining the Hong Kong Police Force in 2016 was one of the exciting events for the Gurkha community.

The Gurkha community has no shortage of writers, poets, singers, musicians, artists, filmmakers, reporters, thinkers, social workers and photographers in Hong Kong. Similarly, there are good sportspeople and entertainers. Gurkhas are not only brave, loyal and hardworking but also cheerful and self-reliant. Adaptability is the Gurkhas' middle name, and despite all their in-house bickering and shortcomings, they still find enough reasons to make a decent living and carry on. We are always happy and easygoing, busy in our small world, and don't give a damn about the world around us. That's Gurkhas for you, for the uninitiated!

One of the most prominent legacies that the Gurkhas established during their time in Hong Kong is the famous Trailwalker Race on the MacLehose Trail, a gruelling, 100-kilometre-long route with over 4,000 metres of ascent and descent, covering various terrains in the New Territories countryside and named after the former Hong Kong governor, Sir Murray MacLehose. It attracts famous trail runners from around the world, and the locals mark it as one of the most anticipated events in the Hong Kong calendar.

CHAPTER 17

THE GORKHAS IN THE INDIAN ARMY

'We were still fighting the Japanese in the jungle 40 km away from Rangoon when they finally surrendered. Then, we moved to Saigon via Hong Kong and attended the final surrendering parade of the Japanese there. Swords collected from the Japanese were distributed among the British officers, the Japanese were ordered to work for eight hours a day, and we, the Gurkhas, guarded them. Then, we moved to Singapore where the Gurkhas were allowed to have slightly longer hair for the first time and we were issued a comb and oil.'

Rifleman Jwala Singh Gurung (93), 1/2nd GR, from Char Ghare Syangja, joined the army in 1943, fought in Burma in WWII, went to Saigon, Vietnam, via Hong Kong, moved to Singapore and New Zealand, and returned home in 1948.

Although the focus of this book is on the two main players in Gurkha history, Britain and Nepal, and the relationship between them, it would not be complete without looking briefly at the history of the Gorkha units which joined the new Indian Army after India's independence.

As mentioned previously, six out of ten Gorkha regiments from the Indian Gorkha Brigade remained in India and became part of the newly formed Indian Army. Those were the 1st, 3rd, 4th, 5th, 8th and 9th Gorkha Rifles. All of them were prominent and famous regiments within the Indian Gorkha Brigade and it raised eyebrows when the British side did not choose them, especially regiments like the 1st, 5th and 8th Gorkhas, which had strong connections with the British. The decision to leave them behind somehow baffled the whole institution.

During the partition of 1947, a referendum was held among the soldiers of the four regiments (2nd, 6th, 7th and 10th Gurkhas) selected for the British side, and they were given a choice of whether to transfer to the British side on a voluntary basis. The outcome was unprecedented, at least to the British. One entire battalion of the 2nd Gurkha opted to join the Indian Army and became the 5th battalion of the 8th Gorkha Rifles. Similarly, a large number of men from the 7th and the 10th Gurkhas, which predominantly recruit from eastern Nepal, opted to join the Indian Army. To retain a specific contingent from this part of Nepal, the decision of re-raising the 11th Gorkha Rifles was made, and men from the 7th and 10th Gurkhas, who had decided against following the British side, were then allocated to this newly formed regiment.

Raising the 11th Gorkha Rifles in 1948 brought the total number of Gorkha regiments in the Indian Army up to seven. Although the old 11th Gorkhas was raised in 1918 during WWI and disbanded in 1922, the wartime regiment had no connection with the new regiment. Similarly, the 3/6th Gurkhas raised on 1 October 1940, which was the original battalion of the VC winner Tul Bahadur Pun, was then designated as the 5/5th Gurkhas on 1 January 1948, hence this battalion in India still celebrates his VC.

Since the British Raj in India raised all the Gurkha regiments, they shared the same history as described in the previous chapters of the book. This chapter will look at the history of Indian Gorkhas in the post-independence era. Readers might already have noticed the word 'Gorkha' instead of 'Gurkha' that I am using in this chapter, and there is an excellent reason for that. In 1949, the Indian Army changed the spelling from 'Gurkha' to the original 'Gorkha', and it has been using it as the official spelling since then. Once India was declared a republic in 1950, all the royal titles of the Gorkha regiments were dropped, and they were only designated as the 1st, 3rd, 5th, 8th, 9th and 11th Gorkha Rifles of the Indian Army.

The Indian Gorkhas have a long, distinguished and proud history of their own. They have established themselves as an integral part of the Indian Army since independence and played a significant role in safeguarding the security and integrity of the country. Trying to write about such colossal historic importance in a mere chapter might look impolite or even disrespectful to some extent, but given the situation, my hands are tied. I have to write the history of more than 200 years in a single book and understandably, that's not easy. I sincerely hope that readers will understand my position.

If the Gurkhas had ever felt abandoned, even betrayed to some extent by the British, it was in that awkward period of independence, and by opting to remain in India, the Gurkhas had chosen stability over uncertainty. Malaya and Singapore, where the newly formed Brigade of Gurkhas was to relocate, were somewhat new and unfamiliar places for them. In contrast, India, where they had been stationed since the very beginning, was like their backyard, and it gave them some much-needed assurance. Most importantly, everything remained the same as before. The only thing that had changed was the replacement of the British officers by Indian officers and just like other things in life, they got accustomed to it over time.

The Gorkha soldiers serving in the Indian Army are not entirely from Nepal. There are Indian Gorkhas of Nepalese origin from places like Dehradun, Simla, Sikkim, Darjeeling and Assam.

The 1st Gorkha Rifles (the Malaun Regiment) is a Gorkha infantry regiment of the Indian Army with six battalions composed mostly of men of Nepalese origin and stationed at Subathu, Himachal Pradesh. The oldest Gorkha regiment has a long and distinguished history before and after India's independence and *'Better to die than live like a coward'* is its motto. Since 1947, the regiment has participated in campaigns against Pakistan in 1965 and 1971, as well as undertaking peacekeeping duties around the globe as part of the United Nations. Men from the regiment have been awarded one Param Vir Chakra, seven Maha Vir Chakra, 16 Vir Chakra, one Kirti Chakra, three Shaurya Chakras and dozens of army medals for gallantry.

The 3rd Gorkha Rifles is also an infantry regiment of the Indian Army with five battalions. It is headquartered at Varanasi, Uttar Pradesh, and mostly comprised of men of Nepalese origin. The regiment, made famous by the storming of the Dargai Heights in 1897 during the Tirah Campaign of the Northwest Frontier, was in action again right after independence and fought in the Uri sector during the 1947-48 Kashmir War. The 1/3rd Gorkha Rifles was the first battalion to carry out amphibious operations during the Indo-Pakistan War in 1971. The regiment has won various gallantry awards, including one Ashoka Chakra, one Kirti Chakra, five Vir Chakras, five Saurya Chakras, and dozens more. Sir Ralph Turner, the professor of Sanskrit, director of the London School of Oriental Studies and the compiler of the famous English-Nepali dictionary, was an officer of the 3rd Gorkha Regiment and fought with them in World War I. It was he, of course, who coined the famous quote, 'Bravest of the brave, most generous of the generous, never had country more faithful friends than you', that has adorned many pages of books about the Gurkhas, and, since 3 December 1997, the legend below the larger-than-life Gurkha statue that is the Gurkha Memorial in London.

The 4th Gorkha Rifles is a light infantry regiment of the Indian Army with five battalions based at Subathu, Himachal Pradesh, and comprised of men of Nepalese origin. The regiment has a long and distinguished history, and the British author John Masters, who served with the regiment during World War II and on the Northwest Frontier, was one of them. The regiment served in the 1947-48 Kashmir War, the Siachen Glacier and Punjab in 1965, and Jammu and Kashmir in 1971. It has also served in various theatres of the world as a peacekeeping force under the United Nations. In the post-independence era, it has won three Param Vishisht Seva medals, one Maha Vir Chakra, one Kirti Chakra, three Vir Chakras, two Shaurya Chakras, twenty-four Sena medals and many more. The regimental day of the 4th Gorkha is 11 March and it commemorates the first battalion's actions in the battle of Neuve-Chapelle in France and the second battalion's entry into Baghdad (in different years, of course) during World War I.

The 5th Gorkha Rifles is undoubtedly one of the most popular Gorkha infantry regiments since the very beginning. The regiment is also known as the 'Frontier Force' since most of its earlier days were spent at the frontier and it is currently based at Shillong, Meghalaya. The regiment also won the most VCs (four in total) among the Gorkhas, and the 2/5th Gurkha was deployed in Japan as part of the British Occupation Force in May 1946. The regiment currently has six battalions of its own and has an association with the 33 Rashtriya Rifles and the *INS Khukri* of the Indian Navy. The regiment has participated in all significant actions that the Indian Army has undertaken since independence including the 1947-48 Kashmir War, the Indo-Pakistan War of 1965, and the Battle of Atgram, Sylhet and Gazipur in East Pakistan in 1971, and it fought against the Tamil Tigers in Sri Lanka as part of the Indian Peacekeeping Force. It has won one Ashoka Chakra, eight Maha Vir Chakras, and dozens of gallantry awards during many operations. The 5th Gorkha was one of the few regiments that shocked all military fraternities when it wasn't included by the British and the ripples are still felt today.

The 8th Gorkha Rifles, also known as the 'Shiny Eight', is one of the crack Gorkha regiments of the Indian Army, and is currently based in Shillong, Meghalaya, with six infantry battalions and a mechanized infantry battalion. Since the days of the British Raj, the Gorkhas had always been at the forefront of wars, and the 8th Gorkhas were no different. The 2/8th Gorkhas took part in the Leh operation of the 1947-48 Kashmir war, and the regiment was heavily involved in both Indo-Pakistan wars of 1965 and 1971, and the Kargil War in 1999. The regiment is also actively engaged in operations in Sri Lanka as part of the Indian Peacekeeping Force, and has won various gallantry medals. But it was in the Sino-Indian War of 1962 when one member of the regiment earned the Param Vir Chakra, the highest honour for valour in the Indian Army, and made the regiment proud.

According to the citation from the *Indian Gazette*, Major Dhan Singh Thapa of the 1/8th Gorkhas was in command of a forward post in Ladakh when the position was attacked by the Chinese on 20 October 1962 with overwhelming strength after they had been subjected to intensive artillery and mortar bombardment. Under his gallant command, the greatly outnumbered post repulsed the enemy's attack not once but twice, inflicting heavy casualties on the aggressors. The enemy attacked for the third time, now with tanks to support their infantry, and despite sustaining heavy losses from earlier attacks, they fought until the end. When overwhelming numbers of the enemy finally overran the post, Major Thapa came out of his trench and killed several enemies in hand-to-hand battle before he was eventually overpowered and killed. He was posthumously awarded the Param Vir Chakra for his gallantry and his wife received the medal from the Indian president on his behalf on 26 January 1963. She was pregnant at that time with a son. The boy was named Param Vir Thapa and later served in the Indian Army as an officer.

The story doesn't end there. It has a sweet ending because Major Thapa returned from China as a prisoner of war in March 1963. Since he was officially dead, he had to go through the rituals of renaming as well as remarrying his wife as required by his religious and traditional beliefs. He went on to serve in different battalions and eventually retired as a lieutenant colonel. He hailed from Dhankuta, East Nepal, moved to Shimla, India, and passed away on 5 September 2005. Out of respect, roads in Shillong and Assam are named after him, the Shipping Corporation of India named a ship after him, and I had the chance to watch a documentary on him made by Doordarshan.

Moreover, the regiment has won four Ashoka Chakras, one Padma Vibhushan, one Padma Bhushan, seven Maha Vir Chakras and dozens of other medals for its valour. Chief of Army Staff Field Marshal Sam Makenshaw MC, whose contribution in the 1971 Indo-Pakistan War

Living VC Ram Bahadur Limbu at his home at Kathmandu, 2018

The author interviews Gurkha veterans in Gorkha, Midwest Nepal

Balaram Gurung, WWII veteran, 94 years old

Former Nepal Army Chief, General Chhetraman Singh Gurung, at his home

The author on the metal bridge over the Mahakaali River, Far West Nepal

At the Rapti River, West Nepal

Gurkha wife Khar Kumari Pun, 80 years old, at Tatopani Myagdi, West Nepal

Gurkha wife Lalita Rai, 79 years old, at Dharan GWT, East Nepal

The author with friends at the Taukkyan War Cemetery, Yangon, Myanmar

Makawanpur Gadhi Fort, the last fort of the 1814-16 Anglo-Gorkha war

The author (back row, 2nd from right) in the Hong Kong Army Education Wing in 1992

Gurkha veterans in front of the statue at the Memorial to the Brigade of Gurkhas on Horseguards Avenue, Whitehall, London; photo courtesy of Maj (Retd) Tikendradal Dewan, JP

With the family of 100-year-old WWII veteran Tahal Singh Rana in Tutung, Palpa, West Nepal

In Pokhara with Maj. (Retd) Yam Bahadur Gurung, 2nd GR; Maj. (Retd) Lachhimi Prasad Gurung; Capt. (Retd) Bhuwansing Gurung, 6th GR; and Lt (Retd) Arjun Kumar Gurung

Gurkha Memorial Service in Ipoh, Malaysia, 10 June 2017

The Gurkha Garden at Kranji War Memorial, Singapore

was legendary, was from the 8th Gorkha and the regiment is famous for producing high-ranking army commanders within the Indian Army.

The 9th Gorkha Rifles is another Gorkha regiment of the Indian Army originally from the old British Raj, comprising men of Nepalese origin and currently based in Varanasi, Uttar Pradesh, with five battalions. The regiment has a unique tradition of recruiting men mostly from the Chhetri and Thakuri clans of Nepal, and it's known as the '*Khas Paltan*' among the Indian Gorkhas. (*Khas* is a word used to describe the Brahmins and Chhetris in Nepal). In modern days, domiciled Indian Gorkhas who originate from Nepal are also taken, and the ratio is about 20 per cent of the regiment's total strength. Since independence, the regiment has fought in the Sino-Indian War of 1962, the Indo-Pakistan War in 1965 and in various theatres such as Kumarkhali, Jammu and Kashmir, and Punjab during the Indo-Pakistan War of 1971. It has won one Ashoka Chakra, five Maha Vir Chakras and dozens of medals of gallantry during those operations.

As already described at the beginning of this chapter, the 11th Gorkha Rifles was re-raised in post-independence India and has no affiliation with the old 11th Gurkha Rifles, which was raised amid World War I and subsequently disbanded in 1922. The youngest Gorkha regiment of the Indian Army is located in Lucknow, Uttar Pradesh, with six battalions, plus a territorial army battalion based in Darjeeling, West Bengal. The regiment is affiliated with a newly formed regiment called the Sikkim Scouts Regiment. The regiment was involved in the 1947-48 Kashmir War, the Indo-Pakistan wars in 1965 and 1971, and the Kargil War of 1999.

It was in Kargil when Capt. Manoj Kumar Pandey of the 1/11th Gorkha Rifles won the Param Vir Chakra on the night of 2-3 July 1999. He was posthumously awarded the medal for his bravery, and his father received the award from the president of India on behalf of his son. In his honour, a new auditorium for Sainik (Army) School, a block for the National Defence Academy, a roundabout in his home town and a gallery in the Kargil War Museum in India are named after him. Furthermore, a major Bollywood movie has been made based on his story.

Birba or Bir Bahadur Gurung of the 1st Assam Regiment won two bravery awards as a young man and subsequently as a soldier in his brief but meaningful life. First, he won the President's Bravery Award for children at the age of fourteen when he jumped into the Brahmaputra River and saved many people from a capsized ferry. Later, Rifleman Bir Bahadur Gurung was posthumously awarded a Shaurya Chakra for an act of gallantry in Mizoram in 1966.

Since the Indian Gorkha Army originated from the British Raj, some of the old practices remain intact in the present day, and sending the Gorkhas to the forefront of action in both peace and war is one of them. As loyal, committed and professional as they have always been, the Gorkhas were right there from the very first day of partition and wholeheartedly contributed to every significant event that the newly independent nation would see in its history. The 1947-48 Kashmir war, the Sino-Indian war of 1962, the Bangladesh war of 1971, skirmishes on the Siachen Glacier with China, the Sri Lankan interlude, and the Kargil War in 1999, the Gorkhas were always there. But it has been the never-ending rivalry between the two nations of India and Pakistan, which are continuously at loggerheads with the risk of a war breaking out any moment, that keeps the Indian Army busy. Guarding those precarious borders is not an easy task, but the tough Gorkhas have always been at the front.

Safeguarding the long, unmarked and difficult borders with China along the inhospitable Himalayan range is another main task of the Gorkhas in the Indian Army. They have been performing well in such harsh, cold conditions since the beginning.

According to records that I found, the ratio of men joining the Indian Army has changed to 60:40 (directly from Nepal versus Indian Gorkhas of Nepali origin) and plans are in place to change that to 40:60 soon. The Indian Army's preference for domiciled Gorkhas over Nepali Gorkhas is changing with time.

There are currently about 42,000 men serving in the force. However, these numbers are only from the current seven regular infantry regiments. If we were to include all other regiments or corps, regulars or irregulars (for instance, the Assam Rifles, Garhwal, Kumaon and Naaga regiments, and Jammu and Kashmir border security forces) and the Indian Gorkhas who have been living in India for generations, the number could easily reach over 100,000 men. The Gurkha tradition might be more than 200 years old, but it's as familiar and robust today as it was two centuries ago. No matter what the future holds, the Gorkha legacy will live on forever.

CHAPTER 18

THE GURKHAS IN THE UK

'The UK is a country surrounded by sea on all sides. London is clean and tidy, shops are decorated in shiny glass boxes, the railroad is underground, nights are as bright as days, people are kind and civilized, the country has various industries, and we very much enjoyed our stay in the UK. The King was kind enough to give us an audience, all 1,500 of us, who had come from Hindustan to attend the ceremony and we were genuinely honoured.' – From the journal of Subedar Major Gambhir Singh Gurung, June 1911

Subedar Major Gambhir Singh Gurung (1871-1940) IOM, OBI and Bahadur, 2/3rd GR, from Sirubari, Aandikhola, Syangja, served in WWI and attended the coronation of King George V in 1911 in London, UK. *Photo © Ex-WO2 Chandra Bahadur Gurung, 2nd GR*

After the British government's groundbreaking decision of 21 May 2009 to grant right of abode, the Gurkha communities celebrated with joy and entered the UK in large numbers. Many packed their bags, sold their properties in Nepal and moved to the UK. Before long, Heathrow Airport was inundated with ex-Gurkhas and their families. The Gurkhas had arrived in such a hurry and in such great numbers that the local councils of areas like Aldershot, Farnborough and Basingstoke, where Gurkhas had initially settled, were stretched to their limits. They struggled to accommodate the new arrivals and cried foul. It was a phenomenon that the British had not seen for quite some time, and it felt like the whole nation of Nepal had moved in all at once.

Modern British life was a challenge for the simple village people the Gurkhas were, and the sudden changes were just too much for many. Many were lost and needed guidance. The media didn't help at all and followed them as if there was a circus in town. Opportunists found excuses to criticize. Few sympathized with them while others became spectators.

The Gurkhas, being the way they had always been, were indeed confused but soon recovered. People had forgotten that they were the same Gurkhas who had faced and prevailed over much harsher situations in their lives. The Gurkhas are renowned not only for bravery but also for tenacity, adaptability and perseverance. Most importantly, they are quick learners, and it didn't take too long before they adjusted to their new-found life in the UK. For the old and uneducated village folks especially, the new life was hard, but the young and educated Gurkha children helped them.

Although the Gurkhas have been serving the British since 1815, it was only in the mid-twentieth century that Nepalis started migrating to the UK through various routes. The recent phenomenon of the Gurkhas relocating to the UK also makes them one of the fastest-growing ethnic minorities there. Today we have a vibrant Gurkha community living throughout England, Scotland and Wales who have already become an integral part of the British population. It was almost unimaginable just a decade back.

Before I write about the Gurkhas' civilian community, let's go back to the Gurkhas in the British Army first, and we will close the chapter with more details about the private side of the Gurkha community in the UK.

Before Hong Kong – the home of the Brigade of Gurkhas since 1971 – was to revert to Chinese rule on 1 July 1997, the Brigade of Gurkhas initiated a great reduction in men during the early 1990s. By the time the reduction was completed in early 1994, only 2,500 out of the previous 10,000 force remained in the Brigade, and the trimmed-down version of the Brigade of Gurkhas was moved to the UK. Although the terms of redundancy were better than in 1969, the massive cutback had different effects on those affected Gurkhas this time around. As the intention of this chapter is not to concentrate on that part, it will be explained in other sections of this book.

The Brigade of Gurkhas has now been stationed in the UK for more than two decades, but not much has changed in its structure since it left Hong Kong. As I write, the Brigade of Gurkhas is currently made up of the following units as part of the British Army.

The Royal Gurkha Rifles is an infantry regiment of the British Army with two battalions: the 1st Royal Gurkha Rifles (1 RGR) and the 2nd Royal Gurkha Rifles (2 RGR), and was formed on 1 July 1994 by the amalgamation of the 2nd, 6th, 7th and 10th Gurkha Rifles in Hong Kong. One of the battalions is based in Shorncliffe, Kent, the other in Brunei, and they change every three years. The regiment has taken part in operations in Kosovo, Bosnia, East Timor, Sierra Leone, Ivory Coast and Afghanistan. Gurkha companies have also been deployed to Iraq.

The HQ of the Brigade of Gurkhas is based at the Royal Military Academy, Sandhurst. The Queen's Gurkha Engineers (QGE) has 69 and 70 Gurkha Field Squadrons based at Invicta Park Barracks in Maidstone. The Queen's Gurkha Signals (QGS) has its headquarters at Gamecock Barracks in Bramcote with 246 Signal Squadron at York, 248 Signal Squadron at Stafford and 250 Signal Squadron which provides command support to the Commander Joint Forces Operation and his staff when deployed. Besides, the QGS has the Brunei Signal Troop, the Nepal Signal Troop, and many small teams supporting the army around the world. The 10 Queen's Own Gurkha Logistic Regiment (10 QOGLR), previously the Gurkha Transport Regiment (GTR), forms part of the Royal Logistics Corps (RLC) and was created on 5 April 2001, and is currently based at Gale Barracks in Aldershot with its regimental HQ and three squadrons.

A company of Gurkha Staff and Personal Support (GSPS) is based at Camberley in Surrey. They are the official clerks of the Brigade of Gurkhas and were formed on 30 June 2011. The Band of the Brigade of Gurkhas is based at Shorncliffe. In addition, a Gurkha Company is based at the Infantry Training Centre, Catterick, North Yorkshire; the Gurkha Company (Sittang) at Royal Military Academy Sandhurst; the Gurkha Company (Mandalay) at Infantry Battle School, Brecon; and the Brigade Training Team and the Gurkha Language Wing are also based at Catterick.

The total strength of the Brigade of Gurkhas currently is around 3,500. New blood is directly recruited from Nepal and around 170-270 recruits join them each year. As British citizens, the children of the Gurkhas can join any regiment or corps of the British Army nowadays, and it doesn't necessarily have to be the Gurkha regiments any more. The qualified ones can directly apply to be an officer cadet and become an officer in the British Army.

Since the Brigade of Gurkhas moved to the UK, it has seen action in Iraq, Afghanistan, Kosovo and other parts of the world. In the Afghanistan war alone, the Gurkhas have had 15 killed and 154 wounded, of whom more than 100 were disabled. The Gurkhas have won several military bravery awards in Afghanistan, including one Conspicuous Gallantry Cross (CGC), which is the second-highest military honour after the Victoria Cross (VC).

Corporal (acting Sergeant at the time of the incident) Dip Prashad Pun of the 1st RGR who single-handedly defeated 12-30 Taliban insurgents storming his control post near Babaji in Helmand province, Afghanistan, was awarded the prestigious CGC for bravery.

According to the *London Gazette* citation, on the evening of 17 September 2010, Sergeant Pun was on duty when he heard a clinking noise to the south of the checkpoint. 'I thought at first maybe it was a cow,' he said, 'but my suspicions arose when I saw the Taliban digging to lay down an IED in front of our gate.' Sergeant Pun had the presence of mind to gather two radios, which would enable him to both speak to his commander and to call in artillery support, his weapon and a general-purpose machine gun. Realizing that he was about to be attacked, he quickly informed his commander on one of the radios and launched a grenade at the enemy. Sergeant Pun single-handedly fought off an enemy attack on his lightly manned position. In the dark, he tackled the enemy head-on as he moved around his position to fend off the attack from three sides, killing three assailants and causing the others to flee. 'I thought there might have been around 20 to 30, but later locals told me there were probably about 15. The firing went on continually for about 17 minutes,' said Sergeant Pun. 'At first, I was a bit scared, and I thought they were going to kill me. But as soon as I started firing, that feeling went away.'

He received his medal from the Queen at Buckingham Palace alongside other medal winners from the British Army. After Honorary Captain Ram Bahadur Limbu VC of the 10th GR, Sergeant Dip Prasad Pun is the only British Gurkha to be decorated with such a high honour in the post-WWII era, something the whole Gurkha community is proud of.

The Gurkhas were deployed as a supporting team in Iraq and thus suffered no casualties.

In Kosovo, Sergeant Bala Ram Rai of 69th Gurkha Field Squadron, QGE, was the only unfortunate Gurkha who was killed in the village of Negrovce, about 16 miles west of the capital, Pristina, while clearing an unexploded NATO bomb.

According to a well-placed source, in the period of 2001-2014, there were 13 operational tours of Afghanistan between the two Royal Gurkha Rifles battalions. The Gurkha Reserve Companies completed an additional 18 operational tours. QGE had ten and QGS had 22, and QOGLR had 16 operational tours in Afghanistan. Twelve Gurkhas were killed and 16 were wounded during those operations, and the Gurkhas won 91 bravery awards, including the CGC won by Dip Prasad Pun, and 48 commendations in Afghanistan alone.

After the Brigade of Gurkhas moved to the UK, slight changes to ranking and promotion structure occurred. The journey of a British Gurkha used to start as a recruit, then rifleman, lance corporal, corporal, sergeant, staff sergeant, warrant officer (Class 2), warrant officer (Class 1, also called regimental sergeant major or RSM, and there is only one RSM in a battalion), Gurkha lieutenant, captain and finally major. One had to follow all the steps as he got promoted, but in some individual cases, a staff/colour sergeant could be directly promoted to a Gurkha lieutenant, bypassing the post of a warrant officer. In the new promotion system, the rank of lieutenant is now missing, and warrant officers are directly promoted to the position of captain instead. The Gurkha officers who were called Queen's Gurkha Officers (QGOs) before and were titled Lt (QGO), Capt. (QGO) and Maj. (QGO) respectively, have ceased as well and they are called merely captain and major now. The distinctions between the Gurkha and the British officers that we had before don't exist any more, and both are known as officers of their respective ranks.

By the time a Gurkha soldier reached the rank of a Gurkha major, he would have already served the regiment for at least 28 years, and a battalion always had only one Gurkha major. In the early days, once a soldier had joined a regiment, he would serve that regiment for his entire career, and Gurkha major was the highest possible rank a Gurkha could attain. Nowadays, an officer must serve in different regiments during his army career, and the same rules also apply to the officers of Gurkha origin.

In the name of British superiority, or shall I say anarchy, a young British 2nd lieutenant was above the Gurkha major who was almost the age of the 2nd lieutenant's father, and still had to salute the immature brat. But that has changed for good now, and there are no longer any differences between the British and Gurkha officers. The restriction on the promotion side also seems to have been lifted, and Gurkha officers can now attain ranks higher than major. Altogether, four Gurkha officers have achieved the highest level of colonel so far in British Gurkha history, and they are Lt Col Lal Bahadur Pun of 2nd GR, Lt Col Bijay Kumar

Rawat of 7th GR, Lt Col Yam Bahadur Rana of QGE and Lt Col Tol Bahadur Khamcha of QGS.

The British royal family has always been an admirer of the Gurkhas. They have always included the Gurkhas in their special occasions, and Prince Harry, who was famously known within the Gurkha regiments as 'Harry Bahadur', is no exception. He served with the Gurkhas during his tour of duty in Afghanistan and is said to have been very fond of the Gurkha curry. A team of Gurkhas from the 1st RGR provided ceremonial guards during the fiery-haired prince's wedding. It is also a long tradition that two of the most senior Gurkha captains of the Brigade of Gurkhas serve as the Queen's orderly officer for a year before they become the Gurkha major of their respective battalion.

Ex-British Gurkhas also serve in the British Territorial Army (TA) in the capacity of both officers and other ranks. Many others serve in the Military Provost Guard Service (MPGS) and the Ministry of Defence Guard Service (MGS). The MPGS is an extension of guard service, which was established to relieve full-time soldiers on operational tours and training. They are armed guards and follow similar terms and conditions of service as the regulars. They have a rank structure, the same pension scheme and are recruited from the ex-service personnel community. The MGS is open for both civilian and ex-service personnel. They are civil servants and are never armed.

Now, we return to the story of the Gurkhas and their children who have been living in the UK since the British government's policy changes concerning the Gurkhas. Jang Bahadur Rana, the PM of Nepal who visited the UK in July 1850 with his entourage of 24 members, was widely believed to be the first Nepali to visit the UK. But according to the Centre for Nepal Studies UK (CNSUK), Moti Lal Singh, who had participated in the Anglo-Gorkha War of 1814-1816, was the first Nepali to visit as well as live in the UK, and he was living in London when he met and joined the Nepali prime minister in 1850.

By 2001, about 5,943 Nepali were estimated to be living in the UK. But after the decision of 2009, the population reached a staggering number of around 80,000. By 2018, 110,000 Nepali were living in the UK, and 68.5 per cent are Gurkhas and their dependents. Apart from the

British Army, the civilian Gurkhas started in low-paid, unprofessional and manual jobs. But slowly and firmly, they began venturing into self-employment, as professionals and private businesspeople and helped to improve their livelihood as well as image. The new generations of Gurkha children, who are not only well-educated but also were brought up in a modern and civilized society, are breaking ground and finding success on their merit that was almost unimaginable for their forefathers.

Although progress is being made on a steady basis, integrating into mainstream society will take time. Gurkhas prefer to stay in small groups and with their own type, hence hindering actual integration. Besides the strong Gurkha community, there is a substantial Nepali diaspora in the UK, and the doctors' community is among them. The UK has more than 300 Nepali doctors and many qualified nurses.

One example is Rajendra Chhetri. His mother was a veteran midwife of the Brigade of Gurkhas in Malaysia, taking care of the wives and children of the Gurkhas for 34 years and nine months. Rajendra became a qualified nurse in the UK in 1973. After finishing his General Nursing Training at St Peter's Hospital, Surrey, he underwent the State Registered Nurse (SRN) training for 18 months and qualified as the first Nepalese psychiatric nurse in the UK in 1975. Then, he was promoted to ward manager, probably the first Nepali to achieve this in the National Health Service (NHS) in the UK, and served for the next 44 years, two months and twenty days before retiring in April 2013. Now, his days are mostly occupied with voluntary and charity work in his community, and he has no plans whatsoever of stopping.

Over time, the Gurkhas have established themselves in the UK by venturing into new enterprises, such as small businesses, eateries and community service facilities. Among them is GnERGY, a utility firm based in Farnborough, solely owned and run by Gurkhas. GnERGY provides gas and electricity supplies not only to the Gurkha communities but also nationwide, and it's the only community-led energy company that competes with other big companies in this industry. GnERGY has been featured in various TV programmes and national newspapers and is the first Gurkha business success story in the UK. GnERGY had a turnover of 12 million pounds (as of 2018) with a workforce of 24 graduates, all

Bhanjas and *Bhanjis* (children of ex-Gurkhas). Furthermore, the success of GnERGY reflects a positive picture, while dispelling myths that the Farnborough area is overcrowded by benefit-chasing ex-Gurkhas. It has not only highlighted the Gurkhas' hardworking ethos but also helped set an example to the broader community. Major (Retd) Tikendra Dewan J. P. and his team have made all Gurkhas very proud, and they certainly deserve respect and kudos from all the Gurkha communities.

Gurkhas are already working in many fields, such as security, restaurants, cab companies, cash-and-carry firms, travel agencies, jewellery and fashion, home construction and decoration, old-age homes, flowers and groceries, service and consultant firms, and tasting success as they learn the new trades and improve along the way. They also have their newspapers, online TV and radio stations, and online video makers. Just like any other community, they have intellectuals, lawyers and many other professionals. Such ventures uplift the local economy and generate employment. Before too long, the contribution of the Gurkha community in the nation's economy will be felt.

The Gurkhas have set up around 400 organizations and communities. They arrange social, cultural and formal gatherings during particular festive periods and help keep the communities together. Tamu Dhee UK (Gurung's Home) is one of the biggest among them and organizes two main yearly events for the Gurkha communities in the UK. The Gurkha Cup, a community football competition, which is held on the Sunday of the May bank holiday each year, is participated in and enjoyed by all the Gurkha communities. The one-day Gurkha Mela (bazaar) is an event held on the August bank holiday weekend each year which showcases Gurkhas' traditional, cultural and festival shows; it is visited by almost 100,000 locals and Nepalis who celebrate the whole event with great enthusiasm, joy and fanfare. According to David Gurung, the founding vice-chairman of Tamu Dhee UK, such events are organized with the purpose of carrying on the old and long Gurkha traditions and helping to bring the communities together.

The Gurkhas in the UK are also testing the waters in politics and already becoming candidates in local council elections.

When I visited the UK in late 2017 for research, I intentionally spent a few solid hours walking the streets of Aldershot, and I was not disappointed. Aldershot is known as a military town, as it hosts one of the most significant army garrisons in Southeast England, and Aldershot is called the home of the British Army. Needless to say, the Gurkhas have known this town for a long time. As I walked along the street on a misty and cold October morning, I saw Gurkhas at each corner, and they were tending to their usual errands as locals. What's more, there were Gurkha-owned shops, eateries and neighbourhood stores on each street, and it felt like I was walking on the streets of Kathmandu or Pokhara back in Nepal.

Then I recalled something Major (Retd) Tikendra Dewan J. P. had said to me. 'It's Aldershot that now thrives on Gurkhas and not the other way around.' Indeed, I said to myself. It wasn't that long ago when Aldershot was overwhelmed by the newly arrived Gurkhas, and the town councillors shouted themselves hoarse and asked for more money from the government. How have things changed since then for the Gurkhas? Being a Gurkha myself, I was not only happy but also proud. Although it took almost 200 years, the Johnny Gurkhas have finally arrived in the UK, and it isn't bad after all.

By 2018, a total of seven Gurkha councillors had already been elected, and it clearly shows the community's commitment, contribution and service to their local area. They were Maj. (Retd) Chitra Bahadur Rana, Bishnu Bahadur Gurung, Lachhya Bahadur Gurung, Lt (Retd) Nabin Siwa, Dhan Bahadur Gurung, Gam Bahadur Gurung and Tashi Lama. According to the newly elected councillor Lachhya Gurung, who has become the vice-mayor of Barnet, London, there are two main levels of government in the UK – central government (including Parliament) and local government (the Councils), and despite being elected through a ward, the councillors' overriding duty is to all residents of the borough. In his case, the Borough of Barnet has more than 400,000 residents, and it is run through 40 different committees. The Gurkha community is looking forward to more such successes.

Last but not least, a true and heart-warming story of a Gurkha who has not only touched the heart but also inspired many people. The tale of

Hari Budha Magar is indeed remarkable. He is a modern-day Gurkha, and the community can learn a lot from him. Despite losing both legs above the knee and sustaining multiple injuries from an improvised explosive device (IED) while serving in Afghanistan, he simply refused to be tied down to a wheelchair and he lives a life full of adventure that would put able-bodied men to shame. After becoming disabled, he has become a skydiver, learnt Alpine skiing and Nordic skiing, and ran a biathlon in Canada. He won a gold medal in archery, a bronze medal in wheelchair table tennis, and did rock-climbing and kayaking. Then, he became an avid cyclist, rode a 100-kilometre course and raised money for disabled veterans. Also, he learnt to golf, played wheelchair rugby, basketball and sled hockey, and took up javelin throwing. His biggest challenge of all is to climb Mount Everest. The Nepali government put a ban on his climb due to his disability, but he successfully appealed against the ban. Since the lifting of the ban, he has tirelessly trained for the mission. The main reason for the expedition is to show the world that any disability, any hardship, can be overcome, and disability may be physical but not in the mind. We wish him all the best.

If anyone among the ethnic minorities deserves to live in the UK, it's the Gurkhas, and they have earned their place through sweat, tears and blood.

CHAPTER 19

THE GURKHA JUSTICE CAMPAIGNS

'I fought in Iraq for four days, in Iran for a week, and then moved to Egypt and Palestine. We fought against the Germans in Libya, Tunis, and then in Taranto, Cassino and Naples for two more years. I was saved from a bomb as I was covered with sand. I had 17 friends, but they are all gone now. If you are not sure of your own life, you have no time to think about anything else.'

Rifleman Tahal Singh Rana (100), 2/8th GR, from Tutung, Palpa, joined the army in 1940 and returned home in 1947. He won seven war medals in WW2, has no army pension and lives on a welfare pension.

Before the Gurkha Army Ex-Servicemen's Organization (GAESO) was formed in July 1990, some organizations for the Gurkhas already existed in Nepal. But they were mostly run by former Gurkha officers from both the British and Indian Armies and labelled as elitist in a rather unflattering way. They were somehow related to the mainstream political parties of the nation and thus lacked independence as well as credibility. The trust between the officers and the other ranks of Gurkhas had always been somewhat professional and not personal. Once they left the army, the gloves automatically came off, and the trust or respect between the two became slightly subjective. What's more, officers are notoriously renowned for always taking the superior side, and they have not done much to improve their image.

Unlike those organizations for officers, the GAESO was the club for the other ranks. It had two founders. Chairman Padam Bahadur Gurung was an ex-corporal from the 2nd GR, and Chandra Bahadur Gurung, the general secretary, was an Indian Army man with one year of service. Most importantly, the GAESO was formed to fight for the rights and welfare of the other ranks without being associated with any political parties. As long as it remained true to its primary goal, it was going to work out pretty well.

Initially, the GAESO prepared a manifesto with 16 points, and they were all related to the injustice and discrimination that the Gurkhas had faced until then. Just like children, it took some time before they could learn to walk and face the many difficulties along the way. As the GAESO gained momentum with time, its popularity grew, and people started associating themselves with it. Gadflies like politicians, activists and intellectuals came in, and before too long the GAESO had become the leading organization of the British, Indian and Nepalese ex-servicemen. One of them was Professor Om Gurung, who, as one of the advisers to the GAESO, helped provide the much-needed international connections with media, human rights and army-related organizations with which the GAESO was able to launch its international campaigns.

The GAESO's first of many beautiful moments came in 1994, when they managed to submit an eight-point request to the British PM John Major through the British Embassy in Kathmandu. Its main points were: providing severance pay to those who were let go empty-handed in the 1969 rundown; equal pensions for the Gurkhas as for their British counterparts; equality between the British and Gurkha soldiers in the British Army; freedom of choice of religion; the British government should make arrangements to search for those lost or missing in the wars, and provide financial aid to their families.

In the period 1995-2004, the GAESO had become not only a national but also an international organization. It had become not only a Gurkhas issue but a national one as well. The campaign had become a human rights issue, with many high-profile individuals from the UK itself joining the cause, and it was internationally known as the 'Gurkha Justice Campaign'. Despite all the odds, the GAESO-led Gurkha campaign had come a very long way since its humble beginning and had finally arrived in the UK.

Various Gurkha-related organizations popped up at the same time and played significant roles during the ongoing Gurkha Justice Campaign. The Nepal Ex-Servicemen's Association (NESA) was one of them, formed in 1990 and serving all the retired personnel of the Nepal, Indian and British Armies. Being associated with the senior political leaders of the Nepali Congress Party, it tried to solve Gurkha-related issues through political and diplomatic channels. It is based in Nepal with a branch in the UK.

The Nepal Ex-Servicemen Organization (NESO) also was formed in 1990, carrying out small-scale activities in Nepal in its earlier days, and was associated with an ethnic political party.

The United British Gurkha Ex-Servicemen's Association (UBGEA), also known as United British Gurkha Nepal (UBGN), was established in 2001. Initially, UBGN was in for the mobilization of political-diplomatic mechanisms and exerting public pressure, but in recent years it has been leading the campaign for equal pay, pension and compensation issues.

The British Gurkha Welfare Society (BGWS) was formed in the UK in 2004 out of necessity. As many Gurkhas had already migrated to the

UK through various illegal means, they were treated, ironically given the Gurkha role in Hong Kong, as ordinary illegal immigrants (IIs) and were deported when captured by the immigration police. This very reason led the ex-Gurkhas in the UK to establish the BGWS to fight for their cause. The first Gurkha organization to take the fight to the streets had been instrumental in convincing the UK government to grant the ex-Gurkha citizenship rights as applied to all Commonwealth soldiers. This was the door opener when, in September 2004, the UK government relented, and Gurkhas were given the right to settle. Though this was only an automatic right for the post-1997 Gurkhas, its extension to those who served earlier was achieved on 21 May 2009 via the Joanna Lumley-led campaign. The BGWS is the only Gurkha organization and the first Nepali community in the UK to own its office building, aptly named 'Gurkha Bhawan' in Farnborough. The society has a significant number of followers and dedicates itself to serving the Gurkha communities in the UK. It provides services such as immigration and welfare advice, information about local offices, translation of official documents and information related to schools. It also liaises with local communities, helps in investment projects in Nepal (like the Shardi Khola hydro project), runs charity projects and offers support in all Gurkha-related issues. Besides, it also runs its community FM Radio and is led by a very capable visionary and well-informed leader, Major (Retd) Tikendra Dewan J. P. from the 6th GR.

The British Council of Gurkhas (BCG), established in the UK in 2005, mostly caters to veterans. Unlike other ex-Gurkha organizations, the BCG is led by Major (Retd) David Owen and has a substantially smaller membership base. The British Gurkha Ex-Servicemen's Organization (BGESO), established in 2009 in the UK, is a breakaway group from the GAESO and has bases in both Nepal and the UK.

In the course of the Gurkha Justice Campaign, they all participated in one way or another and contributed to the primary cause. They all deserve mention here.

Tul Bahadur Pun VC saved the life of James Lumley, a major in the 6th Gurkha Rifles and the father of actress and activist Joanna Lumley, during a battle in the Burma campaign in WWII. Joanna was the leading light of the Gurkha Justice Campaign and fought hard right through to the end for the Gurkhas' cause. She was fully supported by Gurkha admirers like Peter Carroll, a Liberal Democrat councillor in Folkestone, where Gurkhas are based; solicitors Martin Howe and Edward Cooper, who led the legal teams; and the millionaire Sir Jack Hayward, the former RAF flight lieutenant and philanthropist who was one of the leading financiers of the campaign. Various forces helped support the campaign through their websites, public support was garnered through multiple mediums, and a 250,000 signature petition was handed over to the British government during the campaign.

In 2004, the Labour government of PM Tony Blair succumbed to public pressure and changed the law to allow those Gurkhas who had retired after 1997 the right of abode in the UK. The initial victory was sweet, but it wasn't good enough, and the battle continued.

While GAESO was leading the Gurkha Justice Campaign, their main aim was fighting for equal rights for ex-Gurkhas, and they already had more than two dozen pending court cases against the British government. The real architect of the Gurkha settlement in the UK was the BGWS. Their campaign was supported by Carroll, and it really took off when the BGWS was invited to the Liberal Democrats' national conference in Bournemouth. A refined, emotional and to-the-point speech delivered by BGWS chairman, Maj (Retd) Tikendra Dewan J. P., was not only welcomed by a roaring crowd, but in fact he received three standing ovations, but also made history by himself. Major Dewan was not only the first Gurkha to deliver a speech to a national party conference but also the first to do that as an outsider. It is only in the most exceptional circumstances that non-party-members are given the opportunity to address the national conference of any mainstream political parties in the UK.

'We are simply asking for the right to live in the society that we have served over generations. I want to thank the great British public, the Liberal Democrats, Charles Kennedy and Peter Carroll for their help and support.' When Major Dewan finished his speech with these words, he had already made his point, and Kennedy, the then-leader of the Liberal Democrats, took the very unusual step of personally thanking him.

Major Dewan, who at that time was a civil servant in the British government, had assumed the chairmanship of the BGWS only after an overwhelming request by its members. He felt very proud and vindicated. However, for making this speech, Major Dewan was not only accused of wrongdoing while still in government service but was also suspended from service and unceremoniously marched out of the office to the gate by security guards as if he was a criminal. He appealed against this heavy-handed treatment by the Ministry of Defence (MoD) and successfully cleared his name.

Right after the conference of the Liberal Democrats, PM Tony Blair promised that the end of that month would decide the Gurkhas' fate. On 30 September 2004, his Labour government announced the right of settlement pact for the Gurkhas, as promised. But the first hard-fought victory came with a condition – only those Gurkhas who had retired after 1997 were eligible for resettlement in the UK. As a result, the vast majority of ex-Gurkhas were left out. Disappointed but undeterred, the fight for settlement rights for all the Gurkhas continued and the whole direction of the Gurkha Justice Campaign, including the GAESO, had to be focused on this central point. The sudden changeover caused internal discontentment within the GAESO, and top leaders were accused of abandoning the fight for Gurkha rights; this would eventually result in the formation of the breakaway BGESO in 2009.

The Gurkha Justice Campaign continued with its new goal and final justice came in 2009 when 267 votes supported the motion put by Nick Clegg of the Liberal Democrats to the House of Commons, and on 21 May 2009 the Home Secretary Jacqui Smith formally agreed that all the Gurkha veterans who retired before 1997 with at least four years of service would be allowed to settle in the UK. The long and hard-fought battle was won, and justice for the long-suffering Gurkhas was finally delivered.

For the sake of the Gurkha justice campaign, Major Dewan took the helm of the BGWS, and he can proudly claim that had it not been for the BGWS, there would have been no question of Gurkha settlement in the UK. The first success orchestrated by the BGWS made other established Gurkha organizations change their tune accordingly, and they finally achieved their mutual goal. As far as Major Dewan is concerned, he is happy and proud of what the BGWS managed to do in the name of all the Gurkhas, and he didn't mind others taking the credit.

When Joanna Lumley visited Nepal afterwards, the whole nation came out to welcome her, and wherever she went, a huge crowd followed. She was heralded as a new heroine of the Gurkhas and deservedly so, and the ever-grateful Gurkhas from the Himalayan nation of Nepal affectionately called her the 'Gurkhas' Daughter'. She even had a viewing tower on the hill of Mattikhan, at the border area of Kaski and Syangja in west Nepal, named after her, and she attended the opening ceremony during her visit to Nepal in 2009. When I visited in 2018, I was saddened to find that the villagers had changed the tower's name to the 'Mattikhan Viewing Tower' and I wondered whether anyone had taken the trouble to inform Lumley about the development.

Although the GAESO spearheaded the whole campaign and deserved all the credit and respect, it was a concerted Gurkha effort, and everyone, including the rival Gurkha organizations, pitched in. Despite all the failures and tribulations along the way, Padam Bahadur never lost heart. His vision and perseverance finally paid off.

Around the time the GAESO was born in 1990, another ex-Gurkha named Gyanraj Rai (the son of a former Nepali politician and a former warrant officer of the QGE) started his own battle and created an unprecedented situation in Kathmandu. He took the Nepalese government to the Supreme Court of Nepal for negligence in its solemn duty by not protecting the Gurkhas from inequality, injustice and unfair treatment while serving in the British Army. Despite all his efforts, the case was eventually dismissed by the court. However, the incident gave birth to a diehard activist, and this warrior continues to fight with the mighty British through the Gurkha Satyagraha which was formed under his leadership in 2012.

Once the teething problems of the newly arrived Gurkhas in the UK were overcome, Gyanraj and his team changed course and concentrated on fighting for equal rights for the Gurkhas within the British Army. There have always been huge disparities between the Gurkhas and the British soldiers' pay, pension and other facilities provided by the MoD.

The discrimination between the two existed from the very beginning, and it had always been one of the main grievances of the Gurkha Justice Campaign. The campaign had already succeeded in providing pension equality for those joining the British Army after 1997. But there was still one big group left out from sharing the pie. Those who had joined the British Army right after the end of WWII and retired before 1997 were the most affected ones. The Gurkha Satyagraha solemnly took up their cause as one of the main objectives of their campaign and the struggle continued.

Their first action was to hold a relay protest in front of the Houses of Parliament in London until their demands were heard. Then Gyanraj himself started the great hunger strike that began on 7 November 2013 at Whitehall, near Downing Street, and promised to starve himself to death unless the demands were met. He finally called off the strike on the 15th day, when British MPs agreed to make an inquiry into Gurkhas' pensions, healthcare and welfare. The hunger strike was broken by drinking a bottle of orange juice offered by none other than Joanna Lumley, the heroine of the Gurkha Justice Campaign. The British have worked on the issues and made substantial improvements since then. However, the struggle is not over yet, and discussions are still going on as I write.

I had the opportunity of meeting Gyanraj when I was in the UK and spent almost half a day talking about the Gurkhas. For the sake of his passion and belief, the poor guy sold all of his wealthy father's properties back in Nepal. The place where he was living was quite big but, according to his wife, and I admit, it was more like a transit place than home. He had been providing refuge to newly arrived Gurkhas who had nowhere else to go from the beginning, and the practice had become like a tradition. To make ends meet, he still works as a double-decker bus driver, and his passion, dedication and determination are clear. Activism is indeed not a one-way road; you will not only make friends but also enemies, and he is no different. The warrior of Gurkha justice is here to fight until justice is served. He isn't going anywhere yet. An excellent book about the Gurkhas called *British-Gurkha: From Treaty to Supreme Court* in the Nepali language is based on his story.

While Gyanraj Rai and his team were fighting for the equal rights of the Gurkha veterans, GAESO chairman Padam Bahadur Gurung found a new interest. After 27 years of being at the helm of the GAESO, he finally handed the chairmanship over to Krishna Kumar Rai in 2016. The organization is currently run by a working committee of 129 newly elected members.

Padam Bahadur's new baby is called the Gurkha Memorial Park, currently under construction at Salme Danda (Hill), Phedi Khola, Syangja, and being constructed in five phases. They are: the Gurkha Heaven, the Memorial Museum, the Nepali Cultural Village, the Tower and the Gurkha Rail. By building this park, Padam Bahadur wants the world to know about the 200-year Gurkha history and be aware of the irreparable losses the Gurkhas, as well as Nepal as an independent country, have suffered, and eventually change the world's perception of Nepal and its people.

I revisited this location during my Nepal trip in 2018 but was disheartened to witness the actual situation of the project. Padam Bahadur had been too ambitious. The whole place looked abandoned, not much had been done since the initial construction, and Padam Bahadur looked somewhat like a defeated man, although he tried to appear as enthusiastic, passionate and driven as he was during our first meeting just a year previously. The provincial government is now funding the project, a budget of 5-6 crore rupees was arriving soon, and Padam Bahadur was hoping to finish phase one of the project by 2019 but as of now, it's still under construction. He explained that the local leaders understand the importance of the project and they have more than enough incentives to complete it, but I could see the pain on his face while he was describing the situation to me. Given the nature of Nepali politics, I couldn't help but feel sorry for him. The chances of his pet project being hijacked by Nepali leaders taking all the credit for themselves were all too real.

If you want to know more about this great man, read the book *British Samrajyaka Nepali Mohora* (*Nepali Footprints on the British Empire* – a roughly translated title as the book is written in Nepali) by Jhalak Subedi from Himal Books.

By the first quarter of 2018, most of the major players of the Gurkha campaign had united, and a complete dossier on ex-Gurkha grievances prepared by the team was presented to the MoD. It covered Gurkhas' pay, pensions, human rights, medical facilities, fairness and equality, national insurance and legality issues. According to the report by the CNSUK, approximately 22,000 ex-Gurkhas and widows are still treated unequally in comparison to their British counterparts on a pension; 6,534 Gurkhas were made redundant between the period of 1948-1975 with no pensions and 3,438 who were identified as poor receive a welfare pension from the Gurkha Welfare Trust. And 542 Gurkhas discharged after 1975 do not receive any allowances at all.

The participation of the Nepali Embassy in the Gurkhas' cause was noteworthy, and the chances of solving the problem of the long-suffering Gurkhas had improved. The campaigners also presented a detailed report on grievances of the Gurkhas to the PM of Nepal, K. P. Oli, in Kathmandu in April 2018, and hoped the Nepal government would help support their cause and initiate bilateral talks with the British government.

Decisions by the MoD were still to be made and at the time this book went to press, the talks on equal rights for the Gurkhas were still going on.

CHAPTER 20

THE EFFECTS OF GURKHA RECRUITING POLICY IN NEPAL

'I always wanted to have a bravery medal as I heard a lot about the bravery of the Gurkhas. In the 1971 Pakistan war, in a place called Khadinagar, I went for reconnaissance, got fired upon by the enemy and yet I managed to return safely and led the troops to the enemy position. In Pipial, I was appointed an ambush commander, killed four or five of the enemy and captured an enemy officer during the operation, for which I was awarded a gallantry award, the Vir Chakra.'

Hon. Capt. Bal Bahadur Gurung (77), 5/5th GR, from Butwal, joined the Indian Army in 1960 and retired in 1988. He fought in both the 1965 and 1971 Pakistan wars and won the Vir Chakra.

Besides the Himalayas and Lord Buddha, the one other thing that makes Nepal famous in the world is the Gurkhas. The Gurkha history goes back to the same important period as the birth of the nation. Modern Nepal was virtually built on each brick of local princely estate, one by one. The land was won by the fighting skills, bravery and determination of the men from the winning army. By the time the British East India Company and the Gorkha Army eventually met in the Anglo-Gorkha War of 1814-16, both were considered significant powers in the region, and almost all of the northern parts of India were under Gorkhali rule.

In reality, it was the pay system of the Gorkha Army that forced the men to march on. Since the newly formed nation of Nepal had no deep pockets, the country couldn't pay them directly from its treasury. The land taxes paid the army commanders and soldiers and the more lands they won, the more they got. To keep the machine (the Gorkha Army) moving and the army happy and motivated, they needed to gain more land. Human greed and lust for power also played a part, and the British and the Gorkhas eventually had to cross each other's path one way or another. The result was the Anglo-Gorkha War.

After victory in the war, the British managed to clip Nepal's expanding wings and confined it within its defined boundaries. The fighting was over, and the chances of conquering new lands were gone. The British had requested enlisting the Gorkhas into their army, but the humiliated government of Nepal was in no mood to entertain that request, at least not yet. As a result, the nation of brave Gorkhas ended up with vast numbers of idle soldiers with no work. Nepal was still an unknown and unexplored country in the high Himalayas. Fighting was the new trade its men had recently discovered and taking that skill out of their lives made them almost useless again. The last thing they wanted was to go back to the same old dull nomadic life of farming. So they joined the British-Indian Army by coming down from the hills illegally, but they did so of their own choice. The PM of Nepal (1806-1837), Bhim

Sen Thapa, was a wise and experienced leader. He fully understood the ulterior motive of the British and always wanted to keep them at arm's length. Allowing the British to enlist the Gorkhas into their army openly was almost impossible in his reign, and he had always resented the British Resident in Kathmandu.

Although the recruitment of the Gorkhas into the British Army started after the end of the first phase of the Anglo-Gorkha war and the eventual signing of the Sugauli treaty, the tradition of '*Muglan Pasne*' or venturing abroad for a better life was nothing new for the men from the hills. As already described, Gorkhas were already serving in the Sikh-Khalsa Army of Maharaja Ranjit Singh of Punjab at Lahore and hence the origin of the famous term '*Lahure*', which is still in use. Although the enlistment of the Gorkhas into the British-Indian Army was one of the principal terms agreed between the two generals – Ochterlony and Amarsing – there was no mention of that particular point in the actual treaty signed by the two nations. It gives reason to doubt those who believe that the original agreement was perhaps meant to be only for the soldiers then under the command of the Gorkhali general, and somehow got twisted to a whole new level over time.

After the downfall of Bhim Sen Thapa in 1839, the political situation of Nepal became unstable and the country reeled from several unfavourable incidents. On one occasion, the King took refuge in the British Residency, and the British Raj was accused of stirring trouble within the country. Brian Hodgson, the then British Resident in Nepal, somehow managed to defuse the situation. The perpetrators (the senior queen and the Nepalese commander-in-chief) were dismissed, the King drew up a list of ministers for Hodgson's approval, and the relationship between the two nations improved. In return for Hodgson's help, the Maharaja of Nepal offered Nepalese troops to assist the East India Company in both Burma and Afghanistan, but the then Governor-General of India gracefully refused the offer.

Despite their good relationship, the direct enlistment in Nepal of Gorkhas into the British-Indian Army wasn't established during those periods. Hodgson had great influence with the Nepal Durbar. His writing about Nepal's flora and fauna, its laws and administration and Buddhism were remarkable. He resigned in 1843 and moved to Darjeeling. After his departure, Nepal fell into a state of confusion and turmoil until the strongman Jang Bahadur Rana came to power as the most powerful prime minister of Nepal.

Jang Bahadur Rana wasn't in favour of the Gorkhas being recruited into the British-Indian Army. He was even said to have called them 'traitors' and applied different approaches to appease the British. Instead of sanctioning the Gurkha recruiting, he offered to send his troops to assist the British against the Sikhs in 1848, which was gracefully refused. Jang Bahadur Rana was an Anglophile, at least in the eyes of the British. But his actions suggested otherwise. He had not only arrested those agents who had entered Nepal to encourage and facilitate new recruiting, but also issued executive orders to the villages prohibiting new recruiting, and offenders were to lose the rights to their lands immediately. His idea of supporting the British was not through allowing the direct recruiting but by providing his army whenever the British were in trouble. He was an intelligent man and fully understood the consequences of allowing direct recruitment. He didn't want to have a black mark on his legacy. That was the main reason why the British had not been able to raise more regiments than the three they had already had since 1815.

But all that changed after his visit to the UK in 1850. His admiration for Queen Victoria was legendary, and he is said to have pledged the whole power of Nepal to support the British in India. The establishment of the 4th Gurkha Regiment was made possible with his endorsement. Jang Bahadur Rana and the Nepalese Army played a significant role during the Sepoy Mutiny of 1857-58, which was a difficult time for the British, and he probably saved British rule in India.

Jang Bahadur suddenly resigned in 1856 and became the Maharaja of Kaski and Lamjung before resuming the premiership again after his brother Bum Bahadur died. The reason behind Jang Bahadur's unprecedented move was to control the flow of Gurkha recruits from those two areas, which happened to be the hotbed of Gurkhas, as they had heavy Gurung residency and still do.

Nevertheless, the recruiting continued, albeit at a slow pace. Young men from the hillsides continued descending in groups, crossed the border quietly, and joined the newly formed Gurkha Army in the south. In those days, connections made through villages, through uncles from either fathers' or mothers' sides, or through distant relatives, were significant. If you had one, you just had to find his regiment and tell his name to the recruiting officer. Then your job was done.

Basic recruiting was an internal matter of the regiments in those days. Since there were no separate training depots, each regiment had their training wing and recruits were trained by the respective regiments.

After the Sepoy Mutiny, the Gurkhas had already established themselves as a crack force of the British-Indian Army and were affectionately called the 'Gurkha Legion'. Most importantly, the loyalty of the Gurkhas was never questioned again. After leading the Gurkhas in the Afghan Wars, Lord Roberts had great respect for them, and he wanted to raise more Gurkha regiments.

The Nepal Durbar policy on the Gurkha recruiting frustrated the British as they were not able to get as many Gurkhas as they wanted. It was the main reason why the British encouraged the Gurkhas to settle in India, and many Gurkha families migrated to India during those times. The British had also introduced a new law that allowed Gurkhas to buy and own land in India and many had settled there since then. The 'Gurkha Charter', which was introduced in 1860, granted the right for Gurkhas from existing regiments to have their families with them in India, and the reason was to avoid punishment for the returning Gurkhas by the regime in Nepal. Those mobilizations are the reason why the northern hill regions of today's India have people of Nepali origin living there now.

After Jang Bahadur's death, Ranodip Singh became Nepal's prime minister in 1877, and the British requested 1,000 recruits in 1878. According to the book *British Samrajyaka Nepali Mohora* by Nepali author Jhalak Sebedi, to keep the relationship healthy, in return he asked for more arms from the British to fight the Tibetan threat. He accepted the British request and sent 559 men. Surprisingly, 339 out of the 559 men were disabled, blind or frail and were rejected by the British as they were unfit for the army.

When Bir Shumsher took over the premiership of Nepal by assassinating Ranodip Singh in 1885, members of the rival faction took refuge in the British Residence, and they were eventually allowed to live in India under British protection. Bir Shumsher was always wary of the rival faction that someday they might garner enough support from the British and plot against his regime. Besides, he desperately wanted British approval for his premiership too. When Lord Roberts managed to persuade the War Office for a substantial expansion of the Gurkha regiments and initiated a talk with the Nepali Durbar, Bir Shumsher agreed and removed all the restrictions on the Gurkha recruiting policy. The policy of direct recruiting was eventually sanctioned in 1886 and British officers were allowed into Nepal for the very first time to supervise the permanent system of recruitment. After the regime had resisted for 71 years, the direct recruiting of the Gurkhas by the British-Indian Army was finally allowed, and it's still going strong even today.

Before WWI, a peacetime strength of around 26,000 Gurkhas served in ten regiments (20 battalions), but due to the open recruitment, WWI and WWII changed everything. More than 200,000 men (including regulars, irregulars and Nepal Army) came down and fought for the British in WWI alone. In 1914 during WWI, fresh battalions were raised including the 11th Gurkha Rifles with four battalions, and the number of recruits drastically went up. According to the official figures, 57,000 new recruits were enlisted during WWI alone; 63 per cent of them were from western Nepal, and the rest came from eastern Nepal. By order of PM Chandra Shumsher, almost a dozen collection centres were established along the border and men were herded off from there and sent to the training centres in India. Among them, one in ten never returned. The total population of Nepal was a little more than five million and if children, women and old folks were eliminated from the equation, about 20 per cent of the able men of Nepal fought alongside the British.

The unfortunate event repeated itself in 1939 when the Germans and the Japanese started WWII. Despite not being one of the warring nations, Nepal paid a heavy price. The ten Gurkha regiments were brought back to their wartime strength. An extra four battalions were raised for each regiment while some regiments even had five battalions and all the available men from the hills of Nepal were called up again. According to the official figures, 23,000 men were annually enlisted, and about 161,000 joined the Brigade during WWII. Almost 250,280 men fought for the British cause, and about 32,000 were killed, wounded or missing. According to official figures, 66,000 men were released after WWI and WWII; 24,000 men were killed, wounded or lost and, by 1947, the number of pensioners had reached 50,000 from 20,000 before the war.

During WWI and WWII, the Rana government put the whole nation and its resources at Britain's disposal, and men from all the castes of Nepal were duly affected. The demands of fighting men for both WWI and WWII were so high that it depleted the youth from the whole nation and hardly a young man was to be found in the villages. Even criminals serving prison terms were not spared and were sent to the war. The whole nation was robbed of its men. Women and children were left to survive on their own. Life became a never-ending nightmare. Even worse, the worry of whether their loved ones would return or not always hung over their neck like a guillotine, and the fear never went away. During both WWI and WWII, everything stood still regarding development for both country and society. It was a lost time for the stunted nation. Nepal paid a heavy price for the sake of friendship with the British, and the country never recovered.

After the end of the Great War, all the wounded, handicapped and crippled from the war were discharged from the army and sent home without proper treatment or compensation. The suffering nation of Nepal was burdened again by having to look after them. Emptied by the audacity and short-sightedness of its proud, selfish and ingratiating rulers, the country had no choice but to toil on and suffer unimaginable indignity. All the paths heading north from the Terai plains were crowded with men carrying those wounded sons on their tired backs; some had no legs, others had no hands. Mother Nepal couldn't see her children in such unbearable agony and looked away while trying to hold in her own tears. Those were undoubtedly the darkest days of Nepal's history, and her loss was immeasurable. The saddest part of that unfortunate event was that there was nobody to see it, let alone appreciate it.

The social, mental and economic effects on Nepal caused by WWI and WWII were so immense that no words could describe them. The emotional scars it inflicted on the lives of the Nepali people were almost unimaginable, especially the sufferings of the Gurkha families, which were beyond repair. A family lost its capable son, a village lost its strong man, and a nation lost its solid rock upon which it was built. In brief, the future of the whole country was lost in cold European trenches, hot African deserts and the Burmese jungles.

Before and during both WWI and WWII, due to the lack of qualified officers/NCOs, all the Gurkhas who were on leave, as well as those who were recently retired, were immediately called back for duty. The basic recruit training was also shortened to seven months from the usual nine, and temporary training camps were established in various parts of northern India. For office work, men from the Newari tribe of Kathmandu were enlisted in the early days, and they were known as *Babuji* (clerks) in the army. After the partition of India, most of the clerks were enlisted from Darjeeling. In addition, teachers for Gurkha children as well as midwives and nurses for the Gurkha families also came from Darjeeling. As Nepal's standard of education improved by the 1970s and 80s, those posts were gradually filled by candidates from Nepal.

At the beginning of the post-independence period, the recruits for the Brigade of Gurkhas were mostly enlisted from two recruiting depots, Lehra and Jalapahar/Ghoom. The recruitment of Gurkhas from India into the new Brigade of Gurkhas had already ceased. Once they were selected, the recruits were issued with their 'Transit Mufti' (black trousers, white shirt and a Nepali hat) and they were to wear it throughout the journey to Calcutta. The Calcutta transit camp was Barrackpore. They waited there for the ship and eventually disembarked at Penang in Malaysia or Singapore after a ten-day sea journey.

The British had their strategy in recruiting Gurkhas from Nepal. They had initially divided the nation into five zones: the far west, western Nepal, central Nepal, the valley, and eastern Nepal. But it had to be revised later, once the Rais, Limbus and Sunuwars were recruited from eastern Nepal. The far west zone had no Gurkhas of the Mongolian characteristics except the Dotiyals, who had served as porters during wars. The valley zone was forbidden for recruiting as it was home to ruling families and aristocrats, skilled artisans and merchants. No. 1 west and No. 1 east were also restricted as they were reserved for the Nepal Army. The central Nepal region – Gulmi, Palpa, Gorkha, Lamjung, Kaski, Tanhu and Parbat districts – was undoubtedly the most heavily recruited zone as the tribes of Magars and Gurungs mostly inhabited those areas.

Eastern Nepal was divided into No. 2 East Ramechhap, No. 3 East Okhaldunga, No. 4 Bhojpur, Dhankuta and Ilam. The Arun River running between No. 4 and Dhankuta can be taken as the dividing line between Rais and Limbus. Further eastward from Nepal, Darjeeling and Sikkim are mainly populated by Gurkhas of all tribes, but Bhutan was never considered for recruiting Gurkhas.

Beside Magars and Gurungs from West Nepal and Rais and Limbus from East Nepal, Tamangs and Sunuwars were freely recruited to the British Army while recruits from other mixed races of Nepal are also recruited nowadays, albeit in small numbers. Besides, the Damai (tailors), the Kaami (blacksmiths), the Saarki (shoemakers) and the Sunaar (goldsmiths) were also enlisted in the army, and each regiment had a few individuals. A pandit (religious guru) for each regiment was also provided to perform Hindu rites and rituals.

The *Gallawalas*, or the local recruiting officers, who were usually senior Gurkha NCOs, were sent out in groups to those zones. Their responsibility was to select the best potential recruits from their respective areas and bring them to the recruiting camps for the final selection. The recruiting officer (RO) was always British, a colonel or a major, and he was assisted by a group of extra assistant recruiting officers (EAROs) who were mostly Gurkha officers (GOs). The recruiting would generally start in early December, followed by final selection and eventually being sent to the training depots by January. The basic recruit training would begin by January or February of the year, so, after the nine months' training, they could join their respective battalion right before the Dussehra for a timely celebration.

Kunraghat in Gorakhpur has remained the main central recruiting centre of the Indian Gurkha Army and young men from various villages of Nepal still travel there to join up. Kathmandu, Pokhara and Dharan have pension camps serving the pensioners of the Indian Army, and they also have seasonal camps around Nepal. They come in for the recruiting rally each year, make the selection in many places and go back to India. The recruit training for the Indian Army is held in the regiment, but they combine the recruits for two or three regiments together and arrange the training.

Initially, the existing five Gurkha regiments were to have added one more battalion each, and Gorakhpur was established as a central recruiting depot in 1886. Gorakhpur was chosen due to its proximity to Nepal's border. A Central Railway station nearby made the dispatching of recruits to regiments a lot easier, and a new residence called the 'Gurkha Village' was set up to house those recruits. Men from Magar and Gurung tribes were recruited from west-central Nepal in groups and sent down to Gorakhpur for the final selection. By 1932, Kunraghat operated as both recruitment and pension centre, had sheds for 12,000 pensioners, an officers' mess and quarters, and a military hospital.

By the turn of the century, the British-Indian Gurkhas already had ten regular regiments with a total of twenty battalions. When the British started recruiting men from the Rai and Limbu tribes of east Nepal, especially for the 7th and 10th Gurkha Rifles, a new recruiting depot was opened in Darjeeling in 1890 where a small room was lent for a few hours daily in the Kacheri. Initially, the depot was responsible for recruiting men for Burma and Assam. In 1902, part of the British Mountain Battery lines at Ghoom were taken over and with considerable alterations and repairs, new buildings were made in 1930 and 1935. The final expansion took place in 1943.

A temporary depot was made at Purnea (1891-1909) and then in Sakri when the Sunuwars tribe was first enlisted. A further move to Lahera Sarai was established in 1912, and the sub-depot functioned most years until 1929. A sub-depot was opened at Pithoragarh near the western borders of Nepal to serve the Dotiyals.

Since the British had just four regiments with them after independence, the number of recruits decreased drastically. Besides, when choosing the four regiments for the British Army, they had considered the recruiting availability areas back in Nepal, and the so-called martial races played a significant role in their final decision. The 'martial race' term is a creation of the British themselves, and after working with the Gurkhas for a century and a half, they concluded that only a few castes of the Nepali people fall into this class. They were Magar and Gurung tribes from the west of Nepal and the tribes of Rais and Limbus from the east. As far as the British were concerned, only men from those tribes make the best soldiers in the world. The British wanted two regiments of the Magars and Gurungs and two regiments from the Rais and Limbus, making a total of four regiments in the newly formed Brigade of Gurkhas.

The changes in the British position in Asia also changed the fate of the Gurkhas. Once they moved out of India, the recruiting of the Gurkhas was moved into Nepal, and the British were operating directly from Nepal by the late fifties. Two recruiting camps were to be built within Nepal: the Paklihawa camp was to serve the west, and the Dharan camp was for the east. As the tribes of Gurungs and Magars are mostly found in central western Nepal, a new camp was built to serve them in Pokhara by the late seventies. The Pokhara camp is the only recruiting centre that is still in operation as I write.

With the establishment of two new camps (Pokhara and Dharan), activities related to the British Gurkhas are mostly concentrated in those two areas, and the transformation of the surrounding areas was remarkable. Dharan and Pokhara are known as the town of the *Lahures*. Every big new house built in Pokhara belonged to a *Lahure's* family, and had it not been for the *Lahures*, there would not have been a Pokhara, at least not as vibrant and promising as it is now. Kaski, Syangja, Gorkha and Lamjung are the areas where the Gurungs mostly live, and they have come down from the nearby villages to Pokhara as town-dwellers. Unlike their forefathers, the modern Gurkhas don't go to their communities any more and have mostly settled in the nearby towns or the capital.

Before we proceed, I have to discuss the role played by religious beliefs within our societies in Nepal. According to Hindu mythology, the people are divided into four main groups, and your position within the community is determined by the group into which you were born. The hierarchical groups consist of Brahmins – for studying scriptures, performing religious rites and rituals; Kshatriyas – the warriors and protectors; Vaisyas – the farmers, traders and other tribals; and the Sudras – the untouchables and manual labourers. Since the societies were structured into the stringent conformity of the hierarchical religious system and strictly observed, leaving the system and doing something else was almost unimaginable. As a result, regardless of talent, interest or opportunity, the fate of the people was decided by their birth, and they were bound to play their roles as the community would allow them.

In a society ruled by religious belief and a primitive mindset where destiny betrayed them before birth and people were restricted by the certain boundaries of their religious beliefs, progress was almost non-existent. The Gurkhas found themselves limited to farming and herding jobs as Vaisya. Soldiering offered them a new opportunity, a sort of escape route, and they grabbed the chance wholeheartedly. Being warriors by nature, they learned the new trade fast and excelled like no others.

Over time, nothing much changed from the Indian side, while the appearance of the British side improved a great deal. When the British Gurkhas moved to Hong Kong in 1971, the gap between the two had become quite apparent, and that affected people's views within the communities. Since India was conveniently near Nepal, the Indian Gorkhas could go home on a yearly basis, while the British Gurkhas only came back every three years. Most importantly, the Indian Gorkhas were always paid in Indian rupees while the British Gurkhas got paid in Malaysian or Singapore dollars and then in Hong Kong dollars. Although both Indian and British Gurkhas applied the same pay code, the value of the dollars fluctuated, especially against the weak currencies of Nepal and India, where the dollars were always valued high.

For a new, landlocked and primitive nation like Nepal, trade was restricted to the Kathmandu Valley people, and the rest depended entirely on farming. Money earned by soldiering was the only means of income for the tribes from the hills, and they could buy many household things such as clothes, blankets and other necessities with that money. The most common practice was, and still is, to build a beautiful house on a large area of land. Initially, they bought everyday items such as tea, sugar, cigarettes, salt, sweets and clothes as they returned home on leave. Gradually, that list changed to a rather nice variety of household items, which were still luxuries in those days. Those families with more members serving as *Lahures* brought in more money, enabling them to buy more land, build bigger houses, and greatly increase their family assets. With money came power and status in the villages.

The disparity between the two types of *Lahures* grew in such a way that they could be differentiated right away by looks alone as they entered the village. The Indian *Lahures* usually had one porter carrying an army-issued suitcase or bedding and hardly got noticed by the villagers. In contrast, the men of the Malayan *Lahures* (later on, the Hong Kong *Lahures* to some extent), especially if they were returning with the family, had a line of porters, some carrying colourful suitcases and others the children, with loud songs blaring from big and shiny tape recorders. Everyone, including the village dogs, would notice their arrival. The over-enthusiastic village children would have already crowded the path, and before too long, the whole village gathered around the house. The crowd wouldn't disperse until they got their prizes – candies for the children, biscuits for the old ones and gifts for the relatives. At the main house, every family member was busy like in a beehive. Unique dishes were made, and the serving of glasses of hot tea never stopped. The suitcase containing special gifts for the family members would only open when all the villagers had gone home, and everyone was then showered with expensive gifts such as new watches, gold rings and chains, clothes, shoes and much more. I still remember the special night when I had returned home for the very first time after three and a half years, and the sheer joy it brought to the family.

The disparity certainly created a rift within the community. The practices of favouring the British Gurkhas were pretty evident and prevalent, especially in a Gurung village like the one I hailed from. Gurungs are a very tightly knit community. They only marry within their population, and the *Malayako Lahure* was always the first choice of those parents with daughters of marriageable age. The British Gurkhas looked clean and disciplined, wore nice, expensive clothes and had enough money to buy land and gold. The status of the family grew as well and being a British Gurkha had always been the priority of all the young boys in the Gurung village. The grandfather, father, uncle or brother had served as a

Gurkha, and when you count members from both paternal and maternal sides, the chance of finding a family without a Gurkha connection is zero. To continue the status and position, new generations had to follow their family tradition and try to join the Gurkhas as soon as possible. The families without a member serving in the British Gurkhas were the ones who suffered the most in the community.

The new generations of boys saw all those phenomena as they grew up. Becoming a British Gurkha had been their goal since the moment they learned to dream, and everything else became insignificant. The moment the young man meets the basic physical requirements of the Gurkhas (height, 5 feet 2 inches; weight, 50 kgs or 110 pounds; and chest, 30-32 inches), he would line up in front of the *Gallawala* recruiting agent and try his luck. The arrival of the *Gallawala* in the village was a yearly event. All the young men from the village would gather in front of him, and a curious crowd of onlookers would form around them. Those selected were given a number and a date to report for the final selection: Pokhara for the west and Dharan for the east were the places where more tests were conducted before the youngsters finally got the chance to become a British Gurkha. Once selected, they were issued army numbers and a small kit of uniform before having an army haircut and then practising for the new recruit's swearing-in ceremony on a daily basis. Recruits from both Pokhara and Dharan camps were assembled in Kathmandu and then flew out to Hong Kong (nowadays, to the UK) where they went through the basic recruit training for nine months before they could join their regiments as a new Gurkha soldier.

Those not selected waited for the next chance and kept on trying while they had the slightest opportunity. Only after they had tried and failed in Nepal, did youths from the village go on to become Indian Gorkhas. The whole process of becoming an Indian Gorkha was a completely different affair – at least in our village. No recruiting agents visited our communities. There were no gatherings of youths, no selection process and no crowds of spectators. Those who planned to join the Indian Gorkhas slipped away quietly from the village on their own, went to Kunraghat in a small group, and joined the Indian Army. The journey was carried out in such a discreet way that nobody from the village noticed it until they were told so by the family. Those youths who couldn't make it to the British or Indian Gurkhas were to some extent even stigmatized as failures and experienced humiliation. In brief, the Gurung community could be characterized and dictated by three choices: the British Gurkhas – first choice, the Indian Gorkhas – second choice, and the non-Gurkhas (also known as Dhakres) – the third and last choice.

The other three so-called martial races, Magars, Rais and Limbus, had more or less similar situations as the Gurungs, and the recruiting policy played a crucial role in their livelihood for the last 200-plus years.

By the turn of the 21st century, most of the Gurkhas were living in the towns and in the Kathmandu Valley. As their living standards improved, more luxurious items such as TVs, refrigerators, washing machines, ovens and electronic appliances were brought in, and the disparity between Gurkha families and others grew even further. In many towns and cities, the British Gurkhas were also blamed for making land and houses too expensive, which created unnecessary tiffs or resentments out of envy and to some extent divided the community.

These days, only a few hundred recruits are joining the British Gurkhas each year, while a few thousand go to the Indian Gorkhas, and that counts as almost nothing in a country of around 30 million people. Still, 20,000 British ex-Gurkhas are receiving a pension from the UK government, and nearly double that number live in Nepal without a pension. The numbers of Indian Gorkha veterans must be double that of those from the British side. If we add up the new generations of Gurkha veterans, the final numbers will be pretty big. It might be insignificant if we were to take the whole nation in this equation. However, especially in those areas where the martial races are mostly living, the overall effect is enormous. The Gurkhas policy was so ingrained in our societies that its effects can be felt in every walk of our lives. The Gurkha policy has outlived all of us. It was already there before many of us were born, and it will be there even after many of us are gone, and we will never be able to take the Gurkha policy out of our lives.

An exact evaluation of the Gurkha recruiting policy within Nepal is impossible to measure. Perhaps it will never be done, but one thing is sure. The Gurkha policy has had significant effects on our social, economic and political lives. The Gurkha policy has been not only a centuries-long tradition but also a way of life as well as our very identity.

Due to the policy, Nepali people inevitably had to venture outside Nepal, with the Gurkhas being the first ones to cross the borders and step outside. Modern youths and families of Nepal have spread to various parts of the globe. They go out as students, labourers and new migrants, and the substantial size of Nepali diaspora communities already exist in various countries around the world. They have benefited the country through sharing their necessary skills, and their newly acquired knowledge. The money they bring in will help improve their families' lives, the new skills they learn will create new businesses and their expertise in human development as well as civility will help develop a better community. As a result, the country's economy, as well as image, will grow and the whole nation will eventually prosper.

After the announcement of the UK government on 21 May 2009, many British Gurkha veterans and their families moved to the UK, and over 76,000 of them are currently living there. This new trend might have affected the inflow of foreign money to Nepal. Others have even suggested the opposite flow as Gurkha veterans sold their properties in Nepal before settling in the UK. But that is not the truth. According to researchers (the Centre for Nepal Studies UK) and leaders of Gurkha-related organizations (Gyanraj Rai, the convenor of British Satyagraha Committee and Major (Retd) Tikendradal Dewan J. P., the chairman of the British Gurkha Welfare Society), who have conducted detailed research involving various Gurkha veterans and their families, the main reason why Gurkha veterans moved to the UK is for the future of their children; and once that's settled, and the policy changes for the Gurkha pensions, they will return. The land of their '*Gora sahibs*' is too cold and unforgiving for the old folks, and they will never forget their homeland. If they cannot be in Nepal forever, they will keep coming back again and again, and will always do something good whenever they visit their homeland.

Years of living abroad and serving the British has made the Gurkhas' love and admiration for their own country stronger. After the British Gurkhas and their children return to Nepal, they contribute to the development of their old villages by either helping in the construction of the village school, community hall, ancestral temple, water-point, electricity station, or a bridge or a road that connects the villagers to the nearby town. The Gurkha veterans also share their knowledge about financial and economic issues along with educational advice. The sentiment is to improve their own and the community's quality of living through shared contributions.

If you take a look at the town of Pokhara, for instance, which is known as the town of the *Lahures*, each area has its community group. They not only help solve security issues, problems related to the collection of trash and other daily issues, but also deal with the social and religious needs of the community and carry out all the tasks that the municipal authority does in most developed nations. That's why the streets of Pokhara are much cleaner and organized than other cities in the country. The Nepali diaspora communities have various organizations of their own, mostly based on their village, area, caste, school, hobby, regiment, intake and so on. They seem to be always busy raising funds for this or that cause and social media, mostly Facebook, plays a significant role in driving support. When the earthquake struck the nation in 2015, the concern shown by the people was genuine and heart-warming, and the contribution made by the Nepali diaspora was enormous.

On the flip side, the Gurkha policy made us, especially these four races (Magars, Gurungs, Rais and Limbus), seem like horses with blinkers and the only thing we saw was the finishing point. We self-inflicted ourselves with this handicap, didn't look for alternatives and restricted ourselves to the only-one-goal option. We never realized there were other options. We could study hard and become doctors, engineers, lawyers, businessmen, civil servants or mechanics. But we just refused to look around and kept forging ahead stubbornly with only one intention. In pursuit of our dream, many of us neglected our studies. We only knew two things for the last two centuries: either join the Gurkhas or be a farmer, and unfortunately, not much has changed.

While chasing our one-sided dream, we neglected other aspects of our lives in society and ended up like outsiders. We are newcomers in every commercial, social and political field. People from other tribes have already perfected those trades and run them as experts. Wherever we go, we find ourselves at the end of the line, and we cannot even complete a small task without having to beg the officials in our own country. While the others already moved ahead, our community didn't and was left behind. At the same time, we have become one of the most backward and neglected communities within the nation, we have no genuine representatives in higher positions, and we get almost nothing from the government. The deep-rooted resentments of the other communities towards the Gurkhas also doesn't help. As a result, despite being one of the most prominent tribal peoples and contributors in Nepal, we have become the most marginalized community of our nation. There is no sign of things changing for the better any time soon.

The 1990s were a difficult period for Nepal. The new government was weak and the political instability gave room for brewing troubles. The Maoist insurgency was on the rise, forcibly dividing the otherwise peace-loving people of Nepal in the name of a falsified revolution that would eventually plunge the nation into utter turmoil. Due to the British handover of Hong Kong back to the Chinese in 1997, the Brigade of Gurkhas saw one of its most significant run-downs, and almost 7,000 Gurkhas were sent packing back to Nepal before the British left Hong Kong. It wasn't the first time that the British had acted in such a cruel way, though, as the consequences of WWI, WWII and the 1969 incidents were even more prominent. The ramification of this mass cutback was to end with significant effects for one reason. Unlike their grandfathers, the Gurkhas had changed with time. They had already learned to fight for their rights if necessary. They were not prepared to go quietly this time around.

The British failed to heed the changes and acted as they had always done before. Dissatisfaction and disappointment turned to grievances, and grievances to anger. The public outcry of the ex-servicemen gradually took shape into an opposition force, and all they needed now was a leader who could represent them. As a result, many pretenders emerged like mushrooms, but only a few lasted. The Gurkha Army Ex-Servicemen's Organisation (GAESO) and the British Gurkha Welfare Society (BGWS) were some that eventually delivered. The Gurkha justice campaigns had finally begun.

CHAPTER 21

WHAT MAKES THE GURKHAS SO SPECIAL?

'After the completion of my recruit training, I got sick, continuously, for the next four years and gave up my army career. Once I returned home, I offered puja to the local god and somehow fully recovered. Then I decided to go back to the army but was captured by the Nepali Congress on my way to the British camp. As a result, I ended up teaching war tactics to the Congress commandos for the next five years.'

Rifleman Man Bahadur Thapa (77), 2/6th GR, from Dodhara/ Chandani, Mahakali, served in the British Army for four years and lives on farming and a welfare pension.

The Gurkha tribesmen from the hills didn't join the British-Indian Army at the beginning. They were mostly Garhwalis, Kumaonis and other tribes from the newly conquered areas of Nepal then, and their loyalty was not to Kathmandu but mostly to their local leaders. Although the Nepal Durbar did not sanction the policy of direct recruiting until 1886, the practice of Gurkhali youths coming down from the hills and joining the army was pretty common and the British-Indian Army already had three Gurkha regiments by 1850. The 4th and the 5th regiments were formed after the Sepoy Mutiny of 1857-58.

By then, enough Gurkhas from the hills had already joined the British-Indian regiments and made their mark as excellent soldiers. The distinction between Gurkhas from the mountains and other native soldiers was first noticed as early as the 1830s by the British. According to British writers, the remarks made by Brian Hodgson proved that point: 'The Company's Indian sepoys must bathe from head to toe, make puja (pray), and only then begin to prepare their dinner. They eat nearly naked only with a ritual dhoti in the coldest weather and thus take three hours over a meal. The Gurkhas, on the other hand, laugh at all this Pharisaical rigour and dispatch their meal in half an hour.' The Sepoy Mutiny of 1857-58 was the turning point for the Gurkhas. Their loyalty was tested and proved for the very first time, and they became a core element of the British-Indian Army after serving the British for a little more than four decades.

The notion of the so-called martial races (the popular theory invented and adopted by the British that professes what makes a good soldier) was already in the making by the end of the 19th century. Due to the Gurkhas' unparalleled bravery, tenacity, loyalty and adaptability, the British were genuinely impressed. The Gurkhas were not only easygoing, humble and loyal but also tough, disciplined and committed. By the end of the 19th century, the Gurkhas had already distinguished themselves from the Indian native soldiers and the watchful eyes of the British could not have missed that. The 'martial race' was the term created to separate them from the mass of native Indians.

Many Gurkhas were already serving not only in the five Gurkha regiments but also in other regiments of the British-Indian Army by then and created an elite Gurkha force. Until then, all castes of Nepali men were accepted in the army and were mostly recruited from the western and central parts of Nepal. Men from the eastern regions of Nepal, mainly, were recruited for the Assam, Bengal and Burmese regiments at first. Regiments consisting of only Gurkhas (Magars and Gurungs) were still known by other names within the British-Indian Army. At the same time, just like the Magars and Gurungs of West Nepal, the tribes of Rais and Limbus of East Nepal were making a name for themselves strictly on their merits.

The theory of so-called martial races was put to further tests in many theatres of WWI and WWII. If WWI had introduced the Gurkhas to the world as one of the bravest, WWII fully confirmed their name and reputation. The great wars of WWI and WWII were testimonies of the Gurkha legacy, and the Gurkhas had to pay a high price to claim that legacy. Against all the odds, the Gurkhas came out on top.

But WWI and WWII were not only tests for the Gurkha legacy but also for the so-called martial race and they didn't disappoint. According to British author Tony Gould, malingering among the native soldiers was so prevalent during WWI that medical officers had to threaten the soldiers with court martials. The medical officers discovered the self-inflicted injuries when they saw that a considerable number of native soldiers had injuries only on their left hands. In contrast, the Gurkhas were always in a hurry to return for duty even before they were fully recovered and the medical officers had to order them to stay in bed.

There are no doubts about the Gurkha fighting skills and bravery. But what makes the Gurkhas so special? Whatever explanations were given so far by many experts are mostly correct. But since they were mainly written by the British (British Gurkha officers), they cannot escape the suspicion of being biased. Even worse, some of the books written by former British Gurkha officers are nothing more than romanticized versions of their fantasy. Many have claimed that the Gurkhas are only as good as their British officers, and without the leadership of the British officers, the Gurkhas are doomed. That's not true, and it's nothing more than self-aggrandizement by the over-confident British. They tend to overestimate themselves. They said the same thing about the strength of Singapore right before the Japanese assault in WWII, and we all know what happened there. We could include mistakes in France and Gallipoli during WWI and in Iraq and Burma in WWII. In reality, it was the Gurkhas who made their *sahibs* look good in both war and peacetime.

According to Gurkha veterans from WWII who fought in Burma, most British officers must thank the Gurkhas for coming back alive. They couldn't even make a fire, let alone cook their meals without the Gurkhas. Had it not been for the canny Gurkhas, many would have starved to death in the soaking wet Burmese jungles. No matter how difficult the situations were, the Gurkhas always found ways out and took excellent care of their British officers during those harsh days so they could come out alive and bask in the glory.

The Gurkhas won ten Victoria Crosses in WWII alone. The VCs were undoubtedly one of the greatest achievements of the Gurkhas, and that certainly helped spread the Gurkha name around the world. Had all the bravery acts been reported, the number of VCs won by the Gurkhas would have been much higher, Gurkha veterans lament. The reason they gave was: To win a bravery award, the immediate officer(s) commanding the soldier(s) involved had to write a recommendation letter, and only a very few ambitious and motivated officers would want to go through that hassle. If a soldier under their command won a bravery award, let's say the VC, for instance, the officers commanding qualified for an award too. Only those officers who wanted a prize for themselves wrote recommendations, while the rest didn't bother. As a result, many brave acts didn't get reported and many veterans did miss out. With an exceptional act of bravery, luck also played a huge role.

There must have been great British officers in their long history, especially during war, and their leadership undoubtedly played a massive role in the making of the Gurkha legacy: General Ochterlony, Lord Roberts, Sir Francis Tucker, Field Marshal Slim and General Walker, to name a few. However, those few names alone cannot justify the claim that the Gurkhas are only as good as their British officers, and it might instead have something to do with the usual British uppity manner. I cannot probe into the past, and I do have great respect for those brave officers, but I can still write from my time served in the army, and I know there was a big difference between claims and realities.

British officers were treated like royals, or at least they behaved that way in the Gurkha regiments. They were an elite group with a separate mess, hardly mingled with Gurkhas and lived in their own world. In those regimental functions and gatherings, they mostly talked with senior Gurkha officers and rarely interacted with the other ranks. The Commanding Officer (CO) of the battalion or the officer commanding (OC) the company would typically make a formal round of talks with groups of soldiers, but they were mostly one-sided. The officer would do all the talking, and the soldiers were just there to nod. The only time a British officer would join the Gurkha rank and file was when he was a new, green 2nd lieutenant and had just entered the regiment. And he had come there for a reason. To serve in a Gurkha regiment, the British officer had to learn Gorkhali, and his Gorkhali language skill was one of the criteria that determined his future in the regiment. What's more, the young guy was ordered by his CO, and he had no choice. Thankfully, youth was at his side, and the fun-loving, easygoing and curious young officers mostly didn't mind.

The only parade the British officers attended was the one in the morning, which was always a fitness parade, and they did their own things for the rest of the day. While the senior British officers had their schedule, young British officers followed the Company's programme and trained with the men in a platoon. The young British officers were friendly and interested in learning in the beginning. They laughed, joked, ran, ate and played sports with the Gurkha soldiers for the next six months as equals. When their future was decided, they either got promoted to lieutenant as platoon commander or were dispatched back to the UK and never seen again. As they got promoted to higher ranks, not only did their responsibilities but also their appearance change. The young and friendly officer would start moulding himself into a rather stern, severe and unsmiling officer who demanded absolute discipline and respect from his men. The unspoken rule of the regiment for those young officers was either be like us or just get lost. The young officer had to learn fast or be doomed.

The senior British officers hardly trained with their men, at least in peacetime. The British officers were not always there, and the primary task of preparing the troops was still on the shoulders of the Gurkha officers and senior NCOs. The commanding officer did come sometimes for the morning call, received the attendance report and went back to his office instructing the Gurkha officers to carry on. The only other time they attended training with the troops was during those main events the whole battalion or the Gurkha Brigade held, and everyone was required to participate. Such big events were mostly held one to three times a year. Like the training, the welfare, promotion and preparedness of the troops were always carried out by the Gurkha officers and NCOs; the British officers always relied on their trusted Gurkha officers. Apart from a few exceptional officers, many of the British didn't know their men very well, and the senior Gurkha officers had a big say in the future of many soldiers. As they held the high position, they alienated themselves from their men and ended up knowing just a few senior members of the company or battalion he commanded. The British officers were only there to take the credit, which had always been the case.

It was not the British officers who made the Gurkhas great, but the other way around and credit must be given where it's due. Many factors might contribute to the real reasons why the martial races of Gurkhas are so good. One of them could be even the leadership of the British officers. But that doesn't make them great, as they used the same leadership methods with other native soldiers from various parts of the world, and they didn't turn out as good as the Gurkhas were. The critical point is how the Gurkhas had total trust, respect and commitment to their *Gora Sahibs* and why the Gurkhas responded in such ways.

To understand this point, one needs to go to the root of the nature and upbringing of those so-called martial races. We Gurungs mostly live in a tightly knit community, a village primarily consisting of the descendants of one single couple, and that's why they are all related. It can be taken as a patriarchal society, but that doesn't mean the matriarchal side is less significant, and both paternal and maternal sides of the family play big roles in our upbringing. It's also a hierarchical society, although we are not as strict as other tribes from Nepal and all efforts are made to create a happy family environment, especially for the children. We all have our list of grievances and shortcomings; we are no exception. But our community works together to have a simple and healthy life. We are simple people, working on the fields all year long and trying our best to provide enough for the family. Gurungs also marry within our limited community, the elders arrange everything, and disobedience has no place. The most important aspects of our upbringing were to respect our elders, honour our family and never bring any disrespect or dishonour to our community. After some unintentional false steps, we even had some members who had chosen to stay away from the village and never return rather than bring shame to the family.

Honour, respect and loyalty play a crucial role in our lives. Our entire upbringing is focused on those virtues, and we never forget them. I am only writing from the experiences of my childhood. The generations of our grandfathers, who had fought in both WWI and WWII, were way ahead of us regarding honour, respect and loyalty. They were raw, pure and the real deal. No wonder they achieved such greatness in both world wars. Whether the new generations can match that feat, I genuinely doubt, but I am not trying to be disrespectful to anyone. We all change with time.

Another Nepali saying that profoundly affects our lives is this: *'Jasko nun khanchau, usko bhalo sochnu',* which roughly translates as, 'Always think good of the hand that feeds you.' We are very respectful and loyal to that person who has given us a job, and to some extent, we even respect him as a father. As a result, we always try to give our best and never think evil about them. Some people might call it naïve, but we take it as pride, and that's the reason why the Gurkhas are different as well as unique.

The other reason, which I have already described in the previous chapter, is our caste system stemming from our religious beliefs, and this plays a significant role in our lives. It's not your talent, preference or opportunity but your birth that determines your future; your surname decides what you do in life, and your community tells you what's right for you. Our villages were no different. As Gurungs, we never tried business, office work or anything else. All we knew was farming, and that was what we all did for a living. When the opportunity of becoming a Gurkha arose, we tried that and surprised ourselves.

The opportunity of becoming a Gurkha gave the Gurungs a choice; it liberated them from the hardship of a farmer's life and gave something of more importance than farming. As a result, they learned to cherish their newfound trade, gave their utmost and made it their own. In brief, it was a way out, from a rather harsh, dull and frustrating life to a new, adventurous and challenging one. Before long, the practice had become a tradition, and so deeply ingrained into the community that life without it became almost unimaginable.

The example I have given here is of the Gurungs but the situations of other so-called martial races, e.g., Magars, Rais and Limbus, are more or less the same. The so-called martial races are naturally brave and daring; our background, tradition, religious faith and upbringing play a huge part in moulding us into good soldiers; and the teachings of respecting our elders make us good listeners. The top-to-bottom disciplined life of the army made us good disciplinarians, the world-famous British organizational skills made us clean and tidy, and our inherited skills of adaptability, tenacity and endurance made us tough. Besides, our attitudes of never giving up, facing difficult times with a smile and always giving our best are the virtues that set us apart from others. Most importantly, our acute sense of responsibility and gratitude make all the difference and anything else is of less importance.

The next and critical factor that makes the Gurkhas excellent soldiers is their religious faith. The Hindu and Buddhist religions go hand in hand in our community and have a deep-rooted effect in our lives. Besides, the rulers from Nepal also made sure that the practices of Hinduism were applied throughout the army. In Hindu mythology, all things – such as the sun, moon, earth, air, rain, fire, a snake, even a boulder on the edge of the ancestral lands – are deemed among deities and are worshipped as gods and goddesses. In that respect, you owe some connection to whoever or whatever provides for you. You should respect those who have offered you a job. Growing up with such a mentality, they learned to appreciate the British as providers and respected them. Had it been other nationals in the place of the British, the situation wouldn't be much different, at least in the beginning, and once the new master had proven his worth, as the British had, they would have earned the same respect and commitment.

The other factor that is hardly mentioned regarding the Gurkhas is the effect of post-traumatic stress disorder (PTSD). Unlike other armies from around the globe, the Gurkhas are free of PTSD and have not suffered from it at all. PTSD has been non-existent among the Gurkhas, at least in the old times, for two reasons. It was foreign and unknown to the Gurkhas. The hardest and most traumatic wars the Gurkhas ever faced were WWI and WWII, and many were sent home right after the wars were over. The veterans might have suffered from PTSD back in their villages had they not been living with their loving families and not had the care and attention that they received after going through such horrible experiences. Even though they might have had PTSD, nobody knew for sure, as it was a foreign thing and was never seen or recorded by the Gurkhas for themselves.

The wars the Gurkhas fought post-WWII, like the ones in Malaya and Borneo, were long, irregular and indirect. They were like games of cat and mouse; the enemy was always in hiding, and the actual encounters were entirely unprecedented, yet brief. The hostilities extended for so long that the Gurkhas became accustomed to the events and were mentally and physically prepared for battle. As a result, the possibility of PTSD was already ruled out for the Gurkhas, and it was never heard of again. However, I have learned that some Gurkhas are suffering from PTSD in the post-Afghanistan tours in the UK, and it might be a new thing that's catching up with the Gurkhas. After all, PTSD is a mental issue, and the modern and educated Gurkhas' minds are also being affected. Everything has to change with time, and the Gurkhas are no exception.

PTSD has been a severe issue for war veterans of the modern armies of many nations. PTSD affects not only the soldiers but also their families and many have suffered a great deal. According to the estimates of the US Department of Veteran Affairs, 31 per cent of Vietnam War veterans, 10 per cent of Gulf War veterans and 11 per cent of Afghan War veterans suffer from PTSD. The British Army had 0.2 per cent rate of PTSD according to a report by the MoD in 2016-17. Although the British

Army had a low PTSD rate in comparison to the US Army, it's said to be increasing as the risks as well as awareness in modern warfare are catching up.

CHAPTER 22

THE GURKHA WOMEN – HEROES OR VICTIMS?

'Joining such a prestigious team as the QAs, and being able to serve our own Gurkha community that comes with such a great deal of respect, admiration and responsibility was undoubtedly an honour for me, and we did our best to help them by example, and with pride and honour.'

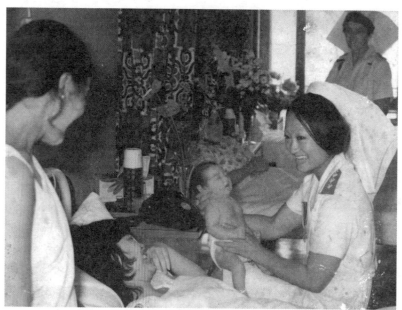

Capt. (Retd) Rukmani Dewan O'Connor, QARANC, one of the very first batches of Gurkha women serving in the QAs in the UK, Hong Kong and Asia. She is seen here with a Gurkha family in the British Military Hospital, Hong Kong. *Photo © Capt. Dewan O'Connor*

Throughout the 200-year Gurkha history, there is hardly a mention of Gurkha women, and that's not only unfair but also unfortunate. The sacrifices those women made for their men, children and the country are paramount. It's so sad that no intellectuals have ever tried to write about or acknowledge them. Not many stories, songs or books were created for them. They always remained in the backdrop of their men like a shadow, but they never stopped supporting them. They took care of the children, the elders and the farms while their men went to fight. Many lost their men in wars, became widows and were forgotten by all in the tens of thousands. They carried on and held the family together. Nobody saw their tears, nobody cared about their anguish, and nobody acknowledged their sorrows.

In such a patriarchal society as Nepal, glories are always reserved for the men, and the women are traditionally consigned to the background. Despite noticeable changes in urban areas, girls in rural areas are still constrained by many rules and prejudices, and society usually overlooks them on the pretext of preserving their traditions. In many places, people accept such practices as a way of life and don't see any problems. The position of the Gurkha women is no different.

It doesn't mean the Gurkha women have no stories to tell. Their contribution, suffering and sacrifices are as significant as the ones made by their men; sometimes, to even a greater extent. If you measure achievements only through the barrel of a gun, or through the blood-tainted sharp edges of the kukri, the Gurkha women will lose. But such an important matter cannot be judged by one method alone. If other factors such as the suffering of emotion and feeling, the burdens of social and family responsibility, and loss of life are used, there will always be only one winner – the women. Their plight is ignored; not many stories of women's sacrifices are written.

We have read about the history of Gurkha women and children fighting alongside the brave Gorkhas on Nalapani in Khalanga during the Anglo-Gorkha War. The historians and writers were too busy glorifying the courage of men while ignoring the contributions of the Gorkha women. There is no better example than this to begin with, and the brave women of the Nalapani fort should be remembered among the first heroes of our nation. Here in the pages of my book, you all have my sincere respect.

One of the glittering stars of the Gurkha women could be found in the history of the Queen Alexandra's Royal Army Nursing Corps (QARANC). The legendary bands of sisters who served on the front lines of both WWI and WWII, nursing the wounded, were subjected to harsh treatment as well as torture by various enemies while being kept as prisoners of war. Known affectionately as the QAs within the British Army, the corps started in 1881, and expanded significantly in 1897, when Queen Victoria's third daughter, Princess Christian, began the Army Nursing Service Reserve and helped treat a vast number of casualties in the Boer War of South Africa two years later. A contingent of nurses from the London Hospital joined them, and the dispatch was organized by Alexandra, the wife of the Prince of Wales, who was to become King Edward VII of England in 1901. On 27 March 1902 the British and the Indian Army Nursing Services were amalgamated, with the new Queen as their patron, and the Queen Alexandra's Imperial Military Nursing Service (QAIMNS) was born.

At the beginning of WWI, the QAs had just 300 nurses, but by the end of the war, they had 10,404 nurses, including reserves, and 200 nurses were killed during their service. During WWII, they served in all theatres of operations and faced horrible treatment as captives by the Japanese in both Hong Kong and Singapore. After the end of the war, the army medical services underwent further reorganization, and the QAIMNS became the QARANC on 1 February 1949.

A rare opportunity for educated Gurkha women came in the early 1960s when enlistment to the QARANC was opened to them for the first time. Initially, they were recruited from Dharan, Nepal; successful candidates were flown to the UK, and basic training for three years was provided in a civilian hospital. On completion of the required training, they would generally acquire one or two specialist training courses for career advancement.

Captain Rukmani Dewan O'Connor, alongside her younger sister Sudhamani Dewan, was one of the most successful. Rukmani, after her nurse's training, worked in six different military hospitals over several years to get more experience before applying for a commission. In peacetime, the QAs were encouraged to specialize in operating theatre work, obstetrics and gynaecology, which would enable them to get posted to hospitals overseas like the British Military Hospitals (BMH) in Hong Kong, Singapore and Dharan. Since no Gurkha battalions were deployed in the UK during that period, the only way to serve the Gurkhas and their families was to work in those hospitals in Asia.

On completion of her six months' commissioned officer training, Capt. Dewan O'Connor was posted to BMH Hong Kong and worked in the obstetrics, paediatrics and midwife line there. Being a Nepali-speaking officer, she was able to explain medical terminology clearly to uneducated Gurkha wives as well as their husbands. Having a Nepali sister around also boosted their morale. As a trained senior staff member, she took charge of a ward where 20 or 30 beds with men, women and children were to be looked after, and had to prepare a daily report to give to the hospital matron. To train the midwives and teach the Gurkhas, their wives and children about health-related issues as well as dental hygiene, she made regular visits to the regimental medical centres in the New Territories of Hong Kong as part of her duties.

'All the recruits selected for the QAs had to go through basic training in BMH Dharan as ward assistants and attend a swearing-in ceremony as a British Army soldier (private) before flying to the UK,' she explained. 'Those weak in English had to go through a competent English course followed by three months' basic recruit training at the QA centres, a three-year course for State Registered Nurse (SRN), and an 18 months' midwifery course in the military hospitals before they could finally become QAs. They had to have SRN as well as other language qualifications before they could apply for the commission and the basic QA officers' six-month training was also conducted at Sandhurst Military Academy, where all British officers are trained. The disciplinary requirements of the QAs are the same as the regular British Army, and they take pride in achieving that high standard.'

After the BMH Dharan was closed in the late 1980s, the recruitment of QAs from Nepal ceased too. By then, almost 50 Gurkha women had already joined the QAs, and seven of them (Major Radha Rawat, Major Saraswati Pandey, Major Bishnu Rai, Captain Doma Lama, Captain Bimla Bangdel, Captain Rukmani Dewan and Captain Sudhamani Dewan) had become commissioned officers of the QAs. Just like their male counterparts, the highest rank a Gurkha QA officer could attain was major and three Gurkha women had managed to obtain that.

As they are living in the UK now, some young Gurkha women have already started joining the service corps of the British forces. Although the total numbers of young Gurkha women joining the British forces are small, some of their success stories made the rounds through social media in the last few years. According to a BBC report of 2018, the Ministry of Defence (MoD) announced a new plan of recruiting the first batch of Gurkha women to the British Army in 2020, and the hopefuls have already started training back in the hills of Nepal. The policy of recruiting Gurkha women to the British forces is still not common practice, and it might take some time before this can be a success. However, as far as Capt. Dewan O'Connor is concerned, having the opportunity to serve her own Gurkha communities was undoubtedly one of the proudest moments of her career, and she will cherish it for life. More importantly, these women were role models not only to their families but also to the whole Gurkha communities. They had proven to the entire world that Gurkha women are as capable and reliable as their men.

The story of the Gurkha women doesn't end here. The Gurkha women (we call them Nepali women, Gurkha wives, or Gorkhali women in Nepal, but as this book is all about the Gurkhas and to align with the story and avoid confusion, I have taken the liberty of calling them the Gurkha women) certainly played a huge role in the making of the Gurkhas and their sacrifices should never be forgotten. However, there is hardly any mention of them in the history, in literature and in records. The only naming of Gurkha women that I could find so far was in *The Book of Gurkhas* by Bob Crew. He wrote about Gurkha women who guarded the beaches of Malaysia with Bren guns, while wearing saris, while their husbands were fighting in the jungle in the 1960s.

After talking with Lt (Retd) Indra Bahadur Gurung, an 86-year-old veteran from 2/6th GR who served in Malaysia as an education officer to the Gurkha Boy Company in the sixties, more details have emerged.

'In 1960, before the end of the Malayan Emergency, the situation was critical for the communist guerrillas and their leader Chin Peng, and he sought help from the Azaharies in neighbouring Borneo and the Indonesians as a last resort,' he explained. 'Intelligence suggested that the enemy had planned to land at Penang beaches by boats, and the Brigade of Gurkhas, including the Gurkha women, had to prepare for possible attacks. Specific army drills such as attending the muster parade, knowing the assembly point, how to take care of themselves and keep their children safe, where to hide, where to get rations and other supplies, and what actions they should do in case of an emergency, were duly provided. They were all parts of the evacuation training, and the Gurkha women provided backup support during those difficult times. Some of the young and brave Gurkha women requested to be trained with arms so they could patrol the beach areas and fight the enemy if necessary. But the enemy never arrived, and hence were saved from the wrath of the Gurkha women.'

According to Lt Gurung, although the whole Brigade of Gurkhas had the same policy, this particular story must relate to the women of the 1/10th Gurkha Rifles who were in Penang at that time, and deserved mention. For the rest, they were always in the shadow of their husbands and quietly let the men take all the glory.

A British Gurkha soldier comes home for a six-month break once every three years, possibly takes the opportunity to get married, and reports to duty again. (On the other hand, the Indian Gorkhas can go back once every year or two for leave varying from one to a few months). A Gurkha below the rank of corporal got to bring his family with him only once in his basic 15 years of service and also had to get to the position of staff sergeant and above before he could bring his family with him on a permanent basis. In a span of 15 years, a Gurkha soldier would be able to stay with his family for five years at the maximum, and during the rest of the period they would have to live separately, regardless of their feelings, desires and needs.

Thankfully, the Gurung community (as well as other communities of the so-called martial races who joined the army) is a tightly knit one, and mostly the women manage the households. The newly married women will never be left alone by her instantly acquired responsibilities. She will have to share the duties of taking care of the elders and children, tending fields and domestic animals and finishing the household chores before she retires to bed. Living in a big joint family is hard but also fun. She will remain so busy that she will hardly have the time to think about anything else. Before long, she will have her children.

Life during peacetime was already difficult. But during WWI and WWII, life was particularly so, and the Gurkha women from those martial races paid the heaviest price of them all. Almost a quarter of a million men took part in both great wars, and one in ten never returned. Many mothers lost their sons, many wives became widows, and many children were orphaned.

Despite not being Nepal's wars, the periods of both WWI and WWII were undoubtedly the darkest times in the country's history, and it was the Gurkha women who suffered the most.

'When our husbands went to fight in World War Two, only women were left behind at the camp, and we were made to watch war movies all the time. After seeing so many people being killed, all we could do was cry.' I recalled one of the Gurkha wives telling us her wartime story back in our village and never thought of having to repeat their story here after so many years. At the time, listening was a mere pastime for us, but it's an honour for me now.

Tales of Gurkha mothers chasing the *Gallawallas* away from their village are legendary. They even used to hide their sons when the *Gallawallas* visited their village. In WWI and WWII, all the men between the ages of 15 to 50 were sent to war by the Nepali government, and avoidance invited severe consequences. The new ruling inflicted such a dire impact that it deprived all the villages of Nepal of men, and only the elderly, women and children were left there to fend for themselves. This was when the Gurkha women took matters into their hands and fought tooth and nail to save their sons. Those families who had to live on without their men were the hardest hit. The society that provides security and togetherness to us all sometimes becomes its enemy, and it had always been too harsh on the women. The households without their men were not only looked down upon, but also bullied (the jackals were always around for easy picking). Men looked at the women with lusty eyes, women watched them with unkind eyes, and even the village children dared to mock them. In the early days, when farming was the only way of living, women were found diligently working in the fields without their men, and they had to learn themselves or seek help from other village men, who were not always free or kind. Without their men, these households had not only less income, but also less respect and were consigned to a harsh life. As a result, their status within the community took a beating.

To add insult to injury in some cases, women who had lost their husbands to the cruelty of war were ostracized by the whole community. In some extreme cases, they were even disowned by the husband's family, kicked out of the village and forced to live a life dependent on their own, rather than their husband's, family. There was nothing more disgraceful or dishonourable than these results for the women. Many would never recover from the humiliation and eventually die before their time.

The other group of women whose lives were ruined by the war were those whose men had returned alive but crippled. These poor women spent their lives taking care of those helpless and broken men. Tens of thousands of men with damaged or lost limbs returned from the war, many still had bullets or metal shrapnel inside their bodies, and needed constant help and support to continue living. They had neither pensions nor a gratuity to support their livelihood. Despite being on the front line and wounded, they returned empty-handed and were forced to live a life of destitution. Had it not been for the Gurkha women, many of those men would have died a terrible death. The hardships and sacrifices our women suffered to care for these broken men are beyond our imagination. The mistakes made by our nation and its leaders became burdens for our Gurkha women.

The children who had lost their fathers to the great wars also suffered a great deal. Growing up without their fathers was like competing in a cockfight with a hand and a leg tied behind their back, and the disadvantages those unfortunate children faced in life were massive. Not by choice but necessity, the women had to fill both roles as a mother and a father, and that was understandably not easy. Life was extraordinarily harsh, but they didn't give up and somehow managed to save our community from disaster. Had it not been for the Gurkha women, the survival of the next generation was in great doubt, and the whole nation must be thankful to them.

The agonies our nation suffered during those difficult times were many, but one of the particular sorrows was the most painful. The families of those killed in the war were at least informed of this. They knew the fate of their sons, and the rites and rituals for the deceased were performed according to their religious and traditional beliefs. Fortunate were those who had returned home alive, despite being wounded or crippled; they had at least returned home, and the whole nation was relieved that the wars were finally over. But those whose sons had neither returned home nor were killed in action had to face the most challenging time of their lives. They were the most unfortunate families of the missing Gurkhas. Their sons did not come home alive, and their deaths were not confirmed. As a result, their families were left in limbo.

The sacrifices Gurkha women made for the cause of the Gurkha legacy are huge. Books and other forms of writing wouldn't be enough to cover their stories, and yet not much has been written about them. Had it not been for the tears and sacrifices of the Gurkha women, there wouldn't be any Gurkha legacy. Without the Gurkha legacy, our nation would not have existed. History can never be forgotten. That we don't have written accounts doesn't necessarily mean it didn't happen, and truth, like the sun and the moon, cannot be hidden for too long. History does not only create heroes and villains, but victims too. There is no better example than the history of the Gurkha women here. Calling these women only victims would be demeaning. As far as this humble author is concerned, I would say the Gurkha women are heroes as well as victims all at the same time.

It's about time we learned from our past mistakes. The whole nation must not only realize but also acknowledge the sacrifices the Gurkha women made for the country and start respecting them. Talk alone is not good enough any more. We must begin writing about their bravery right away and provide some space for them in the glorious pages of our nation's history. Anything less would be a disgrace and would be condemned by our future generations.

CHAPTER 23

THE GURKHAS IN NEPALI LITERATURE

'When we arrived at Ladakh, the 1962 Sino-India war was over, and empty helmets of dead men were found everywhere. In memory of those fallen ones, hills were named "Gurung", "Kanchhaman" and so on by the regiments. There was a cemetery of fallen Gurkhas in the Pounch area after the 1965 Pakistan war. We marched 50 kilometres with only one bottle of water. The bottle was leather and smelly, and yet the water tasted so good.'

The father-son team: Subedar Nar Bahadur Thapa (77), 2/3rd GR, and Hon. Subedar Major Dal Bahadur Thapa, 6/5th GR, from Naya Gaon, Butwal, experienced many actions during wars in India.

The legacy of Gurkhas is undoubtedly the most important part of Nepal's history. The history of Nepal can't be complete without the 200-year history of the Gurkhas. If we take the glorious past of the Gurkhas out of Nepal's history, there won't be much left. And yet, looking in Nepali literature, music and films to find much mention of the Gurkhas, it seems that the country's earlier generations of writers, historians and scholars have somehow forgotten or neglected to write about them.

I've tried to find and read as many books as possible in the researching process of this subject and found that my choices were somewhat limited, which clearly shows Nepal's actual situation concerning literature, and that my views on this subject are not a far-fetched conclusion. The Gurkhas have a vibrant, diverse and distinguished history, especially during WWI and WWII. Unfortunately, the tales are mostly limited to oral history. As we didn't bother to preserve them, they were mostly lost when the storytellers died. The damage is already done. The stories are mostly gone and are never going to be recovered.

The purpose of this chapter is not to find fault in anyone. In my humble view, Nepali writers outside the country were more active than the ones inside. They were the ones who wrote mostly about the Gurkhas. Indra Bahadur Rai, Paari Jaat, Daulat Bikram Bista and Bhupi Serchan were the notable names. The exciting and powerful poems by Bhupi Serchan brought the stories of Gurkhas to the masses and evoked emotions. Many other fine writers might have written about the Gurkhas, but they didn't.

Dr Harka Bahadur Gurung, a geographer, anthropologist, author and artist known for his conservation work, was one of the champions of the Gurkhas. Being a son of an Indian Gurkha himself, he spent his childhood and youth in an army garrison. The Gurung surname also helped. He did a lot of research and writing on the subject and was the leading scholar on Gurkha matters, and any writers who came to Nepal in search of matter on the Gurkhas could not have done his or her job without consulting him. Almost all the books about the Gurkhas that I have seen so far are either foreworded by the eminent Dr Gurung or mention his good name. That clearly shows the influence and respect he had among the writing community. In brief, if anyone had done something for the Gurkhas, it was Dr Gurung.

Encouragingly, though, the interest and endeavour shown by the new generation in this subject are noteworthy. Basanta Thapa of Himal Books has published a trilogy of Gurkha-related books. *Lahureko Katha (The Story of Gurkhas)* is a collection about Gurkha war veterans and compiles a list of 13 real, detailed and heartbreaking stories of Gurkha veterans who had fought in WWII. *British Samrajyaka Nepali Mohora (Nepali Footprints in the British Empire)* by Jhalak Subedi is the second of these detailed and up-to-date books on Gurkhas, and it covers the history of the Gurkhas in general. This book is based on the life of former GAESO president Padam Bahadur Gurung. The third and last book of the trilogy is *Warrior Gentlemen* by Lionel Caplan, a professor at London University and an expert on South Asia's politics, including Nepal. The book is written in English from a rather academic and geopolitical, analytical point of view.

British-Gurkha (From Treaty to the Supreme Court) is another good book on Gurkhas and published by the British-Gurkha Study and Research Centre, Nepal. The book compiles a substantial list of articles, letters and interviews on Gurkha-related issues and provides a great deal of information on Gurkha history. The book is based on the writ submitted by Gyanraj Rai, an ex-Warrant Officer from QGE and a lifetime Gurkha activist, to the Supreme Court of Nepal against the Nepal government, and details of the process and progress of the case form most of the book. If you don't mind reading political writing using diplomatic jargon, you will like this one. The facts, historical details and arguments prepared by the defence lawyers, and the interviews with the diplomats, are good for historical and political lessons. The book can be a useful tool for academic research on Gurkha history.

The singers and musicians of Nepal somehow compensate for the shortcomings found in the written word. Nepal is indeed rich in folk songs. The Gandharwa/Gaaine (the singing caste of Hindus) with their one-size-fits-all type of musical instrument called the Sarangi, must take credit for continuing the old tradition. They did indeed sing a lot about the Gurkhas. Their songs genuinely reflect the actual situation, the pain of separation and the agony of waiting for the Gurkha community as a whole. Listening to their songs was the only way of forgetting the pain within the community, especially in time of war. Crowds would grow wherever they started singing.

Here are some examples of the famous folk songs of Nepal regarding the Gurkhas in the past.

'Cassino attack jandama dekhina ankha dhuwale, chhadyo saathile...'
On the way to the Cassino attack, they couldn't see through the billowing smoke and were left behind by friends.

'Gaai palyo banaiko bhaglai, chhora palyo Germanko dhawalai...'
I raised the cow for the tiger of the jungle, and so were my sons in the battle with the Germans.

'Ghar ta mero Himali pakha beisi ho re, kun dinko sanyogle bane Lahure...'
The Himalayan slopes and valleys are my home, which day's luck made me a Lahure?

'Lahureko relimai feshanai ramro, rato rumal relimai khukuri bhireko...'
The fashion of Lahures makes my dear so lovely, with a red handkerchief for my love and sporting a kukri.

The song is sung by a singer named Jhalakman and heard in the aftermath of the Nepalese revolution of 1950. WWII probably reflected the situation of the country as well as the peoples' position in a very apt manner. The song clearly described the pain, agony and misery of the people whose sons had gone to war and there was no guarantee they would return safely home again.

'Aama basi dharti naroya aama, banche pathaula tasvirai khichera...,
Baba runchan barsha din, aama runchin jindaji bharilai hajura...',
Don't sit on the ground and cry, my dear mother, I will send you a
photo if I survive, Father will cry for a year, and mother will cry for
a lifetime, my dear!

'Hai barai, amale sodhlin ni khwoi chhora bhanlin, ranhai khulyo
bhandias...'
Mother will ask where is my son; tell her the war had just begun.

'Babale sodhlan ni khwoi chhora bhanlan, ranh jitdaichha
bhandias...'
Father will ask where is my son; tell him I am winning the battle.

'Dajaile sodhlan ni khwoi bhai bhanlan, aunsai badhyo bhandias...'
Elder brother will ask where is my brother; tell him his share has
increased.

'Didile shodlin ni khwoi bhai bhanlin, cholinai ghatyo bhandias...'
Elder sister will ask where is my brother; tell her the gift has
decreased.

'Bahinile shodlin ni khwoi bhai bhanlin, maiti ghatyo bhandias...'
Younger sister will ask where is my brother; tell her you've one fewer
brothers now.

'Chhorale shodlan ni khwoi baba bhanlan, topi jhikei bhandias...'
Son will ask where is my father; tell him to take his cap off.

'Chhorile shodlin khwoi baba bhanlin, sunchurako daan diyas...'
Daughter will ask where is my father; tell her to forget about the
gold bangle.

'Priyale shodlin khwoi swami bhanlin, baatai khulyo bhandias...'
Wife will ask where is my husband; tell her the way is cleared.

'Bhaujyule shodlin ni khwoi dewar bhanlin, khasi kaat bhandias...'
Sister-in-law will ask where is my brother-in-law; tell her to celebrate at her will.

'Saathile shodlan khwoi lahure bhanlan, mayamaar bhandias...'
Friend will ask where is my lahure; tell him to forget about me.

The other famous song that every Gurkha must have sung at least a few times in their army career is called *'Resham Fiririri...'* Especially during the recruit training, song and music play a significant role, and a session of dances and songs was held every evening. No one was spared, all had to dance or sing in their turn, and as far as your humble author was concerned, the dancing and singing sessions were ones he would have liked to forget. I was that bad and shy then. But now, I can afford a smile or two at my misery.

'Resham phiriri, resham phiririi'
– the fluttering sounds of my silk handkerchief...

'Udera jaun ki dandai ma bhanjyang, resham phiririri'
– shall we fly over to the mountain pass? The fluttering sounds of my silk handkerchief...

'Eknale banduk dui nale banduk mirgalai takeko'
– one-barrelled rifle, two-barrelled rifle pointing to a deer...

'Mirgalai maile takeko hoina maya lai dakeko'
– my aim is not pointed at the deer but you, my love...

'Resham phiriri resham phiririi'
– the fluttering sounds of my silk handkerchief...

This song was said to have been collected from the villages near Pokhara, composed by Budhi Pariyar, and sung by Sundar Shrestha and Dwarika Lal Joshi through Radio Nepal. Although the official song came out later, the original song was already famous before that, especially with the Gurkhas, among whom this song was undoubtedly the most popular.

Singing and dancing skills were one of the criteria for promotion in the army. Young soldiers with girlish faces and slim bodies were encouraged to dance as *Maaroni* (men dancing in women's attire). They had massive demand for special events, especially at Dussehra and other festivals. Some of them achieved the rank of Gurkha officer or senior NCO through this particular skill, and all the Gurkha battalions had a few such talents of their own. The senior officers were quite fond of these dancers.

Although there must have been a hundred songs and poems, those listed above were the most popular. As it would be almost impossible to list them all here, I must be content with just a few and wished I had a better choice. There must be some new songs about the Gurkhas too, but they may be small in number. Moreover, the times have changed. New generations don't make those old sorts of songs any more, and the songs about the *Lahures* are few and getting fewer.

The film industry of Nepal is still at an early stage, and most of the films they make are not about the Gurkhas for some reason.

Peter J. Karthak, the writer, musician and veteran journalist, is not only an avid Gurkha fan but also an authority on Gurkha-related subjects. He writes about the Gurkhas on a regular basis. He has written more than 20 articles about the Gurkhas in Nepal's leading newspaper. His mother's side of the family suffered a tragic fate in both Burma and Singapore during WWII, and those sad sagas somehow became the main inspiration for his writing. His writing hugely contributed to building awareness among the general public of the Gurkha Justice Campaign and played a significant role in the cause.

Karthak addressed the high-ranking officials and civil servants of Brunei in 1985, and highlighted the virtues and distinction of the Gurkhas, among others. His knowledge, passion and influence concerning Gurkha matters are second to none. Those writing about Gurkhas would be wise to seek out his advice, and your humble author did so.

Lt Col (Retd) J. P. Cross is another enlightened author who has tried to bring the Gurkha legacy to the world through his various books. All are written in English, but given the significance they have had in highlighting

Gurkha history, I couldn't help but dedicate at least a paragraph to his works. During the process of researching this book, I read some of his books as references and found them to be very helpful.

Cross *sahib* is renowned for his Gorkhali *bhasa*, and he must be the only foreigner who has not only adopted Nepal as his home but has also contributed to it in the fields of history, education and literature. I still hear people talking about his remarks on Gurkhas from the west and the east of Nepal as being like cats and dogs, but my position is not to give my opinion here. Last but not least, Cross *sahib* was the Commanding Officer of BGC Camp Pokhara when your author joined the British Army as a recruit in 1980, and I still remember the speech that he gave to us in a fluent Gorkhali *bhasa*. All the Gurkhas should appreciate his works.

Other notable authors, scholars and historians who have written about the Gurkhas include Dr D. R. Regmi, Kamal Dixit, S. Gyavali, Kanchanmoy Mazumdar, Kamal Raj Singh Rathaur, Pratyoush Onta, V. K. Kunwor, Dilip Thapa, Jyoti Thapa Mani, Krishna Kumar Limbu and various candidates in their (unpublished) PhD dissertations at Tribhuvan University.

The main problem the intellectuals from Nepal have with the Gurkhas is that they think of them as naïve, thick-headed and even cocky. They don't consider the Gurkhas' stories worthy of their writing. The dislike is so intense that some look down on the Gurkhas with contempt and do not hesitate to mock them. Had they ever tried to understand the vastness and significance of the Gurkha legacy, they would never have done that. Some of them are still blinded by a veil of ignorance, short-sightedness and selfishness. Religious, social, traditional and racial influences also play a huge role in a backward and biased community like Nepal's. As a result, the Gurkha legacy is neglected by all.

The whole nation did forget one crucial fact. The Gurkhas, especially those joining the British Army, were the best of the best from those so-called martial race communities. If you think being a soldier is easy, you know nothing about the army. Those who have achieved high ranks in the military must not only work very hard but also need a lot of luck, skill and discipline. Besides, they have to go through a variety of training, always remain fit and be on top of their game, and must learn good management skills before they can become officers. Moreover, living a disciplined life and still being able to achieve the highest possible standards is not easy. The Gurkhas have not only done a great job in the army but also in civilian life after they have retired. We have doctors, engineers, professors, PhDs, politicians, businesspeople and many high achievers in the Gurkha communities, and labelling them as naïve and thick-headed is nothing more than stupidity as well as being out-of-date. It's about time that such stereotyped perceptions are changed. We need to start treating the Gurkha community with equality and respect.

Had the intellectuals' view actually been true, you would not be reading this book at all. After all, your humble author is also an ex-Gurkha, and the Gurkhas have come a very long way.

The real problem between Gurkhas and the general public is that we act like feuding siblings. The Gurkhas sometimes tend to flaunt their newly acquired wealth, attitude and way of life in front of other people back in Nepal, which creates a little bit of jealousy and discomfort in the house. The Gurkhas only show the good things and hide their struggles as if there were none. This tiff is caused by a misunderstanding that could easily be solved with a little more caring, respect and understanding on both sides.

The elites, intellectuals and general public of the nation must stop this stereotyped, misguided and short-sighted perception of the Gurkhas and start treating them as their own. They must learn to see the Gurkhas' hardships, respect their legacy and appreciate their contributions and sacrifices for the nation. Most importantly, they must accept the Gurkhas as their brothers, provide equality in both social and practical terms and give them due credit for what they have done for the people, society and country. And start working on the records of Gurkha history before it's all lost.

By putting our differences aside, we must work together for the future and well-being of the nation. The beautiful country of Nepal, the home of the brave Gurkhas, Lord Buddha and the majestic Himalayas, can shine as the brightest star of the universe again. Talk is cheap, deeds must support words and only then can we achieve miracles for ourselves and the nation.

CHAPTER 24

THE ORIGINAL GURKHAS – THE NEPAL ARMY

'In Gujarat during the 1965 Pakistan war, we were surrounded by 39 enemy tanks. But we were ordered to follow a strict policy of "one bullet one enemy" that pissed me off. So I confronted my commander, a major, by pointing a pistol at his head. I genuinely thought that he was a spy, I told that to all of my superiors, and wanted to kill him right there. My subedar major held me back; the suspected officer was taken away and was never seen again. It turned out that the suspect was in fact a spy and I was recommended for an award but somehow didn't get it.'

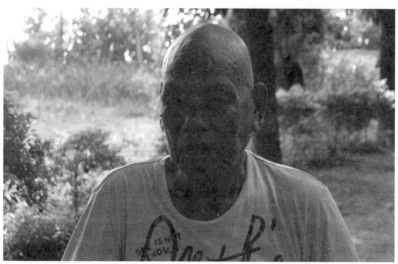

Rifleman Hari Bahadur Budha/Magar (82), 2/4th GR, from Dodhara/Chandani, Mahakali, fought in the 1965 Pakistan war, got hit by shrapnel, and won five war medals.

The name of the Gorkhali Army was derived from the tiny state of Gorkha before the unification of Nepal. The name of the Gorkha state was based on the God of Gorkhanath; one of the tens of thousands of gods in Hindu mythology. The sacred temple of the Gorkhanath still exists today in Gorkha. When the unification of modern Nepal was started with the annexation of Nuwakot in 1744 by the Gorkha King, Prithvi Narayan Shah, also known as the founding father of the nation, the official title of the Gorkhali Army was changed to the Royal Nepalese Army (RNA) and it remained so throughout the monarchy's rule in Nepal. However, it was still known to the outsiders and its enemies as the Gorkhali Army throughout the century and respected as one of the bravest in the world.

At the end of the 238-year monarchy in Nepal, the RNA was renamed the Nepalese Army (NA) on 28 May 2008.

The first battle the Gorkhali Army fought against an outsider was the battle against Mir Qassim, the Nawab of Bengal, in 1763. The Nawab of Bengal had invaded Nepal but was severely defeated by the Gorkhali Army as it had many advantages, including terrain, climate and ethical leadership. The next battle was at Pauwa Gadhi in 1767 against Capt. Kinloch of the British East India Company that had come to aid the Malla kings from Kathmandu Valley. The British suffered a humiliating defeat at the hands of the Gorkhali Army. During the process of unification, the Gorkhali Army had to fight three difficult wars against the Limbuwan before the signing of a treaty in 1774, and the representatives of both the Gorkhali and Limbuwan kings had to swear in *noon-paani* (salt water) and declare Limbuwan as the Limbu's Kipat Lands (self-autonomous lands).

The First Sino-Gorkha War of 1788-1792, caused by trade disputes, was initially fought between the Gorkhali and the Tibetan Army. The victory of the Gorkhali Army forced the Tibetans to sign the Kerung Treaty that required the Tibetans to pay an annual tribute to Nepal. Upon the Tibetans' request, the Qing Emperor of China intervened, and a robust Chinese force of 70,000 men under General Fuk'anggan invaded Nepal. As the Chinese troops arrived at Betrawati River, Nuwakot, just outside the capital Kathmandu, the Gorkhas signed a treaty that required Nepal, among other obligations, to send tributes to the Qing Emperor every five years. The agreement, known as the Betrawati Treaty, became obsolete by the early 19th century as the Qing dynasty in China was weakened.

The Gorkhali Army advanced mainly on two fronts, invading and annexing states along the way. In the east, the Gorkhali Army reached Sikkim by 1780. The Raja of Sikkim fought against the Gorkhali Army with the help of the British. The Gorkhas did finally overrun Sikkim, including Darjeeling and the plains of Terai by the early 19th century, and reached the Tista River. In the west, the Gorkhali Army invaded and annexed the Kumaon Kingdom in 1791, followed by the Garhwal Kingdom in 1804, and absorbed all the small kingdoms nearby, including Hindur, Besahar and Sirmudh. The Gorkhali Army also controlled the hill regions of Nainital, Almora and Dehradun. When the Gorkhali Army finally crossed the Sutlej River and attacked Kangra in 1809, it was repelled by the Sikh Khalsa Army of Punjab's Maharaja Ranjit Singh. The Gorkhali Army absorbed Kangra later on, but that was to be the last post of the Gorkhali Army in the west as the Anglo-Gorkha War was to break out soon.

The Anglo-Gorkha War of 1814-1816 broke out between the British East India Company and the Gorkha Kingdom due to border disputes and ambitious expansion by both sides. The war was fought in two phases. The first phase started in 1814 and occurred mostly in the newly acquired lands of the Gorkhali Army, and General Ochterlony was the head of the opposition force. Despite being outgunned and outnumbered, the Gorkhali Army fought with such courage, honour and bravery that the enemy was hugely impressed and, as we all know, the Gurkha legacy was to begin from here on. After the defeat, the Gorkhali Army had no option but to agree to the terms dictated by the Sugauli Treaty, and hostilities ceased while waiting for the final seal of the Nepal Durbar on the treaty. The Durbar hesitated on approving the definitive agreement which prompted the starting of the second phase of the war. The Nepali

Durbar finally relented and ratified the treaty when the enemy troops had arrived at Makawanpur, and the invasion of the Kathmandu Valley by the British force became imminent. Nepal lost most of its newly acquired lands, including the plains of Terai, and its borders were set at the Mechi River in the east and Mahakaali in the west. Since the events of the Anglo-Gorkha War were already described in previous chapters, only a short detail is inserted here to smoothen the Gorkha story. Readers are advised to refer to the previous sections for more information.

Jang Bahadur Rana initiated the Nepali-Tibetan War of 1855-56. The Gorkhali forces were led by commanders such as Bam Bahadur Kunwar, Dhir Shamsher, Krishna Dhoj and Prithvi Dhoj Kunwar. The conflict ended after the treaty of Thapathali was signed. The Tibetans agreed to pay an annual subsidy of ten thousand rupees to the Nepali Durbar and allow a Nepali trade station and agency to be established in Lhasa.

During the Sepoy Mutiny of 1857-58, PM and commander-in-chief Jang Bahadur Rana led the Gorkhali Army himself with help from Col Pahal Man Singh Basnyat and Col Bhairab Narsingh Rana, and they went down to India together. His brother, General Dhir Shamsher, led another group of the Gorkhali Army and helped quell the mutiny that had already spread across India. Around 17,000 men from the Gorkhali Army took part, almost 5,000 mutineers were killed, and a further 500 were captured in Gorakhpur, Lucknow, Balewa, Jalalpur, Jompur and Shish Gunj. Had it not been for the Gorkhali Army, the history of the British Raj in India would have been very different from then on, and as a return favour, the plains of Terai lying between the Mahakali and Rapti rivers, which were lost by Nepal in the 1816 Sugauli Treaty, were returned to Nepal by the grateful British in 1860.

As the regular troops of the British Raj in India were sent to fight in Europe and the Middle East throughout WWI, the Gorkhali Army was called in for help during their absence. It was deployed along the Indian north, west and east borders and guarded the empty army barracks and vital installations. Under the superb leadership of General Babar Shumsher, General Tej Shumsher and General Padam Shumsher, around 14,000 men with Martini-Henry and Enfield rifles came down to India and helped keep the house clean and tidy while battles in Europe raged on. The battalions involved in the WWI expedition were Kalibox, Shumsher Dal, Pashupati Prashad, Bhairab Nath, Jabbar Jung, Bhairung and Srinath.

In the absence of the British troops, the Masuds from Waziristan, Northwest frontier, revolted against British rule and the Gorkhali force of Nepal was mobilized at the request of the Raj. The campaign, known as the Waziristan War of 1917, was a joint military operation. The Nepalese 1st Rifle, the British 43rd Brigade and the Mahindra Dal battalion with 45th Brigade, which were the British and Nepalese Army, suffered many casualties, and many soldiers from the NA were awarded British medals.

Similarly, the assistance of the NA was needed again in 1919 when the British Raj had decided to go to war in Afghanistan, and the NA troops led by General Babar Shumsher reached India by May 1919. The Amir of Afghanistan had sought help from the Russians, who were unable to provide, and he was bound to accept a peace treaty. The Nepalese troops were stationed in India for three months.

In WWII, the NA was not only mobilized as a backup force but also fought alongside the British as combat troops. In addition to the jobs they did in WWI, such as marshalling the long and tough borders of the northwest and east frontiers and guarding the empty barracks and installations in the absence of the regular troops, they also fought against the enemy. The NA units such as Kalibox, Surya Dal, Naya Gorakh, Sri Nath, Second Rifle, Kali Bahadur, Mahindra Dal, Barda Bahadur, Shumsher Dal, Devi Dutta, Bhairab Nath, Jagan Nath and Purano Gorakh were involved. Many high-ranking NA officers, including late commander-in-chief Kiran Shumsher Rana, ex-commander-in-chief and Field Marshal Nir Shumsher Rana, were deployed during the long and harsh operations of WWII. The NA fought with distinction in the 14th Army under General Slim against the Japanese in the famous Kohima/ Imphal battle. The NA battalions Mahindra Dal, Sher Dal, Kali Bahadur and Jagan Nath were deployed on the Burma front. The Jagan Nath battalion worked as engineers to construct tracks, bridges and water points for the Allied forces.

Once WWII was over, the NA troops returned to Kathmandu, and a grand victory parade was held there on 28 October 1945, where many soldiers and officers were honoured for their works, contributions and sacrifices.

In post-independence India, the whole nation was roiled with religious violence between the Hindus and the Muslims, and the NA was called upon again by Indian PM Jawahar Lal Nehru to assist in controlling the situation. The incident was to be known as the Hyderabad Action of 1948, and the NA troops (units of Kali Prasad, Bhairung, Sri Nath, Barda Bahadur, Devi Dutta, Sher, Bhawani Dal, Bhairab Nath, Mahindra Dal, Kalibox, Kali Bahadur, Ganesh Dal, Shumsher Dal, Mahindra Dal, Second Rifle, Gorakh Nath, Narshima Dal and Jabbar Jung) under Major General Sharada Shumsher Rana were dispatched to many parts of India like Hyderabad, Ranchi, Dehradun, Ramgarh and Calcutta. After successful operations that lasted for almost eight months, the NA returned home in March 1949. The NA contributed a great deal to the stabilization of the situation in India, and history will always remember them.

The NA underwent a significant overhaul in the post-WWII period, reinventing itself as a modern and professional institution and providing necessary assistance to the nation during natural disasters.

Around 9,000 Khampas (Tibetan tribesmen resisting Chinese authority) crossed over to Nepal and established camps to be used as launchpads for operations into the Chinese Autonomous Region of Tibet. The NA was mobilized after various diplomatic initiatives failed, and efforts to clear the Khampas out of Nepal's territory began. The NA units of Sri Nath, Raj Dal, Bhairab Nath, Kali Prashad, Ganesh Dal and 1st Rifle, and companies of Indra Dhoj, Ahridaman and Chandan Nath were involved. The NA Air Corps played a crucial role during the operation. The Khampas agreed to disarm on 31 July 1974, just before the NA was about to strike, and a big stockpile of arms and ammunition was captured. The Khampas' leader, General Wangdi, managed to escape with a party of 50-60 followers and was subsequently killed by army personnel in an ambush when he tried to rob a police post in Mugu in the far west of Nepal. The Khampas who opted to remain in Nepal were provided land and have since settled peacefully in the country as Nepali citizens.

The NA fought a bitter war against a Maoist insurgency which was formed in 1994 and started campaigning against the monarchy in 1996. Initially, the Maoists launched a low-intensity insurgency and targeted the ill-trained and poorly armed police. But they attacked army barracks and stole modern weapons in 2001 and dragged the army into a conflict that turned into a full-scale guerrilla war. The infighting lasted until 2005, killing more than 13,000 people with many more missing. Hostilities ended in 2006 with the renaming the nation as the Federal Democratic Republic of Nepal and the end of the monarchy. The Maoist fighters, also known as the People's Liberation Army Nepal, were eventually integrated into the Nepalese Army under the supervision of the United Nations (UN) and have become a part of the NA. Since the Maoist insurgency, the nation has not been embroiled in further internal conflicts, and the NA is mostly carrying out peacetime missions.

The NA is one of the regular contributors to UN peacekeeping forces and has carried out missions in various countries including Lebanon, Somalia, Haiti, Sierra Leone, Sudan and Mali. The NA headquarters is in Kathmandu; it has major base camps in all the districts of the country and each area has at least 9,500 troops. The NA also runs almost a dozen military schools within the nation.

According to the tradition of the Nepal Army, only generals hailing from the noble families such as Thapa, Pandey, Basnyat, Kunwor, Shah, Shumsher and Rana were appointed army chief. That tradition has been broken only three times, and General Chhetra Man Singh Gurung is one of these exceptions, after General Rookmangad Katawal and General Rajendra Chhetri. He is the first and only Gurung chief of the Nepal Army, so we Gurungs should be proud of him.

General Gurung was born in Tanahu district of Nepal on 18 July 1952, was a graduate of the Dehradun-based Indian Military Academy, and joined the Nepal Army in 1971. He was appointed chief of the Nepal Army on 9 September 2009 and served until 5 September 2012. Gen. Gurung served as Nepal Military Attache in the UK and France, led the UN Mission in Lebanon, commanded an infantry brigade, special forces brigade and an infantry division, and is decorated with Tri-Shakti Patta Class-III and many other medals. He also holds the honorary rank of general in the Indian Army, as all former Nepal Army chiefs do. This tradition has been going on for years.

The NA currently has about 95,000 army and air service personnel on active duty, and both men and women of Nepali origin are accepted.

The current NA chief, appointed on 9 September 2018, is General Purna Chandra Thapa.

CHAPTER 25

OTHER INTERESTING SNIPPETS ABOUT THE GURKHAS

'I saw the first Jammu and Kashmir war in 1948. The army wasn't fully prepared for the 1962 war. I was trapped in crossfire for 16 days in the 1965 war, and helped train the Mujahideen and worked in civil dress as a local during the 1971 war. The key to my survival: I could estimate the bomb dropping area by its sounds alone and help guide us to a safe place.'

Subedar Man Singh Thapa (87), 6th and 6/5th GR, from Naya Gaon, Butwal, joined the army in 1946 and has witnessed almost all the major wars in India since then. He has won 14 war medals.

Subedar Major Singbir Thapa, who joined the 2nd Sirmoor Battalion when it was raised in 1815 as a sepoy and served the regiment for the next 53 years before retiring as subedar major, was the longest-serving member of the regiment. He died in 1868.

– Logbook of the 2nd KEO Gurkha Rifles/The Gurkha Museum

By August 1888, the Snider-Enfield was replaced by the Martini-Henry as the primary firearm used by the Gurkhas in India.

– Logbook of the 2nd KEO Gurkha Rifles/The Gurkha Museum

The Gurkha hat – During the Waziristan Blockade in 1901 the 1/2nd Gurkha Rifles tried out a new cap advocated by one of its officers, Lt Bechar. It consisted of several layers of cloth covered on both sides with puttoo, or homespun tweed, the criss-cross machine stitching giving it a certain amount of stiffness to help maintain its shape, and sometimes known as the Kashmir hat, fitted with a light puggaree, ventilating holes and a chin strap. The whole effect resembled a slouch hat, affording protection both from the sun and the rain. The 2nd Gurkha Rifles subsequently adopted the cap for field services. A similar headdress was introduced into other Gurkha regiments during the same period. Initially procured from unofficial sources, it was eventually sanctioned by the Army headquarters and issued through ordinance channels under the nomenclature of Hats, Felt, Gurkhas.

– A blog post from the site of SIR KUKRI & CO. by V. K. Kunwor

The Gurkhas were not only known for bravery but also for gambling. While fighting near Baghdad during WWI, when the leading gunner was shot through the head, the #2 gunner taking over was also hit on the shoulder, and he had to be replaced by the #3 gunner. The whole incident had been observed by the Gurkha riflemen, who were nearby, and they watched with great interest. There was a roar of laughter from them when

the #3 gunner was unfortunate enough to stop a bullet. They had laid bets on how long he would last, and the winners were highly delighted.
  – From various books on the Gurkhas

The Gurkhas are known for their sense of humour. Stories include one in which they decided to take some armed Tibetan soldiers prisoner by tying their pigtails together while they were asleep. Disturbed in this act of comic daring when the Tibetans woke up, the Gurkhas hotfooted it back to their camp, laughing their heads off like naughty schoolboys.
  – From various books on the Gurkhas

When four Gurkha officers went to the UK to mount a guard at King Edward VII's lying-in-state in 1910, they were forced to stand guard for one hour with bowed heads, whereas the British Grenadier guards stood for only half an hour since they had many more of them to relieve one another. Besides, they had to wear higher collars than those they were accustomed to, and these cut into their short necks. And to add insult to injury, they had no opportunity to prepare their food, so they had to live on uncooked grain, washed down with water, because their religion forbade them to eat English food. When three of the four Gurkhas were to deliver a wreath to the deceased king, the fourth officer had to stand for four gruelling hours. They did the disciplined and honourable thing and endured all this without a word.
  – According to Rudyard Kipling from various books

Subedar Major Gambhir Singh Gurung IOM (Indian Order of Merit), OBI (Order of British India) with the title of 'Bahadur', who hailed from the village of Shirubari, Aundhi Khola, Syangja, West Nepal, and belonged to the 2/3rd GR, was one of the officers who attended the coronation of King George V in London on 22 June 1911. According to the notes written in his handwriting and provided by his family, they had around 1,500 people from the Indian subcontinent who attended the ceremony and had plenty of time to visit the city of London. Subedar Major Gambhir Singh Gurung and his team were awestruck by the development and glamour of city life. He wrote about the shiny glass facades of the shops, the vastness of the seaport and the big ships and the railway stations. Even more, he wrote about the brick houses in the countryside, the lush grasslands and the animals grazing there. The unusual timing of sunset and sunrise during the summers amazed them the most, and he wrote about this phenomenon in detail. Subedar Major Gurung later fought in Europe during WWI and won the battle honour of Neuve Chapelle – March 1915. In his honour, he had a school (Bhasa Pathasala) and a temple (Shibalaya Mandir) established in his village, and his villagers much respected him.

– From ex-WO2 Chandra Bahadur Gurung, 2/2nd GR, and his family

One of the Gurkha officers, Santabir Gurung, who had forgotten to ask for the Rana Maharaja's permission before his UK trip, was excommunicated from his religion and banished from his country by the Raj Guru. Even a royal request from King George V couldn't budge the religious authority, and his appeals were repeatedly rejected. He could only enter Nepal after the death of PM Chandra Shumsher at the age of 83, and he had to undergo all the purification rituals again, so he didn't die an outcast.

– Various books

There were some distinct differences among the Gurkha regiments. For instance, only the 5th Gurkha had the privilege of keeping arms in the barracks; the 7th Gurkha alone among the Gurkha regiments flew the national flag of Nepal on special occasions; unlike other regiments, the 10th Gurkha combined the kukris and the bugle horn of rifle on its badge; and the 2nd Gurkha wore brown boots while other regiments had black and retained the spelling 'Gorkha' in their title.

– From *Warrior Gentleman* by Lionel Caplan

Scrimshanking was so prevalent during WWI and WWII, the native soldiers, including Sikhs, were flagrant self-mutilators, and when the medical officers found a rash of a wound on the left hand, the soldiers had to be threatened with court-martials to stop self-inflicted wounds.

The Gurkhas were utterly disgusted and they were always ready to go back to the battleground as soon as their injuries were treated.

— From *Imperial Warriors: Britain and the Gurkhas* by Tony Gould

In the early days of the Sepoy mutiny, only once had a Gurkha regiment mutinied against the British, that too on a tiny scale. In Almira, the 3rd Gurkha took great exception to a proposed reduction in their already paltry pay and expenses, but the matter was swiftly sorted out by the British, who conceded that the Gurkhas had a point, and removed their commanding officer.

— From *Gurkha Warriors* by Bob Crew

Parbir Thapa of the 5th GR was the first Gurkha Rifleman to visit the UK when he went with Brigadier Charles Bruce en route to Switzerland for an alpine mountaineering expedition in 1891.

— From *Imperial Warriors* by Tony Gould

The incident of 13 April 1919, at Jallianwala Bagh, Amritsar, where 1,650 rounds were fired into a crowd, killing 379 and wounding 1,200, is taken by many as a black mark on the Gurkhas' otherwise brilliant 200-year history. The film *Gandhi* (1982) also pointed a finger at the Gurkhas. A column of 25 men, each from the 9th Gurkhas and 59th Scinde Rifles, were involved under the command of Capt. G. Crampton. Members of the crowd were not killed by the rounds fired, but mostly killed or wounded by the panic-stricken stampede in an attempt to escape through a single narrow exit. Besides, those were young soldiers who had recently finished their recruit training and were obeying orders from their commanders. Although his actions were praised by the governor of Punjab, Sir Michael O'Dwyer, Brigadier General R. Dyer was widely criticized for his cruelty at both the national and international levels. Sir Michael, the mastermind of the incident, was assassinated by a Sikh revolutionary in London in 1940.

— From *Valour: A History of the Gurkhas* by E. D. Smith; *Imperial Warriors* by Tony Gould

After the 8th Gurkha introduced boxing as an unlikely sport, one 17-year-old Gurkha NCO, Naik Lal Bahadur Thapa, won the All India Flyweight Championship in 1944, and he was the first Gurkha soldier to achieve such a distinction.

– From *Valour: A History of the Gurkhas* by E. D. Smith

The 4/10th Gurkha was named the 'Non-Stop Gurkha' by the military correspondent of the *Times*, earned by their independent mission at the end of 1944 when they crossed the Wainggyo Gorge in Burma at unbelievable speed during WWII carrying the Union Jack.

– From *Valour: A History of the Gurkhas* by E. D. Smith

The famous Chindits only consisted of the British, the Gurkhas and the 2nd Battalion Burma Rifles, and the Gurkhas were responsible for taking care of the herd of mules. Brigadier Wingate had no respect for the Gurkhas and is said to have cared more about the number of mules. He even ordered to leave the wounded ones at the nearest villages, which the officers didn't like at all.

– From *Imperial Warriors* by Tony Gould

In 1918, a small detachment of Gurkha volunteers was seen in a somewhat unfamiliar role: they mounted camels and served under the famous Lawrence of Arabia in Palestine. (In the 1962 movie, the British archaeologist and writer T. E. Lawrence was played by actor Peter O' Toole).

– From *Gurkhas* by David Bolt

In the aftermath of WWI, the Gurkhas were moved to Persia (Iran), to the shores of the Caspian, and saved the British consul and his staff from rebels who had besieged the consulate and had set it ablaze. They stayed on for operations against the Turks and fought against the Bolsheviks during 1920-21. Other Gurkha units, meanwhile, were committed to putting down the Arab revolt in the newly formed Iraq.

– From *Gurkhas* by David Bolt

The 2/6th Gurkha baked and froze in the wastes of Iraq and Persia, the 3/6th Gurkha began its career on India's Northwest Frontiers before changing to its historical and romantic role with the 'Chindits' and the 4/6th and 1/6th Gurkhas were now part of the 19th Indian Division to be known the world over as the Dagger Division.

    – Logbook of the 6th QEO Gurkha Rifles/Gurkha Museum

The Gurkhas demonstrated their uncanny skill in producing fire in all and any circumstances and many British soldiers had occasions to bless our men for saving them in sodden wet and shivering conditions.

    – Logbook of the 6th QEO Gurkha Rifles/Gurkha Museum

During the Burma campaign in WWII, the Indian forces were not only opposed by the Japanese but also their own, like the Indian National Army (INA) led by Subhas Chandra Bose. (The INA was created mostly from deserters from the British forces after their initial defeats in Malaya, Singapore and Burma). While in Japanese captivity, they were subjected first to propaganda, then to stronger forms of persuasion, starvation, solitary confinement and torture. Most of the Gurkhas resisted. One defector, Jemadar Puran Singh of the 2/1st Gurkhas, however, was later to become inspector general of police in Nepal.

    – Various books on the Gurkhas

The Gurkha major of 1/6th Gurkha, Major Lachhiman Gurung, was the only high-ranking officer who played throughout every round and in the finals of the Nepal Cup for the second year in a row and managed to set a new record within the Brigade of Gurkhas.

    – Editor, *The Kukri*, No. 3, July 1951

The Brigade of Gurkhas has its journals, *The Kukri* (started in 1949) and *Parbate*. It also has the BFBS (British Forces Broadcasting Services) which provides radio/TV programmes to the armed forces.

    – The author

In 1951, two ex-Gurkhas of the old British-Indian Army made it into the first democratic cabinet led by Nepali Congress PM M. P. Koirala. They were Capt. Narbahadur Gurung of the 4th GR, Minister of State for Health, and Mr Naradmuni Rai of the 7th GR, Minister for Local Self-Government.

    – *The Kukri*, No. 4, August 1952

During the Everest Expedition of 1953, five Gurkhas were included in the group, and their duties were to supervise the porters and guard the expedition and its supplies. They hired 388 porters. Each received a disc with a serial number and was contracted to carry a load to Thyangboche in 17 days for Rs 60 plus half this sum for the return trip. Since the expenses for the whole expedition were to be paid in coin, boxes full of coins were to be carried up the hills, and to protect the treasure boxes, the Gurkhas spread blankets over them and slept on top of them at night with rifles at hand.

    – *The Kukri*, No.5, September 1953

The *Sangola*, the *Sirdana* and the *Santhia* are the three leading ships of the British India Steam Navigation Company which have carried the Gurkhas and their families to and from Malaya since the Brigade was formed on 1 January 1948.

    – *The Kukri*, No. 5, September 1953

In search of Gurkha soldiers in Burma during WWII, the Japanese sent regular troops to villages and used to make the same gesture using both hands – one hand on the head with the index finger pointing upward and another hand at the back making a curved shape. It represented the two symbols of the Gurkhas, the toupi (a long thread of hair from the top of a bald head) and the kukri. The Japanese had invented a straightforward way to depict them.

    – Various books on the Gurkhas

The British propaganda machine didn't even leave the poor Gurkha toupi alone during the wars. They tried to fool the enemies by informing them that it was a wireless cord enabling the Gurkhas to receive and send actual messages without any devices. From the start to the end of WWII, the Gurkhas were required to have a clean shaved head with a toupi, and the practice was abolished only after WWII when the Gurkhas' grievances were passed over to the visiting Army Chief.

– Various books on the Gurkhas

To improve the livelihood of the Gurkhas, the British Raj issued a charter in 1864 that allowed the Gurkhas to have their families with them for the first time. Besides, it also permitted the Gurkhas (both in service and retired) the right to buy land, receive the government's subsidized land and settle in India. The ordinance was later known as the Gurkha Charter, and the charter is the main reason for the heavy presence of Gurkhas in the areas of Dharamsala, Dehradun and Almora.

– Various books on the Gurkhas

Permission was given to enlist the Gurkhas in the Burma Military Police and Kashmir State Forces right after the end of WWI, and the same order was extended in 1935 to recruitment for the five battalions of the Assam Rifles.

– *The Kukri*, No. 2, July 1950

The Brigade of Gurkhas had four Gurkha boxers representing Nepal in the XVIII Summer Olympic Games of 1964 in Tokyo, Japan. Ex-Capt. (QGO) Nam Sing Thapa of 6th GR, Ex-Capt. (QGO) Ram Prashad Gurung of 6th GR, Corporal Om Prashad Pun 6th GR and Rifleman Bhim Bahadur Gurung 6th GR made up the four-man boxing team. Two marathon runners, Ganga Bahadur Thapa Magar and Bhupendra Silawal, from the Nepal Army, completed the national Olympic team and it was the first-ever participation of a Nepali team in the Olympic Games. Both Ram Prashad Gurung and Bhim Bahadur Gurung were knocked out in the round of 32. Nam Sing Thapa got a bye at the first round and moved to the next round without having to fight, but was defeated by an American boxer in the round of 16. Om Prashad Pun defeated an Ethiopian fighter in the first round and lost to a Tunisian boxer in the next. The whole expedition was managed by Major James Keen of the 2/6th GR in Hong Kong. The boxing team didn't win any medals, but given that it was their first participation on such a vast stage, their overall performance was excellent. The other two runners didn't finish the race, and the Nepal Olympic team returned home without a medal. The experience they gained from their participation was invaluable, and they were told to be prepared for the next Olympics in 1968. Unfortunately, it didn't happen as Nepal didn't send any athletes to the next Olympic Games.

– From Ex-Capt. (QGO) Nam Sing Thapa of the 6th GR

The other time Gurkhas were in trouble was in 1986, also known as the Hawaii incident, when an arrogant and insensitive British officer insulted the Gurkhas in front of the Americans by using derogatory words. The British officer was beaten up by a group of enraged Gurkhas and ended up with some 15 stitches on his head while another Gurkha officer was knocked unconscious during the melee. The whole company was rounded up on their arrival in Hong Kong, caged like animals and treated as criminals, while they tried to find the ringleader. The Gurkhas felt extremely offended by the treatment. They closed ranks and didn't cooperate with the authorities. As a result, all 111 men were dismissed from service and sent back to Nepal.

– From *Imperial Warriors* by Tony Gould

On Sunday, 4 December 1988, there was an unfortunate incident in the office of D Company of the 2nd Gurkha in Hong Kong. Someone had fixed a grenade in Major Richford's desk, which exploded when he opened the drawer. Major Richford was murdered and Lt (QGO) Lal Bahadur Pun was severely wounded in both legs. The murder had a long-lasting effect on everyone in the battalion as the killer was never caught. There was an intense and prolonged investigation by the special investigation branch of the Military Police. Suspicion fell on an ex-soldier who had been discharged sometime before. He was found to have been in Hong Kong on the day of the murder, and had left for Japan soon afterward. He must have been one of the soldiers who had been punished by Major

Richford before. The trail stopped there, and as inquiries showed that the man had not returned to his home in Nepal, the investigation ended with no result. Lt (QGO) Lal Bahadur Pun made a complete recovery, and Major Richford was given a full military funeral at St. Martin's Church, Shek Kong, on 16 December with the presence of his parents and all the members of both battalions and the Regimental Band.

– From the History Page of the 2nd GR

An underground rebel group of Gurkhas was formed in early 1990 in the 10th GR with the purpose of speaking out against injustice as well as anomalies within the Brigade of Gurkhas. The successes that the group is said to have claimed were improvements in the services of BFBS Radio. The forces radio service organized a jeans' night in the battalion's cookhouse against the strict policy of the mufti dress code, and wrote an anonymous letter to every Gurkha major of the Brigade regarding rumoured bribes, nepotism and cronyism within the Brigade. The group also staged a similar revolt in GRU, Brunei, and were said to have been dismissed from service there as well. Those individuals were later associated with the Gurkha movements and became active leaders in Gurkha-related organizations.

– PhD dissertation by Dr Ram Narayan Kandangwa at Tribhuvan University

During WWI, the Gurkhas fought in Europe, West Asia and Africa. A wartime censor's office was located at Boulogne, France, to keep track of the mail sent and received by troops from the subcontinent to France and England. It was the responsibility of the office to seize letters with sensitive information about the war fronts and conditions back at home. Those taken letters written by the soldiers were stored at the India Office of the British Library in London. In more than 20 volumes of the censors' reports, each consisting of more than 200 folios, there were only 50 letters from Gurkhas. Those letters were written in Gorkhali or Hindi and then translated into English. The names of the sender and receiver were deleted and typically marked 'from a Gurkha wounded in France to his friend in India'. Since thousands of Gurkhas fought in France, these letters come from only a tiny percentage of them. Those who couldn't read or write their experiences were lost forever.

– Pratyush Onta/Himalmag.com

CHAPTER 26

THE POSITION OF THE BRITISH GOVERNMENT ON GURKHAS

'We were deployed in the 1962 war, fought with kukris in the 1965 war and defeated the enemy. However, the war I am fighting now is something different. I was wrongly dismissed with another 70 members of the battalion in 1979, and I have been fighting for justice since then. We have written to the Nepal and Indian governments, leaders and embassies. But nobody has responded to my letters. I sincerely hope that people will hear my plight one day and I will get justice in the end.'

Sergeant Major Indra Bahadur Gurung (76), 4/3rd GR, from Lamjung, participated in both the 1962 Sino-Indian war and the 1965 Pakistan war and has been fighting for justice against unfair dismissal for the last 40 years.

'Nepal is one of the poorest countries in the world, the nation survives solely on foreign remittances, and becoming a Gurkha is the best chance they have in life.' Whenever an article about the Gurkhas is written by a Westerner, the first thing he or she will do is to include a brief paragraph conveying a similar view as above, and it's always at the beginning of the article. The perception is not only an old, stereotyped and outdated view but also well-planned propaganda with an ulterior motive. The motive is to send out a clear message to the people of Nepal and make them believe it. The message is loud and clear. 'We, the British have done you a great favour, and you should always be grateful.' The message is not only heard by the Gurkhas and Nepali people but also the general public in Great Britain as well, and we are still hearing the same words even today.

It was the period of winners taking all. History has always been written by the winners, and as the winners, the British got to write about the past as they wanted.

The signing of the Sugauli Treaty of 1815 was undoubtedly the most unfortunate event in Nepal's history. It raised a question on the very sovereignty of Nepal. Especially the problematic Article no. 7 which said, 'Nepal now engages never to take or retain in his service any British subject, nor the subject of any European or American State without the consent of the British government.' Nepal also was restricted from buying arms from other nations without the consent of the British. The only diplomatic relationship Nepal had with nations other than British India was with China and Tibet. Nepal's position itself was unique, she was neither a colony nor a fully independent country, and always had to manoeuvre carefully to preserve her status.

The cost to the defeated nation was huge, and the nation of Nepal is paying the price even today. The government not only lost most of the lands it had acquired but also had to allow the British Resident in Kathmandu to dictate the future of the country. The British got everything they had wished for, and Nepal was made to pay for the British gains. The signing of the Sugauli Treaty reduced the proud country to a toothless tiger.

The policy of recruiting the Gurkhas into the British-Indian force wasn't explicitly included in the Sugauli Treaty. Instead, that agreement was said to have been agreed between the two warring generals, and the policy was meant to be applied only to the deserters from the first phase of the Anglo-Gorkha war. It must be the reason why the plan was not even included in the treaty, and the British were unable to raise more than the three Gurkha regiments that they already had for the next four decades. Even Brian Hodgson, the former British Resident in Nepal, who was credited for recording the flora and fauna of Nepal and natural history, did his best to open up the direct recruiting policy in Nepal but failed.

Hodgson was also said to have taken many original Sanskrit and Buddhist scriptures out of Nepal and given them to British museums and libraries. According to Nepali author Satya Mohan Joshi, Hodgson had 381 sacks of old books divided into five lots with him when he left Nepal for Darjeeling in 1844. One lot was sent to the Oriental Library of Bengal, and another lot ended up at the India Office in London, where well-known German researcher Edward Conze found the famous Buddhist scriptures by Nagarjuna, and subsequently wrote many books on Buddhism. Other noticeable books Hodgson took away from Nepal included books in Sanskrit: *Lalit Bichar* – a book based on Buddha's life, and nine such precious books about Nepal. The famous Indian writer and Nobel laureate, Rabindranath Tagore, also saw them and was an avid fan of those invaluable books.

Despite not being officially sanctioned by the Nepal Durbar, the British kept on recruiting the Gurkhas illegally, and they were mostly smuggled in. The Nepal Durbar was entirely against the policy and didn't allow their men to come down the hills and join the British side. Despite political upheavals, infighting and instability in Nepal around that time, the British couldn't increase the numbers of the Gurkha regiment until 1857. Nepal had a new strongman during this period, Jang Bahadur Rana, and he wasn't a particular fan of the British until his historic visit to the UK in 1850.

The British only valued the work of the Gurkhas but not the Gurkhas themselves. During the siege of the Hindu Rao's house during the Sepoy Mutiny of 1857-58, the Sirmoor Regiment was deployed into the direct range of British artillery so they could be wiped out if they changed sides. The three Gurkha regiments, which were raised during the Anglo-Gorkha war in 1815, were still irregulars after more than four decades of loyal service and were only brought into the regular army after the quelling of that rebellion. Had it not been for the Gorkhali Army of Jang Bahadur Rana, the British would have been hacked to pieces, and the story of the British in India would have come to an end.

According to British author Tony Gould, the Gurkhas were a cheap alternative to Europeans. The Gurkhas provided the same services and values as the European soldiers but cost the British a fraction of what they had to fork out to keep the Europeans. Most importantly, the Gurkhas were unbelievably loyal, disciplined and obedient too. Those were the main reasons why the British had wanted to increase the Gurkha regiments in India, but the Nepal Durbar was entirely against the direct recruiting. After his UK visit, strongman Jang Bahadur Rana was fully aware of the power of the British Empire and applied the policy of friendship with the British.

Nevertheless, he wasn't ready to accept the policy of direct recruiting and favoured a policy of offering the help of the Gorkhali Army instead whenever the British were in trouble. By this, the strongman achieved three main benefits. He saved the Gorkhali Army from depleting its workforce, kept a good relationship with the British, and still managed to get something out of the British whenever he was able to help them as a favour.

The British finally got their opportunity when the reign of Bir Shumsher was threatened by Jang Bahadur's sons, who had taken refuge in the safety of the British Raj as they were hunted down by the ruling Shumsher clan. In return for not supporting the possible revolt by his enemy, Bir Shumsher had no choice but to yield to the demands of the British and sanction the direct recruiting of the Gurkhas in 1886.

As far as the British were concerned, the Gurkhas were not only dispensable but also an experimental force and were always sent to the forefront of the battles at home and abroad. There wasn't a single battle in which the Gurkhas hadn't fought for the British, and needless to say, the Gurkhas were always the ones leading the campaigns. The practice wasn't only limited to wartime but also during peacetime. The British discriminated against the Gurkhas from the very beginning. The aura of superiority and inferiority was always there, and words like equality and fairness didn't exist in the Gurkha-British relationship.

The other tactic the British used to get the best out of the Gurkhas was flattery. It was used to such an extreme absurdity that, as far as the British were concerned, it was nothing more than a show and used merely as a veil to cover the reality. Most importantly, it didn't cost them a penny, and the British also were seen as being generous. The well-conceived scheme was designed for targeting two audiences: the rulers of Nepal and the Gurkhas. The rulers were showered with lavish gifts, honorary titles and nominal awards and positions. The Gurkhas were a simple and easy bunch, and just a few impressive-sounding words of praise were enough to please them. Besides, the Gurkhas were genuinely brave. Thus the British didn't even have to pretend. The world got a new phenomenon, the Gurkhas were *makhkhai* (deliriously happy), and the British got their way without much effort.

The first test of that friendship came in the shape of WWI. Regardless of the British perspective, the Gurkha nation had accepted Britain as their true friend and they readied to sacrifice themselves for the British cause. The number of Gurkhas serving in the British Raj by then had reached 26,000 men with twenty battalions. PM Chandra Shumsher decided to throw almost everything the nation had in support of the British Raj, and the tiny country with a population of little more than five million sent 200,000 men to the war.

According to historians from Nepal, men between the ages of 14 to 50 were forced to go to war. Almost 20 per cent of the able men from the hillsides finally went, and one in ten never returned. In the midst of the war, the hills of Nepal were so depleted that hardly a single man was to be found. Nepal provided not only the workforce, but also arms, ammunition, porters, medical staff and other necessary supplies. The resources of the whole country were at Britain's disposal.

According to author Asad Husain, three lakh rupees were initially provided to buy machine guns for the Gurkhas of the Indian Army in September 1914. On New Year's Day of both 1916 and 1917, three lakh rupees were presented to the Viceroy again for use in the war. A further two lakh rupees were given to the silver wedding anniversary of the King and Queen of the UK. Besides, 40,000 pounds of cardamoms, 84,699 pounds of tea, 200 jackets and 12 great coats were sent to the soldiers. Furthermore, 200,000 deep gauge sleepers and 220 Sisoo logs were supplied free of charge for the railways, and the Maharaja was prepared to send 2,000 Tibetan and Nepali blankets known as Pakhias and Jhum Radhis to the troops as well. Nepal also offered 340 mechanics to repair broken arms, but only 71 were needed and accepted. The country also provided the equivalent of 10.1 million Indian rupees and 2.5 million Nepali coins as a donation to the British war chest in India, which was in severe need of extra funds.

During WWI, the Gurkhas suffered the most unfair and discriminatory treatment from the British, who were supposed to protect them. Due to their religious beliefs, the Gurkhas had never crossed the ocean before WWII, but the British forced the Nepali ruler to twist that rule. When they finally arrived in Europe, a new and unfamiliar place in the harsh European winter, the Gurkhas weren't even provided with proper clothing or equipment and were then thrown into battles without adequate training. Furthermore, they were ordered to occupy the trenches dug by the taller British soldiers, which were too deep for the Gurkhas and brought unnecessary misery during rains. Many Gurkhas were killed or lost their limbs because of frostbite, poor conditions and harsh weather rather than enemy bullets. The Gurkhas suffered a similar fate in the extreme heat of the deserts in the Middle East. They were brought there by the British for the very first time without proper training or equipment. Even worse, the main factor of the fatalities in WWI was the ineptitude of many British commanders (in the Flanders, Gallipoli and Mesopotamia fiascos). Without those blunders, many Gurkhas wouldn't have died.

In both WWI and WWII, Nepal was regularly contacted by the enemies of the British through letters, radio broadcasts and propaganda offices, and offered immense incentives to betray Britain. The Nepal Durbar not only passed that valuable information to the British but also provided necessary suggestions and never left the British side as a true friend. Among the most notable were the letters from the Chancellor of Imperial Germany, the Amir of Afghanistan, and the Japanese Imperial Army.

Just before the final assaults would begin in the battles of both WWI and WWII, the Gurkhas were ordered to drink a substantial amount of rum until they felt hot, and then ordered to fight the enemy under the influence of alcohol. The practice might provide the necessary encouragement for advancing soldiers in battle, but it certainly raised the question of ethics. Such stories were commonly heard during conversations among the war veterans back in Nepal. After hearing them, it didn't take long to decide that many things in this world, including human rights, look nice only on paper.

Similarly, almost 250,000 men from the tiny nation came to fight with their British friends during WWII and suffered nearly 32,640 casualties (including almost 9,000 killed or missing). During WWII, PM Juddha Shumsher sent 50 cigarettes, a photograph of himself with a message on the reverse, a pound of tea, and a pound of sugar to each soldier. Nepal sent one lakh rupees to the Viceroy's fund, 25,000 rupees to London fire victims, 5,000 rupees to Lady Linlithgow's Fund, 15,000 rupees to the St. Joseph Relief Fund, 15,000 more to divide between the widows and orphans of soldiers from the Indian Army, 4,560 pounds sterling to the flying squadron fund, 50,000 rupees to the Red Cross, and many more small contributions to other war funds. Three thousand walnut trees were sent to manufacture rifle butts. They also sent 192 service revolvers, 144 pairs of binoculars, 25 Vickers machine guns, 70 Lewis guns, 800 sal trees and many more items that were provided as gifts from Nepal.

The British were overwhelmingly moved by such generosity from a true friend like Nepal and started praising Nepal as a grateful person would typically do. Unfortunately, they were limited to words, which never transformed into deeds. Before too long, everything was forgotten, and the British again became selfish.

The way the British had treated the Gurkhas in the aftermath of WWI and WWII was not only cruel and inhumane but also a disgrace. Almost half a million young men fought for the British, many died, and others were injured. But instead of being thankful, the British sent them back to Nepal empty-handed, and the tiny nation was burdened with the responsibility of nursing the wounded, crippled and mentally destabilized ones on its own. They were discharged without pensions, medical expenses, gratuities or severance pay. A meagre salary, based on a rate of 24 rupees a month, 150 pounds equivalent of travel money, and a nine-foot piece of white cloth was given to each of them when they were sent home. By doing so, the British made not only a mockery of the Gurkha sacrifices but also insulted the religious beliefs of the whole nation. Giving a piece of white cloth to a Hindu is deemed inauspicious as such a practice is only performed when someone has died in their family, and part of the fabric is meant for covering the dead body on its final journey to the pyre. The British should have known better and been more sensitive. Or was it intentional? Since many were suffering life-threatening wounds, perhaps the British thought they would die anyway and might soon be in need of the white cloth.

More than 60,000 Gurkhas were killed, wounded and missing in both world wars, not to mention the loss, agony and suffering of their families. The sacrifices of the men, women, children and the whole nation were for nothing. If there was no value for life, what chances were there for sweat, hardship and blood? The future of the whole nation was gambled away in the name of friendship, and Nepal lost in a big way.

Neither the British nor the Nepal government kept any records of those who went to the wars and then were killed, injured or missing. Recruits were provided the basic training and were sent away to the front lines throughout the war. Those wounded were hastily treated at the military hospital and sent out to fight again once they had recovered. But those severely injured or badly crippled were discharged and sent home right away, as they were no good for the army any more. As a result, there is no clear, detailed list of those veterans who fought in the wars. The standard practice of having similar names in our society didn't help and further complicated the situation. Due to disabilities and impaired limbs, many veterans lived in absolute poverty. Had the British done their job, they could have easily been found, and helping hands such as NGOs, the War Reparation Fund and other institutions could have helped them. Was it intentional? It doesn't matter. But the way the British treated the Gurkhas was undoubtedly an act of betrayal, and no matter how history might have portrayed it, truth cannot be hidden for too long. The relationship between the British and the Gurkhas was always one-sided.

The next act of betrayal from the British side came in 1947 when the rule of the British Raj ended, and the British had to leave India once and for all. As we know, only four out of ten Gurkha regiments were chosen to go with the British and the decision was made in such a hasty, indifferent and cold way that the feelings, honour and loyalty of the Gurkhas were ignored. Given that the decisions were made by bureaucrats back in London, the final decision clearly showed the value, respect and attitude the British had for the Gurkhas, and it was disgraceful. The Gurkhas were shocked, hurt and utterly disappointed. And they didn't hesitate to show their true feelings through their actions. The Gurkhas' actions shocked the British to the core, the bubble of complacency was burst, and the Gurkhas didn't line up in droves to follow their colonial masters as the British had predicted.

In the end, the British had to retreat to Malaya and Singapore with a severely depleted army (for instance, the 2/6th had less than 200 men in a battalion that generally had more than 1,000 men when in full strength) and had to rebuild them from scratch.

In the name of the 1947 tripartite agreement after partition to retain Gurkha services in the British and Indian armies (a copy of this document is provided in the annexes), a treaty was signed between the British, India and Nepal. This is undoubtedly the most critical document regarding the Gurkhas, and has dictated the future of the Gurkhas since 1947.

The agreement was made in such a dubious way that it clearly showed the British had ulterior motives. All the British wanted was this: no matter where the Gurkhas were deployed in the future, they wanted to pay the Gurkhas the same as those in India were paid. The policy of long and calculated exploitation of the Gurkhas as cheap labour was hence begun. Despite the title of the treaty as being tripartite, it was, in fact, bilateral, and Britain and India had already agreed it before they talked to Nepal. Nepal was approached at the last minute so as to leave no time for further negotiation.

According to a book by the British Gurkha Study and Research Centre, the Nepal team requested equal treatment regarding promotion, welfare and other facilities with other British units so they wouldn't be regarded as mercenaries, and the Gurkhas should also be eligible for the commissioned ranks with no restrictions whatsoever based on qualifications. Given the urgency of the treaty to be signed, the British agreed to Nepal's request, and the agreement was signed on 9 November 1947 by the three nations. ACB Symon from the British, Lt Col Kanwar Dayasingh Bedi from India and Padma Shumsher JB Rana from Nepal represented their respective countries at the signing ceremony. The written agreements provided by the British representative at Nepal's request were added, not in the main treaty, but in its annexes.

Despite the agreement, Britain and India had already agreed on the pay issue on 7 November 1947, and Britain has been using its terms since then. The treaty signed by the three countries was just for show and to get the final signature from Nepal. The British had never thought of honouring it. The pay of the British Gurkhas had been attached to the Indian Pay Code (IPC) since the beginning, and every time questions were raised concerning the Gurkhas' pay, the British used the treaty to silence the critics.

While the Gurkhas were based in Malaysia, Singapore and Hong Kong, they were paid according to the IPC rate. The discrimination in pay between a Gurkha and a British soldier was wide. For instance, a Gurkha soldier was paid 42 dollars a month in Malaysia and Hong Kong while a British soldier drew 450 dollars. In Hong Kong, both the British and the Chinese volunteers were paid a lot more than the Gurkhas, but when it came to work and duty, the Gurkhas were always at the front line.

The discrimination in promotion, welfare and other facilities was also tremendous between the Gurkhas and other British units. The Gurkhas had KGO/QGO (King's Gurkha Officer/Queen's Gurkha Officer) and the highest rank they could achieve was the Gurkha Major. Only a very few able officers were selected as commissioned officers, and that policy had already died down by the early 1980s. Concerning pay, welfare and allowances, there were two separate policies for the Gurkhas and the British. While the British had a variety of benefits, high salaries and severance pay, the Gurkhas only had a monthly salary and nothing else. We had not only different pay, promotion and welfare policies from our British counterparts, but also different rules and regulations from them. We had some British soldiers and NCOs serving in our battalion when I was still in the army, and our battalion's rules and regulations were never applied to them.

When we were in Brunei in 1982, our company commander always used to take our company to the jungle, and we genuinely thought that he was a jungle warfare freak. However, the real reason behind his motive was later discovered to be money. The British officers had extra jungle/field allowances, while we Gurkhas had none.

During the Malayan Emergency, 1948-1960, a total of 208 Gurkhas lost their lives. But unlike their British counterparts, who were entitled to severance pay, gratuity, war pay and many more benefits that could amount to tens of thousands of pounds, the Gurkha families received nothing. When the Malayan Emergency was over, the British were planning for a big cutback. But that plan was put off because Sukarno, the Indonesian president, was about to start guerrilla warfare, later to be known as the Borneo Confrontation. Another 59 Gurkhas lost their lives in that conflict, and their families also received nothing, as before. Once the conflict was over, the rundown plan that had been on hold until then was put back in action in 1968-69.

The autocratic Rana government of Nepal was gone by now, King Mahendra was at the helm, and the *panchayati* partyless political system was in place. But the tactics the British used were the same old trickery and flattery that had served them so well. A high-ranking official was dispatched to Kathmandu for a talk, King Mahendra was made an honorary colonel of the Brigade of Gurkhas, and the biggest cutback of the Brigade in the post-WWII era went ahead as planned. By 1969, the Brigade of Gurkhas was cut by almost half, and about 6,000 men were sent home. Only those who had served more than 10 years received a nominal pension, while those with less than 10 years received a small gratuity, according to their years of service.

Another discriminative policy against the Gurkhas was the years of service for a pension. A Gurkha below the rank of corporal qualified for a pension in 15 years, whereas a Brit in the same position needed 22 years. The British suggested the policy was a favourable one for the Gurkhas, but in reality, the actual motive was something different. The British only wanted the best and youngest blood in the army. The ages 18-35 are the best years of our lives and by applying the policy of 15 years, the British made sure that they only got the best of the Gurkhas. In brief, the Gurkhas were replaced well before they became old and avoided hurting the whole army system.

The same British elitist mentality was to blame for the way they treated our VC winners. After resigning, Bhanubhakta Gurung VC was sent home without a pension. The ill-treatment of Tul Bahadur Pun VC by the British Border Control Agency during his arrival in the UK was disgraceful – the result of an error made by a British consular official in Kathmandu – and prompted a public outcry.

The British even brought one of the VCs (subedar Lal Bahadur Thapa) into the UK after WWII and made him perform, imitating a shrill battle cry in front of a jubilant, clapping British crowd as if he were in a circus. Those actions showed a lack of judgement on their part, and the British ended up disrespecting their greatest honour, the Victoria Cross, the highest award for valour in the British Army.

The British had never accepted the Gurkhas as equals and used many forms of trickery, treachery and flattery to discriminate against them. No matter what they had said or done in the past 200 years or so, it served only one motive, and that was to use the Gurkhas as cheap labour. Thanks to the selfish, foolish and submissive nature of the Nepali rulers, the British easily succeeded, and the Gurkhas were the ones who suffered the most.

The salary of a Gurkha soldier started at Indian Rs 6 per month in 1815. By 1911, just before WWI, it was Rs 11 per month and increased to Rs 16 per month after WWI. By the end of WWII in 1945, the salary was Rs 24 per month. After the British Gurkhas moved to Malaysia in the 1960s, the wages of the Gurkha soldier were increased to Malaysian $42 per month. When I was a recruit in Hong Kong in 1980, the least I ever got paid was HK$716 per month. Unlike our seniors before, we had bank accounts at HSBC, the monthly salary was directly deposited into the bank, and our *guruji* used to help update our bank accounts as recruits were not allowed to go outside. On top of the army-issued kit and equipment, we had to buy some items such as a regimental blazer, ties, badges, emblems and many more things with our own money, and those items were purchased from the private regimental shop. The costs of those necessary items were directly debited from our salary that particular month. I still remember our pay then was less than HK$1,000 a month.

The above pattern shows that the British always had a well-orchestrated plan. The British never intended to pay more than was necessary to the Gurkhas and whenever there was an objection, which happened very rarely, they brought up the IPC. The British did not only apply this mean mentality within their jurisdiction, but also tried to teach others under their influence. I will relate an exciting story to prove this very point. The basic monthly pay of the Gurkha Reserve Unit (GRU) soldier in Brunei started at around 600 Brunei dollars, whereas the British Gurkha soldier serving in Brunei earned about 120 dollars. When a British officer was hired to command a GRU unit, he couldn't abide by it and started plotting a scheme against the high pay. Once that was found out, some Gurkhas in the GRU took action, and the British officer's plan failed. A similar incident happened in the Singapore Gurkha Contingent and the British officers were behind that as well.

The flagrant display of the British elitist mentality was most visible in the Brigade of Gurkhas. A 21-year-old British 2nd lieutenant was above the Gurkha major in terms of seniority. The major had not only more than 28 years of service under his belt, but was also the most senior Gurkha officer of the regiment and that said it all. The British officers in the battalion were treated like royals, the commanding officer was the king, and the rest of us Gurkhas were their subjects. In brief, the relationship between the British and the Gurkhas was always like a boss and a servant. It might sound a little harsh, and I know some readers might not agree with this statement. But reality bites and people usually don't want to hear the truth, as truth can be bitter.

To put more emphasis on the above statement, I want to add a point here that might not have been heard or written about before. To provide necessary support and army-related training demonstrations to the officer cadets at Sandhurst Military Academy, a Gurkha Demonstration Company was permanently based at Sandhurst. I was one of the junior NCOs who served there during 1985-86. Whenever we went to jungle warfare training with the officer cadets, there were always two support teams deployed from the Company. One was the demonstrating team while the other was the administration team. The demonstration job was straightforward as expected, but the administrative job was somewhat ambiguous and involved a lot of manual tasks such as helping the cooks at the cookhouse, serving the officers at the mess and cleaning the dishes at the end. We had to go to the houses of retired and serving regimental officers on weekends and help cook food, serve the guests, and do the cleaning-up during the officers' private parties. We also had to help the officers move into and out of the houses, and all such extra work was done only as a favour.

I found a fascinating story in early editions of *The Kukri*, the Brigade of Gurkhas' journal. When the Gurkhas were deployed in Hong Kong for the first time in 1948, they were initially based at Whitfield Barracks but were then ordered to move to Beas River Stables to make room for the 1st Royal Leicesters. Once they had cleaned the horse stables and settled in, the Gurkhas were ordered to hand over the stables to the 1st Middlesex and moved to San Wai to build a tented camp.

When the Brigade of Gurkhas was stationed in Hong Kong, the five infantry battalions used to take turns for a two-year tour to the UK, and the wives and children of the Gurkhas, including officers and senior NCOs, had to be left behind during the trip. Had this been required of British regiments, they never would have considered accepting such a discriminatory policy.

The final test of the British colonial and elitist mentality came in 1997 when British administration ceased in Hong Kong, which meant the British Garrison stationed in Hong Kong also had to move out. The situation was made trickier by the fact that Hong Kong also happened to be the last major British colonial outpost and the British Garrison had nowhere to move to after Hong Kong. The reality of bringing the British Garrison back to the UK did bite, and as far as the British were concerned, that was a big dilemma. As the old saying goes – patting the back of your hardworking workers for a job done well is one thing, but eating with them at the same table is another. You show such hospitality to your friends, families and fellow tribes as equals, but the British and the Gurkhas were never equals. Taking the Gurkhas to the UK would have been like accepting the Gurkhas, and the British were not comfortable with that situation.

Although the Gurkhas had already served the British for 182 years at that point, the Gurkhas had always been deployed in British colonies outside the UK. Understandably, the cost of the British Garrison was borne by the colony wherever the Garrison was stationed. But the situation had changed by then, and the responsibility of paying the Garrison had now fallen back to the British treasury. The Gurkhas were not going to be paid in Indian rupees, Malaysian, Singapore or Hong Kong dollars but in pounds sterling, and the British had a problem with that. Paying the Gurkhas in sterling meant equal treatment and the British found it very difficult to accept. The British had taken the Gurkhas for granted for almost two centuries; they were accustomed to treating the Gurkhas in that particular way and found it hard to change that old habit. But at the same time, the British didn't want to end the Gurkha legacy either, as that would have been unfortunate since it could have hurt their reputation. It could have given a bad name to the mighty British, hence the dilemma. Luckily for the British, two white knights came just in time to save their skin and the problem that plagued them was solved.

Had it not been for Brunei and Singapore, the shape and formation of the Brigade of Gurkhas would be very different by now. The tiny but oil-rich Sultanate of Brunei has been hosting a Gurkha battalion and a few more British troops since 1970. The defence treaty and the royalty the British earn from the agreement is said to be quite substantial. The British also act as an agency of the Singapore government and help provide facilities, expertise and services on the recruitment of Gurkhas for the Singapore Gurkha Contingent. The income the British receive from those two nations should be enough to pay for the continuation of the Gurkhas in the British Army, and the final number of Gurkhas retained for the UK as part of the British Army might have been determined by that amount. In conclusion, the Gurkhas had to be traded off to secure their future in the British Army and be thankful to the British too, all at the same time.

Although a total of around 3,500 Gurkhas are currently serving in the British Army, only about 2,500 out of more than 10,000-strong forces were retained initially, and the remainder were sent home. The redundancy terms were a bit better than the rundown of the late 1960s, but the same policy of providing the bare amount as the British had always done before was also applied then. Many were made jobless at the stroke of a pen.

A Gurkha battalion was permanently based in Brunei, as it is now, and the two Gurkha battalions take turns to replace each other every three years.

The Gurkha pay scheme was always connected to the Indian Pay Code, and the Gurkha Pension Scheme (GPS), which was created in 1949, handled the pension-related issues for the Gurkha veterans. There was a significant gap in both pay and pension of the Gurkhas in comparison to other members of the British Army. The reasons, as the British had always said, were: parity in pay with the Indian Gurkhas while in service, and the Gurkhas' pension was still at par with living standards back in the villages.

The disparity between the British and the Gurkha soldiers in pay, pension and compensation continued even after the Gurkhas had moved to the UK. The treatment the widow of Sergeant Bala Ram Rai of 69 Squadron, QGE, received from the British was unfair and degrading. Two Gurkha engineers of QGE, Lt Gareth Evans and Sergeant Bala Ram Rai, were killed in Kosovo in 1999 while clearing an enemy mine, and compensation was paid to the fallen soldiers' families. Despite doing the same task and being killed in the same event, the family of Bala Ram Rai was paid just 7.5 per cent of what the family of Gareth Evans was paid, and the unfair treatment of the Gurkha caused a huge public outcry among the British people and sent the British government back-pedalling.

The British Army adopted a new pension policy, the Armed Forces Pension Scheme (AFPS1975) in 1975. But the Gurkhas were not included in the scheme even after they had moved to the UK. Only after the decisions on the Gurkhas' settlement rights in the UK, in 2004 and 2009, were the British forced to make some necessary amendments to Gurkha pensions. As a result, all the serving members of the Gurkhas received equal pay, pension and terms of service on 8 March 2007. But only the Gurkhas who enlisted on or after 1 October 1993 qualified for a pension equal to their British counterparts under the AFPS05. Terms for the Gurkha veterans who went on pension before that date were and are dictated by the old and discriminatory GPS, and although some improvements on Gurkha pensions have been made since then, it still lags a great deal.

According to the Centre for Nepal Studies UK (CNSUK), the discrepancy between the British and the Gurkhas on pensions was about 1,000 per cent. For instance, a British Captain got a yearly pension of 5,269 pounds sterling while a Gurkha Captain was paid a meagre 606 pounds in 1989.

As of 2013, there were about 22,935 pensioners (16,065 retired Gurkhas and 6,870 widows) and thanks to the new changes, the pensioners were divided into two groups – with the new pensions or old pensions. After the Gurkhas had won the right of abode in the UK, the Gurkhas are not living back in the villages of Nepal any more. Despite the outcry from the British public on several occasions as injustices were brought to light, the perspectives of the British establishment towards the Gurkhas have remained the same. For my research for this book, I enquired about the position of the British government through the British consulate in Hong Kong. After a long trail of emails, I was finally guided to a page that showed the same old and outdated statements that had already been available on the internet for quite some time.

The fight for equal pensions for the Gurkha veterans is still on. The Gurkha veterans and related organizations are in talks with the UK government. I was provided with the manifestos, and the details of the discussion. The final agreement was still to be reached as I wrote this book.

The leading team on behalf of the Gurkha veterans has the usual and well-known parties of the Gurkha Justice Campaign on board, with one exception. The Embassy of Nepal in the UK was also included in the team. Still, I could feel the lack of unity in the group and agents from the mainstream political parties of Nepal had infiltrated the organization. I wished they had put all their differences and personal ambitions aside, and come together as a united team to fight for the actual cause.

The British had always taken the Gurkhas for granted. They have used all the tricks, deceptions and cunning ways to pay the Gurkhas as little as they possibly could and exploited the Gurkhas for the last two centuries. The relationship between the British and the Gurkhas was never built on equal terms, no matter what history might have suggested. It was rather like a boss and a servant, and the art of flattery was used to cover that bitter fact.

We used to joke among ourselves whenever we were down, and lamented our position as if we were a piece of tissue or a lemon. A tissue is tossed away after it's used. So is a lemon. After you've squeezed the juice out of it, you can throw it away. Unfortunately, the Gurkha story was a similar one, and the lemon version of the joke was my favourite. We were so naïve and innocent, and knew nothing at all about the history of the Gurkhas that had played such an essential role in our lives. I didn't imagine in my wildest dreams back then that I would be writing a book about the Gurkhas to try my best to highlight their history, their plight and the injustice meted out to them.

In more than 200 years, the position of the British government did not change a bit. But times have changed, the Gurkhas have found their voice, and they will fight for their rights.

I still remember like it was yesterday when I was in the army, and one of the British officers always used to say this to all of us: '*Baau baaje jasto chhaina*' (You are not like your fathers or grandfathers). 'Of course, we are not,' we used to say to ourselves without knowing what had changed. It took a few more years before change could appear on the horizon and a decade or so before it could bear some result. The Gurkha Justice

Campaign was the change that we didn't foresee then. It has restored some respect and dignity for the Gurkhas, and the Gurkhas have changed for good. Now we can proudly respond to the British as well as to the world: 'Of course, we are not like our fathers or grandfathers' and we know our rights. The British officer who had said this to us would not have liked our answer, but he certainly could have afforded a smile for being able to predict the future correctly.

The saying of Sir Arthur Hirtzel, then under-secretary of state for India, on 22 August 1922 summed up the British position very well: 'It is, after all, mainly because of the Gurkha element in the army that we value the friendship of Nepal.' It has not changed since then.

Last but not least, the book *The Gurkhas* by Byron Farwell blatantly called the Gurkhas mercenaries throughout. I was shocked by the flagrant use of the word, given the fact that the tripartite treaty protected the Gurkhas from such abuse.

Even worse, what surprised me the most was the fact that the book had been endorsed by many high-ranking British officers who had served with the Gurkhas. It raises a very obvious but plausible question. Was it the author's opinion alone or had he just been a messenger? Whatever the truth, it showed insensitivity, arrogance and bigotry from the parties involved, and such a lowly opinion shouldn't have been expressed in such a blatant way, at least not by such a highly educated and decorated bunch of people. People cannot blame us for presuming that they were expressing their real opinions.

The Gurkhas have served the British for hundreds of years, fought so many battles and sacrificed tens of thousands of lives. For what? The Gurkhas won neither respect from the country they had fought for, nor had they secured a place in the history of their own country. Instead, they were ridiculed by many as mercenaries.

The Gurkha story is not all about bravery but also about tragedy, and the British were the main perpetrators of the latter. But were they alone? Not at all! They had a very able helping hand, and their partners in crime were, unfortunately, none other than the rulers of Nepal themselves. Had it not been for the rulers of Nepal, the British would never have been successful in exploiting the Gurkhas for so long. The rulers of Nepal were equally to blame as the British.

CHAPTER 27

THE POSITION OF THE NEPAL GOVERNMENT ON GURKHAS

'It took us 18 days and nights at sea from Bombay to Cairo. We trained and fought at the Suez Canal and in Libya after arriving at Cairo. The whole battalion was lost, and only 11 returned. Then, we fought in Italy. I was a signaller, and we took months to capture the final objective. The hardest battle was in Libya: tanks on the ground, bombs from the sky, and Africans were used as porters with mules. We fought, sacrificed and won bravery medals. We should have been given better pensions and welfare than the others, but we weren't. It's not fair.'

Corporal Dil Bahadur Thapa (93), 2/3rd GR, from Chhetrapur, Chitwan, joined the army in 1940 and retired in 1955. He fought in Egypt, Libya, Italy and Cyprus during WWII and won seven war medals.

Some called them 'Nepal's diplomatic currency' and others called them the 'main export of Nepal'. In general, a Gurkha was always regarded as someone who was somewhat naïve and not so well educated. But no matter what, the Gurkhas played a vital role in saving Nepal as a nation. History can be forgiven but never forgotten, and it doesn't lie. The Gurkhas were the main reason for the long history of cooperation between the British and Nepal. Both nations knew very well the importance of the Gurkhas. They both used the Gurkhas for their mutual interests.

The British might have acted in their national interests, but as far as the Nepali rulers were concerned, their actions were personal and self-serving. In many cases, the Gurkhas were the primary tool that had been used by both sides and served the interests of both nations. Had it not been for the Gurkhas, the history of Nepal might have been very different. Whether it would have been good or bad, nobody can say for sure. But we can still study the history of the Gurkhas, find the facts and make up our minds.

When the unification of modern Nepal was initiated by the Gorkha King, Maharaja Prithvi Narayan Shah, the British East India Company was on a similar mission after they had defeated the Nawab of Bengal and his French supporters. By the time Rana Bahadur Shah, the grandson of Prithvi Narayan Shah, took power from his uncle Bahadur Shah in 1795, the boundaries of greater Nepal had reached the Kangra Valley in the west and Bhutan in the east. After the death of King Prithvi Narayan Shah, the Shah dynasty lacked a visionary and robust ruler like him, and mostly regents and their chief councillors ran the country. Due to infighting and rivalries, the Nepal Durbar was severely weakened.

The first treaty the Nepal Durbar signed with the British was the trade treaty of 1792, which levied a 2.5 per cent tax on the imports of luxury goods from Britain to Nepal, and Nepal was forced to sign it in return for Britain helping the Gorkhali Army against the Chinese although that help failed to arrive in time.

The British had already established themselves as one of the leading powers of the region. Nepal, the Marathas and Punjab were other major powers among the few. After the failure of the previous two expeditions (Kinloch and Kirkpatrick), the British were waiting for the right opportunity. According to the book *Gurkhas* by David Bolt, when King Rana Bahadur Shah took a Brahmin girl as his second wife, the Brahmin community was shocked and cursed him. The new queen fell sick, and the king spent heavily on expensive rites to cure her as demanded by the Brahmins. The queen died anyway, and the king went mad. He not only asked for repayment from the Brahmins but also smashed their sacred images to dust with artillery and cursed the gods as well. The people of Nepal revolted and he was sent into exile in Benares.

Rana Bahadur Shah became a *sadhu*, known as Purnacahir Goonanund Swammee Jee, and the Nepal Durbar had to pay his yearly expenses of 'Patna Sicca Rupees': 82,000, of which 72,000 was paid in cash and 10,000 in elephants (half in male and half in female elephants, each elephant being priced at 125 rupees). He was also allowed to retain no more than 100 male or female attendants, but no personal soldiers.

To pay for his luxurious lifestyle, the exiled king borrowed money from his host, the British, and granted them the right to send a British Resident to Kathmandu in exchange. Captain Knox was assigned as the first British Resident, but the Nepal Durbar coldly ignored him, and he finally withdrew after a useless 11 months.

That was, of course, the British side of the story. In reality, the Nepal Durbar was forced to sign a treaty by the British after the deposed King Rana Bahadur Shah had taken refuge with them. The treaty was known as the 'Treaty of 1801', the first of many such agreements based on peace and friendship. It had three main points: the exiled king, the British Resident and trade. But the terms inserted by the British side were not favourable to the Nepal Durbar. Having a British Resident in Kathmandu had only one purpose as far as the British were concerned. They wanted to keep Nepal under their thumb by interfering, manipulating and bribing the Durbar and they could do so only by being there on the spot. The Nepal Durbar used an array of delaying tactics for quite some time before accepting the treaty. The regent of the then-reigning King Girwanyudha

Bikram Shah, Queen Subarna Prabha, was worried that with the help of the British, the exiled king would return and try retaking the throne. In return for keeping the exiled king away from Kathmandu, she finally agreed to the treaty.

Although the treaty didn't last too long, it was the first in which Nepal had officially accepted British supremacy and gave precedence to the advent of more such treaties in the future.

Although the treaty was signed on 28 October 1801, Capt. Knox only reached Kathmandu on 16 April 1802, and left on 19 March 1803. The political scene in the Nepal Durbar had changed since the arrival of the senior queen, Raj Rajeswari Devi from Benares, and internal rivalries among the factions of rulers weakened them. When the British Resident was trying to establish himself in Kathmandu, the exiled king was put under house arrest, and the Durbar was to pay for his expenses. As Capt. Knox left Kathmandu, the exiled king was set free and returned to Nepal. Hostility between the British and Nepal continued for more than a decade and ultimately led to the conflict later known as the Anglo-Gorkha war of 1814-16.

To establish their supremacy in India, the British had to stop the Gorkhali Army that had run wild and conquered many states on its northern border. The British had been trying to achieve three main goals in Nepal: to tame the roaring tiger; open a trade route to Tibet (where they were mining gold); and keep Nepal under its protection. That aim was achieved by the Anglo-Gorkha War of 1814-16. Most unfortunately, the treaty ended up raising a big question about the very sovereignty of the nation itself.

The treaty had terms that were unfavourable to Nepal in many ways. In short, the Sugauli Treaty of 1815 was undoubtedly the most unfortunate event in the history of Nepal, and it is the main reason why the nation hasn't prospered. The government of Nepal is still paying the price, even today, from that fateful treaty. Generations after generations have suffered since then.

John Peter Boileau came into Nepal as an acting British Resident, and Edward Gardner replaced him in 1816 and served until 1829. After the signing of the Sugauli Treaty, the British always applied a friendly policy towards Nepal, and the Gurkhas were the main reason behind that conciliatory approach.

During the reign of Bhimsen Thapa, Brian Hodgson came in 1829 as an assistant first, and then became the British Resident in 1833. Thapa was a capable, intelligent and powerful ruler. Besides, he didn't like the British interfering in Nepali politics and always looked for chances to settle scores. A dangerous diplomatic game of cat and mouse continued between the two able men and ended only when Bhimsen Thapa lost power in 1837. By then, Hodgson already had significant influence in the Nepal Durbar. The noblemen of the Durbar were always fighting, and he knew how to take advantage of them. Understandably, the losing factions sought his patronage and didn't take long to ingratiate themselves with the British. Had it not been for Hodgson, Nepal would have embroiled itself in a bitter battle with the British again, and the then king called him the saviour of Nepal for maintaining peace. At the pinnacle of Hodgson's influence in 1841, King Rajendra Bikram Shah was said to have drawn up a list of ministers for his approval and sanctioned the restarting of the 1792 trade treaty.

The question was: if Hodgson had so much influence in the Nepal Durbar, why didn't he succeed in the official sanctioning of the Gurkha recruitment into the British Indian Army? Wasn't that what they wanted? It could also be possible that he wasn't as influential as he has been portrayed. Because the Nepal Durbar was weak and indecisive then, the British did manage to take advantage of the situation.

The British and Jang Bahadur signed the first extradition treaty on 10 February 1955, and Jang Bahadur's main intention behind the signing of the treaty was to capture his rivals who had been hiding in India.

The British Residents did their best to influence the Nepal Durbar through the schemes of interfering, plotting and dividing the high-ranking officials. The sanctioning of direct recruiting by the Nepal Durbar was their primary goal, but that wasn't possible until Jang Bahadur was in power.

After the death of Jang Bahadur, Ranodhip Singh became the new PM of Nepal in 1878. According to Nepali author Jhalak Subedi, the British started asking for the enlistment of a thousand new Gurkha soldiers under the new regime. To be accepted by the British as the new PM of Nepal, he couldn't refuse, but sent only 559. He also needed some new men for the Gorkhali Army to counter the Tibetan threat.

To remain in power, the rulers of Nepal understood the importance of the mighty British being on their side, and the British took full advantage of the Nepali rulers' weaknesses. Since the British were in the mood of full expansion, they needed more men to fight for them, and Gurkhas were the prize they had always sought. And for good or bad, Nepal had the best soldiers in the world, and both the British and the Nepali rulers used them. After the reign of Bir Shumsher, the Gurkhas had become the anvil on which relations between the two nations were forged and maintained, even today.

During Ranodhip Singh's premiership, the Shumsher faction of the Rana clan also had their aspirations for high office. But if they were to wait their turn, Bir Shumsher was seventh in line by then, and he wasn't ready to wait that long. They had to clear Jang Bahadur's sons out of their way, so they staged a coup, killed the PM Ranodhip and Jagat Jung, the first son of Jang Bahadur, and the other children of Jang Bahadur had to take refuge at the British residence in Kathmandu and eventually were sent to Benares. General Jit Jung, another son of Jang Bahadur, pleaded with the British to replace Bir Shumsher with himself as the ruler of Nepal. He even offered the service of the whole of Nepal and himself to the British in return. Bir Shumsher was fully aware of the situation, and he couldn't sleep at night. He also needed the backing of the British to remain in power. So, in exchange for the guaranteeing of his regime, he agreed to sanction the direct recruiting of the Gurkhas into the British Indian Army in 1886. Nepal also got one rifle per head for the enlisted Gurkhas.

During the reign of Maharaja Chandra Shumsher, the relationship between Britain and Nepal went up to a new level. After the relaxation of the recruiting rules, the British had already established ten Gurkha regiments (twenty battalions with 26,000 men) by 1908, and Chandra Shumsher played a significant role in making it a reality. Just like Jang Bahadur, Chandra Shumsher visited the UK in 1908 and arranged a shooting trip to Nepal for the newly crowned King George V when he visited India in 1911. They were said to have killed 21 tigers, ten rhinos and two bears during that single expedition alone.

Chandra Shumsher wasn't a fan of the British before he came to power. His sudden change of attitude had something to do with the Russian threat via Tibet. According to the Nepal-Tibet treaty of 1856, Nepal was to protect Tibet in case of war, but Chandra Shumsher wasn't ready to keep that promise. The Russian threat to Tibet and then to Nepal was imminent and to counterbalance the Russians, he decided to take Britain's side. It was the main reason why he helped Capt. Younghusband's Tibetan expedition with 8,000 yaks, blankets and porters. The Russian threat was gone after the convention between Great Britain and Russia was signed in St. Petersburg on 18 August 1907.

The First World War knocked on the door, and this was a fight mostly between European nations. Nepal was not a warring nation. What Chandra Shumsher did was beyond logic. Rules were broken to make all the castes available for the army. The Nepalese Army was deployed along the Indian borders to free up soldiers for war. Porters, drivers, stretcher-bearers and men for all kinds of jobs were sent to India. The numbers of men in the regular army were increased from 26,000 to 55,000. Religious rules were changed so soldiers could cross the ocean and go to war, and even inmates from the prisons in Nepal were sent. Almost 200,000 men (20 per cent of the total youth population) from the tiny nation were sent to fight for the British. Added to that, Nepal provided arms, ammunition, food and other supplies, including financial support of Rs 10 million to the British war chest. The resources of the whole nation were at the disposal of its friend in trouble. One in ten never returned. Others returned either wounded or crippled and were sent home, empty-handed, to survive on their own.

In return for all the sacrifices the Gurkhas had made for the British in WWI, Chandra Shumsher was given an array of awards (honorary full general of the British Army, Grand Cross of the Order of St. Michael and St. George, the Imperial Order Par Excellence). He was henceforth called 'His Highness' by the government of India, and the colonial name of 'British Resident' was altered to 'British Envoy' and later to 'British Minister'. He was also made a Grand Commander of the Legion of

Honour by the French. The sacrifices of the Gurkhas also facilitated the treaty of 1923: Nepal was allowed to import arms and ammunition from other countries. Most importantly, the treaty of 1923 gave Nepal the status of an independent nation for the first time in its history. Also, a million rupees as a reward were provided by Britain to Nepal on a yearly basis, and the amounts were to increase later.

In short, the sacrifices of the Gurkhas allowed the dignity and very existence of the nation of Nepal and the whole country should be grateful to them.

As the saying goes, lightning doesn't strike twice in the same place, but for the Gurkhas, that is precisely what happened within the next two decades. Another war, WWII, had encompassed the world. The enemies were more formidable and on more fronts than in WWI, and the British had to fight the Germans and the Italians on the one hand, and the Japanese on the other. No worries, the British had a staunch friend in Nepal, and the tiny nation opened up its doors, hearts and workforce for the British again. They gave everything they had with 250,000 men sent off to fight for Britain, and about 32,000 were killed, wounded or missing. In return, Maharaja Judha Shumsher was showered with honorary titles such as GCB, GCSI, GCIE and so on. Permission to open the Nepali London Embassy was given, and the British Minister in Kathmandu was called the British Ambassador henceforth. The Rana government was said to have expected an enormous favour and rumours such as returning the state of Darjeeling to Nepal circulated in Kathmandu, but they had to be content with a lot less. Britain is said to have offered money as a reward to appease the Rana government. They chose personal before national interest as usual and let the nation suffer.

In brief, 200,000 Gurkhas had to be sacrificed in WWII for the total independence of Nepal. However, the sacrifices of the Gurkhas went down the drain and Nepal got nothing in return except for more advantages for Prime Minister Rana and money for his family.

The money Britain sent after WWI and WWII as royalty is said to have no proper records within the Nepali government. According to various authors from Nepal, it must have been pocketed by the Nepali rulers for personal use.

The Rana regime applied an isolation policy for Nepal, and foreigners were not allowed to enter Nepal during their rule. They also deprived the Nepali people of proper education and kept them in the dark for too long. When the Viceroy of India expressed his desire to visit Nepal, the Rana PM used the Gurkhas' cause as an excuse to refuse. If the British were allowed into Nepal, more outsiders would come, and Nepal wouldn't remain so unique and mysterious. The British would become like ordinary men and the respect the Gurkhas had for them would be gone. As a result, it would create disciplinary problems within the Gurkhas, which was not a good thing for the British or the Ranas. They argued and managed to keep the viceroy away.

Whether it was the royals, Rana maharajas, *panchayati* or the multi-party democrats, the rulers of Nepal always had the same mentality towards the Gurkhas and it continues to this day. Similarly, their attitude toward the British hasn't changed either. The Nepali rulers and the government itself have always been cold, unconcerned and indifferent towards the Gurkhas, whereas the Gurkhas have always been warm, caring and respectful to the British. In some cases, the rulers were ingratiatingly submissive to the British and hardly said a word on behalf of the Gurkhas. Instead, both British and Nepali leaders found the Gurkhas very useful as a bargaining chip for their own political and diplomatic gains, and used them accordingly. The way the British acted was understandable as they were outsiders. But Nepal's leaders were the Gurkhas' own people, and they were supposed to look after their men. Sadly, that almost never happened.

The rulers of the nation fully understood the value of the Gurkhas as a diplomatic chip from the very beginning, and they have been utilizing it ever since. They were not only motivated by political and personal gains but also a racial factor. In a nation like Nepal, where a feudal caste system still plays significant roles in all aspects of life and your profession is determined by your surname, the policy of becoming a Gurkha was like a god-sent boon for the Nepali rulers. The Gurkhas, especially the so-called martial races (Magars, Gurungs, Rais and Limbus) are the doers. Whatever they do they always do with passion, tenacity and heart, and becoming a Gurkha was indeed the perfect job for them. Had men from those four tribes not been Gurkhas, the rulers of Nepal might have had trouble in taming them in the long term, and the history of the country itself might have been different. As the Nepali saying goes, *'Badharnu parne kasingar hawale udai diyo'* ('the dust that needed to be swept was blown away by the wind'). It was a perfect scenario for the Ranas, and they wouldn't have changed it for anything else.

The Gurkha policy did not only save the Nepali rulers from unnecessary headaches but also provided a chance of enriching them. In other words, the Gurkhas were like the hen that lays golden eggs or a milking cow that never dries up, and the rulers of Nepal knew very well how to get the best out of them.

In the name of religion, *Paani Patiya* was one of the practices used to fill up the personal treasury of the *Raj Guru* (Royal Pandit) and the policy didn't end until the late 1960s. Going out of the country was deemed unclean for the Hindus, oceans were called *Kaala Paani* (black water), and all Gurkhas had to go through the ritual of purification or *Paani Patiya* when they returned. If not, they were to lose their religion and to be kicked out of the community – or out of the nation in extreme cases. The ritual lasted for a week. Soldiers were to take one meal a day, drink *Gahut* (cow's urine) a few times a day, and remain inside the camp. Only on the completion of the ritual were they allowed to return home, and the soldiers were to give money as *Guru Dakshina* (teacher's fee) to the Hindu pandits. As all the money received from the ritual went to the *Raj Guru*, you can calculate the total amount that had been amassed over such a long period and who would have benefited from it.

Another practice that reeked of a similar motive was the exchange rate the Nepali government used with the Gurkhas' earnings in the early 1950s. Since the Gurkhas were paid in Indian rupees, their earnings had to be exchanged into Nepali rupees through the government, and the government charged a very high rate: so high that the Gurkhas were getting 40 per cent less than the market value and the government was banking the profits from the poor Gurkhas' earnings. When the Gurkhas found out, they revolted, and the government had to adjust the exchange rate.

In support of the monarchy against the ruling Ranas, the rebels of the Nepali Congress invaded Nepal from India in 1950, and the Gurkhas were involved. The Gurkhas from the western part of the country weren't interested as usual. But the Kiratis (Rais and Limbus) from the east were concerned and took up arms against the Ranas. The Kiratis were mostly ex-Gurkhas of the Indian Army led by their own Gurkha officers. The Gurkhas overran the Nepali Army in no time. The revolt eventually overthrew the autocratic rule of the Ranas and helped establish a new government in Nepal. Although small, it was still a contribution on the Gurkhas' part. But nobody was willing to give them credit, and that has always been the travesty of our people, history and the nation as a whole.

In the fifties and sixties, the British Gurkhas fought a long battle in the jungles of Malaya and Borneo. Hundreds of them lost their lives, and when the war ended, thousands of Gurkhas were sent home empty-handed. But the Nepali rulers, as always, didn't say a word on behalf of the Gurkhas. The British were using their usual trick of flattery again, and King Mahendra was made the Colonel of the Brigade of Gurkhas when the rundown of 1968-69 was carried out. Whatever the British had told them, the Nepali rulers always believed and supported them. Whether it was during the Falklands War, Iraq or Afghanistan, the Nepali rulers never objected to the British and the requests had become no more than a formality. When the Brigade of Gurkhas faced one of the biggest rundowns in its history in the 1990s, they didn't even have to appease the Nepali rulers with embellishments like honorary ranks, and went ahead with the final rundown as they had planned. Thousands of Gurkhas were sent home empty-handed again, but it didn't make any difference to the rulers in their palaces.

The nation and the general public have a biased view of the British Gurkha, which might have been caused by jealousy. They only see the British Gurkhas' clean clothes, nice appearance and money. But they don't see the pain, sweat and blood that the Gurkhas have to sacrifice to become a Gurkha. The Gurkhas don't display their hardships and problems to the general public back in Nepal. Perhaps that's the only mistake the Gurkhas have ever made.

Being a Gurkha is anything but easy. One needs to be physically, mentally and emotionally fit all the time and must learn the necessary skills as the career advances. Gurkhas were always paid less, and the British had never abandoned the policy of 'minimum pay for maximum return' towards the Gurkhas. The only reason why the British Gurkhas looked better off than others was the value of the Nepali currency. For instance, one Hong Kong dollar buys more than ten Nepali rupees, and most Gurkhas are super-savers by nature. If you save HK$1,000 a month, you can save almost HK$36,000 in the space of three years. To maximize the return, Gurkhas used to buy gold in Hong Kong and bring it home.

Whenever there was a Nepal Airlines flight bringing Gurkhas and their families back home from Hong Kong, the customs office at Kathmandu airport would buzz with excitement. I am writing this from my own experience as a Gurkha returning home then. The customs staff at the airport would look at us with a tight smile and a prying eye. They would not talk or deal with you directly. They would use eyes and hand signals, apply a variety of delaying tactics and make indirect suggestions until we got the point. We had to meet with a particular agent, make a deal, and pay him the agreed amount on the spot. Only then would things start moving, and we could go home. It didn't matter whether you had one bag or lots of baggage, a big or small amount of gold, goods to declare or not, you had to make a deal with the agent and pay the dues accordingly. Even the young and single Gurkhas, who didn't have much to declare, were not spared. Those with prominent families and returning from the UK or Brunei were the hardest hit as they had arrived with the most massive loads, and they were always the last ones leaving the airport. We used to talk about the ordeals among ourselves back at the British Transit Camp in the evening, and some of the numbers we used to hear were simply outrageous. The dues could be over 100,000 rupees, and many felt robbed.

As I have described previously, a Gurkha below the rank of a corporal got to bring his family with him only once in his entire career, and that was the only time when we were with our families. Understandably, it was also the only time when we had our children, and the Gurkha family lines had another nickname – the children-making factory. But the funny side also had some truth to it. After three years, we had to return home with our families, and only those promoted above the rank of staff sergeant got to bring their families with them again. When returning to Nepal with our families, we were allowed to bring a few big kits (plywood boxes) with us in which we packed household stuff that we had gathered during our stay in Hong Kong, and they were mostly a mixture of old, used and new items. We had to pay a hefty customs fee as fixed by the customs officers, and we haggled for days. I thought that was unfair and, needless to say, I was not alone. The whole British Gurkha community had the same feelings towards the predatory custom officers from our country.

Perhaps we would not have felt that badly had the money gone directly to the treasury. But it didn't. These were under-the-table deals and only helped enrich the individuals who worked there as government officials. Under the veil of that privilege, it was daylight robbery.

It is an open secret and widely talked about among people in Nepal that there is a scholarship policy arranged by India with the purpose of helping the bright children of the ex-Gurkhas from the Indian Army. However, the system has been hijacked by the top government officials in Nepal, and their children are sent abroad for study instead of Gurkha children. As a result, the rightful beneficiaries always got cheated by the people in power.

Whether it was the old or the new regime, nobody spoke out for the Gurkhas. The Ranas were busy sustaining their own rule and luxurious way of life, happy with the embellishments the British had showered on them, and usurping the money that came in as royalties for the services and sacrifices the Gurkhas had provided to the British. The new regimes don't give a monkey about the Gurkhas; all they care about is the donations and aid money that they receive from the British. No Nepali rulers from old or new regimes ever thought or cared seriously for the welfare and well-being of the Gurkhas from the very early days to the present. They just accepted whatever the British asked for, didn't fight for the rights of the Gurkhas even once, and gave a free hand to the British as far as the Gurkhas were concerned. In short, Gurkhas were used by both sides for their own benefits and sadly, the Gurkhas had no one on their team, including their government and leaders. As a result, the Gurkhas had no respect, dignity or credit, which they so highly deserved. They ended up as the subject of mockery in some cases for far too long.

Had it not been for the selfish, short-sighted and obsequious nature of the Nepali rulers, the Gurkhas would have been treated fairly and lived dignified lives. Seemingly, the rulers from Nepal weren't fully aware of, or were merely ignorant of, the reputation the Gurkhas have around the world. They could have used that reputation for restoring the good name of the Gurkhas, which would have benefited both the Gurkhas and the nation. But they were blinded by a sense of self-importance, pride and selfishness. We have a common saying in Nepali, '*Maal payera chaal napaune*', which means, 'If you don't know the real value of a precious item, you will give it away cheaply'. The position of Nepali rulers and the Gurkhas has been similar since day one and has remained that way. Even worse, the blindfold is not coming off any time soon.

This mercenary tag still tarnishes the name of the Gurkhas, and it has wiped out all the good work the Gurkhas have done so far. It does matter, as I still see people calling and writing about the Gurkhas using that derogatory term even today. Had the Nepali rulers been a little more sensitive, smart and caring, this stigma could have been avoided a long time ago. All they had to do was to follow up the Tripartite Treaty of 1947 and make the British keep their word and implement the treaty properly. Unfortunately, that wasn't the case, and the Gurkhas suffered a great deal.

It took more than 50 years to raise public awareness about this grave issue. The people's uprising of the 1990s in Nepal gave impetus to it, and the Gurkhas had to fight for their rights as others wouldn't do it for them. Many Gurkha-related organizations were born out of necessity. They knew the urgency of the case, and the final result was the Gurkha Justice Campaign. We have already covered the campaign in previous chapters, but we must make one point clear. The Gurkha Justice Campaign was done for, to, and by the Gurkhas. The government of Nepal and its leaders gave nothing more than lip service, and only a very few of the general public supported the campaign. The campaign scored a significant victory by winning settlement rights in the UK for the Gurkhas and their families, but it isn't over yet. The campaign is still going on for equal pensions for Gurkha veterans.

The biggest mistake the government and the Nepali rulers have made so far was not any of the above. It was instead the open policy they had used for the Gurkhas. No government kept any records of the Gurkhas who went overseas, and nor did they keep records on whether they returned or not. The British had and have a monopoly. They came in and took whatever they wanted, and didn't have to check-out at the counter, as if it was an unattended shop. They have been doing it for the last 200 years and more, and still nobody checks on them. Whose fault is that? How foolish is it? How many Gurkhas went to fight for the British, or for India, died in the wars and never returned home? Why does the government have no record of them? Because of the dearth of records, nobody can fight for their cause and help provide justice for them. Had the government been keeping records of those Gurkhas, things would have been a lot easier for all, and the suffering Gurkha families would have benefited too. It is a national issue which should have come before anything else. In a country where personal interests win over national interests, such mistakes are nothing new and easily ignored. However, given the importance and severity of the issue, it was not just a mistake but a crime.

The Gurkhas have come a long way. They are not as weak, naïve and vulnerable as they were before. They have learnt their lesson in a hard way, yet come out strong. They are fighting for their rights and eventually will get them. The Gurkhas and their families can live, work and prosper in the UK. They are getting the same equal pay, welfare and pension as their British counterparts, at least in the British Army, since 2008. The stigma of 'mercenaries' has also become invalid by now, and it should be consigned to history for good.

The number of recruits the British take from Nepal nowadays is a mere 200-250. Fifty to sixty or more out of this group go to the Singapore Gurkha Contingent and the name itself is insignificant in a nation of more than 30 million people. The Gurkha recruiting policy, at least to the British, has become nothing more than a symbolic gesture. It still carries a long and significant history that both the British and the Gurkhas are proud of, and we don't see why the legacy shouldn't continue.

The end of the struggle for the British Gurkhas doesn't mean the end of the story here. The problem remains the same, and only the victims have changed. After the period of the Hong Kong British Garrison, many British Gurkhas returned home, and went to other countries such as Japan, Korea, Malaysia, Qatar, Kuwait and Dubai, and even to war-torn nations like Iraq and Afghanistan in search of jobs. The trend continued for quite some time before they were replaced by other youths from Nepal when the Gurkhas won the right of abode in the UK. Today, hundreds of thousands of Nepali youths are following the same path as the Gurkhas did. They are in almost every part of the world and doing hard labour, searching for a better future. Due to a lack of proper documentation and immigration procedures, they are subject to exploitation and abuse and fall into traps. Social media and news portals are full of such sad and unfortunate stories. Many fall victim to human traffickers and have suffered through inhumane situations. Many have cried out for help; others have sought the government's assistance. But only a lucky few have escaped the ordeal, and their struggles continue as I write.

The government has learned nothing from past experience. They still don't keep proper records of the Nepali youths going abroad, making the same mistake they did before with the Gurkhas. Most importantly, supplying a workforce to one nation by another must be dealt with first and foremost at a national level. Terms and conditions are to be discussed and agreed upon before they are put into action, and both participating governments must be fully aware of the exact details of the deal beforehand. National interests must be considered, the safety and welfare of the people involved must be thoroughly discussed, and emergency or alternative measures must be in place if things don't go as planned. Only then should the deal go ahead. But as far as Nepal is concerned, nobody seems to have followed the basic rules, and individuals or private enterprises play the role of the government. As a result, the future of about five million Nepali youths estimated to be abroad at present is in jeopardy. Nobody seems to care about it, and that's an ominous sign of an irresponsible government.

Furthermore, the government doesn't check on the unscrupulous agents and thugs. Many people have been cheated out of their life savings by such agents and left stranded in a foreign and unwelcoming land. Even worse, the Nepali embassy and consular offices are not much help in those desperate situations. I read a book about consulate officials participating in trafficking Nepali youths in the Middle East. Instead of being helpful, they had become the problem. What could be more unfortunate than this? Public servants should be here to serve the public, but in Nepal, it's the opposite. Unless this mentality is changed, the public's sufferings will continue.

CHAPTER 28

THE GURKHA WELFARE TRUST & THE CWGC GURKHA CEMETERIES

'After walking for four days and nights, we arrived at Maulo, Burma, and dug in. Before too long, the Japanese attacked. I tried to fire back, but my gun jammed. I finally changed the magazine and returned fire. Luckily, it was a small Japanese force, and they withdrew. The Japanese came back with a bigger force, the fight continued for seven days and nights, and my commander was killed right in front of me. Then, I killed three enemies, burnt two trucks full of the enemy on the way back, and lost about 200 men. I should have been awarded the VC, but there was no witness as my commander had already been shot dead.'

Hon. Capt. Kul Bahadur Gurung (99), 2/6th, 3/6th and 5/5th GR, from Dangsing, Pokhara, joined the army in 1938 and retired in 1967. He was awarded the MM (Military Medal) and is the only member of the Chindits, officially known as the Long Range Penetration Groups, who I met during my trip to Nepal.

The Gurkha Welfare Trust (GWT) was established in 1969 by the then major-general, Brigade of Gurkhas, A. G. Peterson, and the primary purpose of the trust was to alleviate poverty and distress among Gurkha veterans and their families. The particular groups of the Gurkhas that needed support were those (or their widows) who served in WWII and didn't serve long enough to qualify for a pension. A massive fundraising appeal was launched in the *Times* newspaper to raise a million pounds sterling, and the trust has been working for the welfare of the ex-Gurkhas for the last 49 years.

According to the chief of staff of the GWT, Nigel Rowe, the trust is an independent charity registered in the UK and run by a board of trustees. The funds they receive are mostly from fundraising within the UK. Additional funds come from the Ministry of Defence for services that the GWT provides to the MoD. The Department for International Development provides funds for water and sanitation projects, and Kadoorie Agricultural Aid (Nepal) funds the medical camps. Serving members of the Gurkhas also donate a day's pay to the trust.

As of July 2018, the GWT provides a monthly allowance of 10,000 Nepali rupees to 7,000-odd Gurkhas and eligible dependents in addition to a comprehensive medical service with free primary health care and medicines. They also provide free mobile health care facilities to more than 32,000 people and run two residential homes in Pokhara and Dharan which each cater for up to 26 residents who have no family to assist them. The GWT also runs eight medical camps a year, each of which can see up to 1,500 patients, and they are open to the whole community. It also builds schools, delivers water and sanitation projects, and it helped reconstruct 1,100 homes for ex-Gurkhas and repaired 60 schools after the 2015 Nepal earthquake.

The GWT is headquartered in the UK with 21 staff members and has its field headquarters in Pokhara with 22 Area Welfare Centres spread throughout Nepal, plus one in Darjeeling, and directly employs around 440 staff in Nepal. The GWT has plans to improve the way it delivers medical services to beneficiaries in Nepal by making it more responsive to the needs of recipients as well as the quality of the service it offers.

The GWT enjoys the patronage of Prince Charles and other dignitaries from the UK. I personally visited some of the GWT offices in Nepal during my recent visit in pursuit of finding the remaining WWII veterans and duly confirmed that most of the veterans were indeed surviving on the generous pension provided by the GWT. The staff working at the GWT offices are ex-servicemen from the British Gurkhas, and most officers and senior NCOs are employed for their management and decision-making skills. Most importantly, they already know the British way of doing things so no retraining was required. Both the Pokhara and Dharan GWT centres provide accommodation for the Gurkha veterans and arranges for free medical check-ups and medicines for the ex-servicemen and their families.

'Working at the GWT not only provides continuity from their regimented life but also a sense of pride and fulfilment, as they mostly work for the welfare of Gurkha veterans,' said one of the Gurkha welfare officers we met in Dharan, and I couldn't agree more.

* * *

The Commonwealth War Graves Commission (CWGC) was formed on 21 May 1917 by Sir Fabian Ware to commemorate the fallen from the Commonwealth nations who fought in WWI for the British crown. The CWGC has its headquarters in Maidenhead, UK, honours 1.7 million men and women, and maintains cemeteries and memorials in 23,000 locations in 150 countries.

Among them are Gurkhas killed in the battles of Flanders, Ypres, Neuve Chapelle, Normandy, Gallipoli, Cassino, Mesopotamia and Africa in both WWI and WWII. The Rimini Gurkha War Cemetery in Italy is one of the most prominent, where Gurkhas under the 4th and 10th Indian Division who fought the enemy at the battle of Rimini in WWII are commemorated. Headstones bearing the names of the fallen Gurkha soldiers are found in various cemeteries and memorials in different countries of Europe.

'When you go home, tell them of us and say, for your tomorrow, we gave our today.' These profound words welcoming all the visitors to the Kohima War Cemetery, in Nagaland, India, need no explanation. The battle of Kohima and Imphal carries great significance in the history of the British-Japanese war in Burma, as it was the turning point for the British. The Japanese were defeated right here at Kohima/Imphal, not at Yangon. The battle of Kohima/Imphal was one of the hardest, most brutal and deadliest fights of the war and many lost their lives here. To bury and commemorate those fallen soldiers, war cemeteries at Kohima in Nagaland and Imphal in Manipur were established, and they are respected as one of the most important memorials of WWII.

The Taukkyan War Cemetery of Yangon, Myanmar, is another huge cemetery where the dead from WWII are buried and commemorated. It honours 27,000 fallen heroes in the graveyard alone, and many among them were Gurkhas. It also must be one of the main memorials abroad where many fallen Gurkhas are buried. During the research process, your humble author had the privilege of visiting it personally, and I was moved by the list of names that adorned the walls, plaques and ceilings of the memorials. They were all too familiar: Gurungs, Magars, Thapas, Rais, Limbus, Puns, Shresthas, Bhandaris, Chhetris, and the list went on and on. If I were to read them all, it would have taken weeks. To fit with my solemn mood, the day was cloudy and damp with light patches of rain, and we strolled along the rows of headstones with my Burmese/Nepali friends. Although I knew none of the fallen personally, I could still feel a pang of sorrow in my heart and decided to leave the place before I became emotional and made a mess of myself in front of my friends.

According to one of my Burmese/Nepali friends, there was a separate cemetery near Yangon where all the graves belonged to the fallen Gurkhas. However, the city authorities had already cleared them, and the place has been transformed into a residential area.

After India's independence in 1947, four Gurkha regiments that followed the British were stationed in Malaya and Singapore and were heavily involved in the Malayan Emergency (1948-1960) and the Borneo Confrontation (1963-1966). According to the records, 204 Gurkhas were killed in the Malayan Emergency and 29 fallen Gurkhas among them are buried and remembered in a Gurkha cemetery in Ipoh, Malaysia. Thanks to Wira – the Warriors' Association of Malaysia – they are honoured on 10 June each year. Dignitaries such as the Nepali ambassador to Malaysia, the British High Commissioner and military attaché, and war veterans from the disciplined national services attend the yearly ceremony and a small team of Gurkha Pipes and Drums from the Gurkha battalion stationed in nearby Brunei provides the military calls. At the invitation of the Wira and its president, your author had the privilege of attending the memorial on 10 June 2017 and will remember the occasion for the rest of his life.

Similarly, other Gurkha cemeteries in Malaysia are located in the Taiping, Perak and Seremban districts. According to the online database of the UK Ministry of Defence, Rolls of Honours, five unidentified graves of Gurkha children are found in Cheras Road Civilian Cemetery, Kuala Lumpur. The Gurkha/Nepali communities of Malaysia visit and commemorate the fallen Gurkhas on a regular basis.

To commemorate the fallen heroes of the British and Allied forces defending Singapore from the invading Japanese troops in WWII, Kranji War Memorial was opened in 1946, and is located at Kranji Woodlands, in northern Singapore. As the cemetery is built on a hill, the headstones of the fallen heroes are erected in rows on both sides of the main entrance, and the graves of the fallen Gurkhas are found on the right-hand slope from the top of the hill. It's aptly called the Gurkha Garden and many rows of headstones bearing the names, ranks and regiments of the fallen are arranged. The familiar surnames can be seen and your author spent a whole morning there listening to the breezes blowing over him while remembering our fallen fellow countrymen. After the completion of my visit to Myanmar and Malaysia, I was in Singapore for two days and visiting the war cemetery was one of the main reasons I had come. I didn't know what to say while there though. Besides, I was too wary of becoming emotional at such a place.

After Malaysia and Singapore became independent, the Gurkhas moved to Hong Kong and remained there until Hong Kong was handed over to China in 1997. According to the records, a total of three Gurkhas lost their lives in duty while serving in Hong Kong and a Gurkha cemetery was built at Ngau Tam Mei in the New Territories. Your author, who served as a member of the Garrison in Hong Kong, was based at the army barracks called Cassino Lines, where the barracks and the family accommodation sandwiched the Gurkha cemetery in the middle. We used to pass by the graves on a daily basis as we went to work but we didn't pay much attention to them then.

The Gurkha Cemeteries Trust Hong Kong runs the Gurkha cemetery on behalf of the CWGC, and all of the Gurkhas/Nepalis and their descendants who died in Hong Kong are buried there. The Gurkha Cemeteries Trust, which is run by a group of avid ex-Gurkhas and their associates, also started a tradition of remembering their ancestors with a memorial ceremony which is known as the *Purkha Diwas*. The memorial is held on 5 April of each year and has been celebrated for several years.

Last but not least, a Gurkha cemetery was found in a remote area of the old British Dharan Camp during my recent visit to Nepal. The cemetery is a small one with fewer than 100 graves. But it is the only such site in Nepal where fallen Gurkhas and their children are buried and carries significant meaning in the history of the Gurkhas.

If anyone wants to find their missing relatives from WWI or WWII, they might want to visit the official website of the CWGC and have a try. You need to have at least the details of name, rank and regiment of the missing person and the wars he had fought in. If the particular person is listed in the database of the CWGC, the details of his burial location will be displayed right away. The job the CWGC is doing in honour of the fallen is indeed commendable. After all, they died for our future and deserve respect and admiration from all of us. May their souls rest in peace and find a place in God's unique garden.

CHAPTER 29

LAST WORDS

It was a family affair. All the people in this picture are my relatives (my uncles, cousin, brothers and close family members), and the only reason I include this photo is to show just how our community is connected to this institution... the Gurkhas!

Capt. (Retd) Rachhe Bahadur Gurung, 6th GR; Capt. (Retd) Birta Prasad Gurung (92), 3/8th GR; Hon. Capt. Buddhiman Gurung, 4/4th GR; Corporal Amal Bahadur Gurung 3/4th GR; Sergeant Padam Bahadur Gurung 2/2nd GR: Hon. Naik Subedar Min Bahadur Gurung, AOCs; and the author, in Pokhara, Kaski.

One thing I have learnt from my experience of the last two years researching and writing this book is that the only thing the Gurkhas wanted to hear was the story of Gurkha bravery, nothing else. I have continuously been using social media platforms during the last few years and have posted my writing on Gurkhas on an almost daily basis. The posts which got the most reactions were the ones related to Gurkha bravery, and the rest of the posts were ignored. The Gurkhas are undoubtedly the bravest soldiers in the world. Their bravery and fighting skills are unparalleled. The Gurkhas with their kukris are renowned for their bravery.

One thing is confirmed. The tale of Gurkhas is not only about bravery but also about tragedy and the cunning British brainwashed the world into believing otherwise. Fate, the British and the Nepali leaders played essential roles in the making of the Gurkha legacy. For good and evil, the trio was responsible. And as they took credit for making the Gurkhas famous, they also must take the blame for the making of a tragedy, and here are the reasons why.

First and foremost, the Gurkhas were betrayed by their destiny. They were born in a place where profession, position and status in the community are determined by your surname, and the merit of your hobbies, skills and abilities have no value. The Gurkhas were destined to be farmers; soldiering was found later on by chance. When they found out they were good at it, they persisted. Being a Gurkha was not only an alternative way of earning a living but also a necessity, and they had to cross borders in pursuit of a better life. It was the main reason why the tradition of soldiering had started well before the British discovered them, and the Gurkhas were already serving in the Khalsa Sikh Army of Maharaja Ranjit Singh in Lahore, Punjab. Although the Gurkhas have served the British since 1815, the official sanctioning of direct recruiting didn't begin until 1886. The British had already amassed a substantial number of Gurkhas in the British-Indian Army and had five ready-made Gurkha regiments by then. Had there been no such rules, traditions or restrictions back at home, the Gurkhas would not have gone abroad for a better life, and the fate of the nation would have certainly been different, if not better, by now.

Understandably, the youth are the main asset of the nation. A brain drain of the youth and its workforce can inflict great harm on any country. But here in Nepal, the best and most capable ones have all gone abroad, and you don't need rocket science to understand the situation of the country as a whole. This land was selling its best to the outside world and selling them cheap. What could be more unfortunate than this? But they did not care then nor do they care now.

The Gurkha legacy that started during the Anglo-Gorkha War of 1814-16 has lasted for more than 200 years and is still going strong. During that history, there was not a single war where the Gurkhas didn't fight alongside the British. They sacrificed tens of thousands of lives for Britain. The Gurkhas served, fought and died. They gave everything they had to the British and willingly died for them: whether it was in the cold, unfriendly and unfamiliar countries of Europe; on the long and inhospitable northeast and northwest frontiers of India; in the hot, unforgiving and unpredictable deserts of the Middle East and Africa; on the thick, swampy and unfriendly jungles of Burma, Malaya and Borneo; or along the porous and unpredictable borders of Hong Kong. They fought harsh, sadistic and numerically superior enemies like the Japanese. Whatever enemy or strange land, the Gurkhas never shirked their duty and always gave their best.

Most importantly, the Gurkhas always trusted and respected the British and remained loyal for two centuries. In return, the British took the Gurkhas for granted and also took full advantage of them all along. In short, they betrayed the Gurkhas and used them.

As already described in the previous chapter, the British used a policy of trickery, treachery and flattery towards the Gurkhas. To weaken and subjugate Nepal, they used unfair and one-sided treaties in the name of trade, and the deals of 1792 and 1801 were just the beginning. However, the Sugauli Treaty of 1815 was the one that eventually fulfilled the British wishes (to open up a trade route to Tibet, establish a British Resident in Kathmandu and start the Gurkha recruiting policy), which they had been seeking for so long. The Sugauli Treaty was undoubtedly the most unfortunate event of Nepal's history, and the country and its people are still paying the price today. Even worse, the last point of the agreement, the recruitment of the Gurkhas into the British Army, turned out to be the most significant loss to the nation of Nepal. Yet, it wasn't even mentioned in the treaty, and it is said to have been based on a verbal agreement between the two wartime generals, Ochterlony and Amarsing Thapa, right before the end of the first phase of the Anglo-Gorkha War in 1815.

More treaties were signed between Britain and Nepal during the next 100 years, but they were mostly forced by situations favouring the British. The British Resident in Kathmandu never stopped meddling in the internal affairs of Nepal. Weaker kings like Rajendra Bikram Shah had to revalidate the treaty of 1792 to please Brian Hodgson, and only Jang Bahadur Rana won big when the plains of Terai between the rivers Mahakali and Rapti were given back to Nepal as a return favour for his help in quelling the Sepoy Mutiny of 1857-58. But it was Bir Shumsher who conceded the rights of direct recruiting to the British to save his premiership and eventually opened up the route of direct recruiting for the British in 1886 that they had coveted so much for so long.

Chandra Shumsher had to make the whole resources of the nation available to the British and eventually sent more than 200,000 men into the mouth of death in WWI, which wasn't even their war. Why? Just to get British backing for his rule in Nepal.

Judha Shumsher did the same and sent more than 250,000 men from Nepal to WWII. Almost 33,000 never returned home. Others who did return were mostly wounded or crippled for life. In return, he only managed to get the legalization of the Nepal Embassy in the UK, and a few million rupees from the British.

After the end of both WWI and WWII, most of the men who had fought for the British were sent home empty-handed, and the nation was left to take care of the wounded and broken ones on its own. After sacrificing more than 20 per cent of the country's youth to the British, the people and the nation as a whole didn't get much in return. What were all those sacrifices for? Why did nobody ask this for those fallen ones? Did their lives have no value?

It was not just the British and the Nepali rulers; even the general public of the country did not understand the Gurkhas very well. The Gurkhas have never been able to separate themselves from the stigmatized word of 'mercenaries' for 200 years. The damage it has done to the good name of the Gurkhas is unhealthy and harmful.

When the Gurkhas came into the limelight again at a recent event, providing the core security for the historic summit between US President Trump and North Korean Chairman Kim in Singapore, the media world was abuzz with the news, and some of the media outlets called the Gurkhas the 'strongest mercenaries'. It doesn't matter whether they are called strongest or weakest or just mercenaries, the damage is done, and the Tripartite Treaty of 1947 was the main reason why the Gurkhas are labelled mercenaries in the world. Thanks to the betrayal by Britain and the indifference and selfishness of the Nepali rulers, the treaty that was supposed to protect the dignity of the Gurkhas ended up giving them a bad name.

Had the British not cheated and had duly honoured the Tripartite Treaty of 1947, which required equal treatment of the Gurkhas to their British counterparts, and had the Nepali rulers been a little bit smarter, more caring and less selfish, and insisted the British honour their words, the Gurkhas would have never experienced this unpleasantness for so long. The treaty did more harm than good to the Gurkha community.

The Nepali rulers never understood the value of the Gurkhas, nor did the general public understand the Gurkha plight or sentiment. The only people who did understand the value and potential of the Gurkhas were the British, and they used the Gurkhas to the maximum.

Self-serving motives that were personal, political and racial certainly played great roles in the decisions of the people in power in Nepal. But the policies of indifference, resentment and isolation applied by those in power were systematic and deliberate. The same reason could be given for the shortage of literary works, textbooks and artwork on the history of the Gurkhas. Despite playing the most important part in the history of Nepal, no part of Gurkha history is taught in textbooks in Nepal. We cannot blame students for not knowing the subject or being ignorant.

It's quite understandable why the British had mistreated the Gurkhas. After all, they were outsiders. But the Gurkhas were essential to Nepal's people and their rulers. They were supposed to respect, protect and care for the Gurkhas. After all, the Gurkhas have saved the nation several times. Had it not been for the Gurkhas, the picture of their country would have been different.

The Gurkhas were made cannon fodder in the hundreds of thousands, but they didn't say a thing. The families of tens of thousands of Gurkhas who went to fight someone else's war neither received dead bodies nor got them back alive, but they didn't utter a word. Thousands of severely wounded and disabled Gurkhas were sent home empty-handed, and they still didn't complain.

Why were their histories, sacrifices and contributions forgotten? Why can't we feel their pain, tears and anguish? Are we people of Nepal made of stone? Have we become so self-centred and selfish that we stopped caring for our history? The people who cannot remember their past have no future. We must never forget that. If we ignore the sacrifices our grandfathers made for this country, we will be cursed by their tears and sorrows, and that will be the most unfortunate history of this nation. We cannot let their sacrifices go to waste for nothing. We just cannot let that happen.

Despite their hard work and unparalleled bravery, the Gurkhas had tough luck from the very beginning, and their destiny seemed to always treat them too harshly.

The Germans, who ran for their lives the moment they saw the Gurkhas with their kukris, are now one of the richest industrialised nations and they donate millions to Nepal in alms. The mighty Japanese, who were soundly defeated by the Gurkhas in Burma and ended their ambitious adventure in WWII, are now considered one of the richest countries in the world. The descendants of the brave Gurkhas live illegally and wash dishes in Japan now. The Indians, who were saved and protected by the Gurkhas on various occasions, have become one of the greatest nations on earth and make the Gurkhas stand at their doors and call them *'Bahadur'*.

The Malaysians, who were saved by the Gurkhas from the grip of the communist rebels, have become one of the most developed nations in the Far East. They lock the Gurkha children in prison and beat them like animals. Hong Kong, one of the richest places in the world, was also saved by the Gurkhas from being overrun by illegal Chinese immigrants and treats its Gurkha community poorly, as if they are simply not there. The Gulf nations, for which the Gurkhas died in their thousands, have become rich by finding oil and gas and treat the Gurkhas' children as a commodity.

Similarly, Singapore, Brunei, Cyprus and Kosovo are just a few more countries where the Gurkhas contributed and helped those nations to prosper. What did the Gurkhas get in return? Why did their bravery have no value? What did Nepal get in return for their sacrifices?

People change with time. So do their values, priorities and perspectives. Now we worship frivolity, fake things and glamour. Celebrities, movie stars and sportspeople are our new idols, and we adore them as demigods, regardless of their nationality. Globalization has made national borders irrelevant, at least in the virtual world. And the Internet has made everything possible. In the process, we have forgotten our real values, traditions and the history of our real heroes, including the Gurkhas who sacrificed their lives for our future and the country. The forgotten Gurkhas are direct victims of the negligence, ignorance and indifference of our modern thinking. If we don't know how to respect our history, we will never know how to preserve our future, and a nation without its history is like a nation without a soul. Unfortunately, we are heading in that direction.

Although they might have acted only in the name of flattery and to show the world, the British have at least done something for the Gurkhas and erected some monuments in their memory. For instance, the monument to the Brigade of Gurkhas on Horse Guards Avenue outside the Ministry of Defence in London, the Gurkha Museum in Winchester, and many more memorials across the UK. In contrast, there isn't even a single monument or memorial that the government of Nepal has created to commemorate the Gurkhas. The Gurkha Memorial Museum in Pokhara was built solely from the donations and contributions of the Gurkha communities themselves. Given the importance of the contribution that the Gurkhas have made to Nepal, the whole country should be strewn with streets, bridges, parks, buildings, institutions, villages, towns and cities named after the brave Gurkhas. Monuments, memorials and museums should have been built around the nation to respect them.

Most importantly, a pair of giant statues of the Gurkhas should have been erected at the arrival entrance to the leading international airport of the country, and Nepal should be introduced to the world as the nation of the brave. This would be not only the right thing to do for all of us but would also help to promote the country's tourism industry a great deal. But sadly, that will never become a reality in Nepal, and if we somehow manage to erect a small and insignificant statue somewhere on the street of the capital city Kathmandu someday, it will be one of the greatest achievements of the country.

The Gurkhas are not a subject of ridicule, nor do they have the submissive or subservient mentality as perceived by some. Being a Gurkha was not a choice but a necessity for many. Nationalism and patriotism are nothing more than empty talk these days. We can keep on talking forever, but nothing can match what the Gurkhas have done for the nation. They have saved the country, for God's sake. Nepal is known to the world for three things: Lord Buddha, the Himalayas and the Gurkhas. If the country can learn, respect and appreciate them, they could help promote the good name of Nepal in the best possible way, and the country could benefit a great deal.

One thing the Gurkhas didn't learn in 200 years was to ask for their rights. The other communities wrote down their contributions, so they could provide proof when the time for the final rewards arrived. Since the Gurkhas were mostly simple folk and not so educated, they couldn't do so by themselves – and those who could, did not help them. Besides, the Gurkhas never had the 'right friends' in the ruling circle. If we are not aware of our history, we cannot ask for our rights, and that's the main reason why the Gurkha community is suffering now. The debt of honour that Britain and Nepal owe to the Gurkhas will probably never be paid back, at least not in this lifetime. But we can certainly do one thing: we can start respecting the Gurkhas. That's the least they deserve after all they have done for the country. We should learn to be grateful.

Jai Gurkhas!

ANNEX I

THE TREATIES

1. THE SUGAULI TREATY OF 1815

TREATY OF PEACE between the HONORABLE EAST INDIA
COMPANY and MAHARAJAH BIKRAM SAH, Rajah of Nipal, settled
between LIEUT.-COLONEL BRADSHAW on the part of the HONOR-
ABLE COMPANY, in virtue of the full powers vested in him by His
Excellency the RIGHT HONORABLE FRANCIS, EARL of MOIRA,
Knight of the Most Noble Order of the Garter, one of His Majesty's Most
Honorable Privy Council, appointed by the Court of Directors of the
said Honorable Company to direct and control all the affairs in the East
Indies, and by SREE GOOROO GUJRAJ MISSER AND CHUNDER
SEEKUR OPEDEEA on the part of MAHARAJAH GIRMAUN JODE
BIKRAM SAH BEHAUDER SHUMSHEER JUNG, in virtue of the
powers to that effect vested in them by the said Rajah of Nipal.

Whereas war has arisen between the Honorable East India Company
and the Rajah of Nipal, and whereas the parties are mutually disposed
to restore the relations of peace and amity which, previously to the
occurrence of the late differences, had long subsisted between the two
States, the following terms of peace have been agreed upon:

ARTICLE 1st
There shall be perpetual peace and friendship between the Honorable
East India Company and the Rajah of Nipal.

ARTICLE 2nd

The Rajah of Nipal renounces all claim to the lands which were the subject of discussion between the two States before the war; and acknowledges the right of the Honorable Company to the sovereignty of those lands.

ARTICLE 3rd

The Rajah of Nipal hereby cedes to the Honorable the East India Company in perpetuity all the undermentioned territories, viz.

First.-The whole of the low lands between the Rivers Kali and Rapti.

Secondly.-The whole of the low lands (with the exception of Bootwul Khass) lying between the Rapti and the Gunduck.

Thirdly.-The whole of the low lands between the Gunduck and Coosah, in which the authority of the British Government has been introduced, or is in actual course of introduction.

Fourthly,-All the low lands between the Rivers Mitchee and the Teestah.

Fifthly.-All the territories within the hills eastward of the River Mitchee, including the fort and lands of Nagree and the Pass of Nagarcote, leading from Morung into the hills, together with the territory lying between that Pass and Nagree, The aforesaid territory shall be evacuated by the Goorkha troops within forty days from this date.

ARTICLE 4th

With a view to indemnify the Chiefs and Barahdars of the State of Nipal, whose interests will suffer by the alienation of the lands ceded by the foregoing Article, the British Government agrees to settle pensions to the aggregate amount of two lakhs of Rupees per annum on such Chiefs as may be selected by the Rajah of Nipal, and in the proportions which the Rajah may fix. As soon as the selection is made, Sunnuds shall be granted under the seal and signature of the Governor-General for the pensions respectively.

ARTICLE 5th

The Rajah of Nipal renounces for himself, his heirs, and successors, all claim to or connexion with the countries lying to the west of the River

Kali, and engages never to have any concern with those countries or the inhabitants thereof.

ARTICLE 6th

The Rajah of Nipal engages never to molest or disturb the Rajah of Sikkim in the possession of the territories; but agrees, if any differences shall arise between the State of Nipal and the Rajah of Sikkim, or the subjects of either, that such differences shall be referred to the arbitration of the British Government, by whose award the Rajah of Nipal engages to abide.

ARTICLE 7th

The Rajah of Nipal hereby engages never to take or retain in his service any British subject, nor the subject of any European or American State, without the consent of the British Government.

ARTICLE 8th

In order to secure and improve the relations of amity and peace hereby established between the two States, it is agreed that accredited Ministers from each shall reside at the Court of the other.

ARTICLE 9th

This Treaty, consisting of nine Articles, shall be ratified by the Rajah of Nipal within fifteen days from this date, and the ratification shall be delivered to Lieut.-Colonel Bradshaw, who engages to obtain and deliver to the Rajah the ratification of the Governor-General within twenty days, or sooner, if practicable.

Done at Segowlee, on the 2nd day of December 1815.

PARIS BRADSHAW, Lt.-Col., P.A.

Seal.

Seal.

Seal.

Received this Treaty from Chunder Seekur Opedeea, Agent on the part of the Rajah of Nipal, in the Valley of Muckwaunpoor, at half-past two o'clock P.M., on the 4th of March 1816, and delivered to him the Counterpart Treaty on behalf of the British Government.

(Signed) DD. OCHTERLONY,

Agent, Governor-General

Source: *British India's Relations With The Kingdom of Nepal* by Asad Husain.

2. THE FRIENDSHIP TREATY OF 1923

TREATY of FRIENDSHIP between Great Britain and Nepal signed at KATMANDU, 21st December 1923, and Note bearing the same date respecting the importation of Arms and Ammunition into NEPAL---1923

(Exchange of ratifications took place at Katmandu on the 8th April 1925)

TREATY

Whereas peace and friendship have now existed between the British Government and the Government of Nepal since the signing of the Treaty of Segowlie on the 2nd day of December 1815; and whereas since that date the Government of Nepal has ever displayed its true friendship for the British Government and the British Government has as constantly shown its good-will towards the Government of Nepal; and whereas the Governments of both the countries are now desirous of still further strengthening and cementing the good relations and friendship which have subsisted between them for more than a century; the two High Contracting Parties having resolved to conclude a new Treaty of Friendship have agreed upon the following Articles:

Article I.---There shall be perpetual peace and friendship between the Governments of Great Britain and Nepal, and the two Governments agree mutually to acknowledge and respect each other's independence, both internal and external.

Article II.---All previous treaties, agreements and engagements, since and including the Treaty of Segowlie of 1815, which have been concluded between the two Governments are hereby confirmed, except so far as they may be altered by the present Treaty.

Article III.---As the preservation of peace and friendly relations with the neighbouring States whose territories adjoin their common frontiers is to the mutual interests of both the High Contracting Parties, they hereby agree to inform each other of any serious friction or misunderstanding with those States likely to rupture such friendly relations, and each to exert its good offices as far ss may be possible to remove such friction and misunderstanding.

Article IV.---Each of the High Contracting Parties will use all such measures as it may deem practicable to prevent its territories being used for purposes inimical to the security of the other.

Article V.---In view of the longstanding friendship that has subsisted between the British Government and the Government of Nepal and for the sake of cordial neighbourly relations between them, the British Government agrees that the Nepal Government shall be free to import from or through British India into Nepal whatever arms, ammunition, machinery, warlike material or stores may be required or desired for the strength and welfare of Nepal, and that this arrangement shall hold good for all time as long as the British Government is satisfied that the intentions of the Nepal Government are friendly and that there is no immediate danger to India from such importations. The Nepal Government, on the other hand, agrees that there shall be no export of such arms, ammunition, etc., across the frontier of Nepal either by the Nepal Government or by private individuals.

If, however, any Convention for the regulation of the Arms Traffic, to which the British Government may be a party, shall come into force, the right of importation of arms and ammunition by the Nepal Government shall be subject to the proviso that the Nepal Government shall first become a party to that Convention, and that such importation shall only be made in accordance with the provisions of that Convention.

Article VI.---No Customs duty shall be levied at British Indian ports on goods imported on behalf of the Nepal Government for immediate transport to that country provided that a certificate from such authority as may from time to time be determined by the two Governments shall be presented at the time of importation to the Chief Customs Officer at the port of import setting forth that the goods are the property of the Nepal Government, are required for the public services of the Nepal Government, are not for the purpose of any State monopoly or State trade, and are being sent to Nepal under orders of the Nepal Government.

The British Government also agrees to the grant in respect of all trade goods, imported at British Indian ports for immediate transmission to Katmandu without breaking bulk en route, of a rebate of the full duty paid, provided that in accordance with arrangements already agreed to, between the two Governments, such goods may break bulk for repacking at the port of entry under Customs supervision in accordance with such rules as may from time to time be laid down in this behalf. The rebate may be claimed on the authority of a certificate signed by the said authority that the goods have arrived at Katmandu with the Customs seals unbroken and otherwise untampered with.

Article VIII.---This Treaty signed on the part of the British Government by Lieutenant-Colonel W.F.T. O'Connor, C.I.E., C.V.O., British Envoy at the Court of Nepal, and on the part of the Nepal Government by General His Highness Maharaja Sir Chandra Shumshere Jung Bahadur Rana, G.C.B., G.C.S.I., G.C.M.H., G.C.V.O., D.C.I., Thong-lin Pimma-Kokang-Wang-Syan, Prime Minister and Marshal of Nepal, shall be ratified and the ratification shall be exchanged at Katmandu as soon as practicable.

Signed and sealed at Katmandu this the twenty-first day of December in the year one thousand nine hundred and twenty-three Anno Domini corresponding with the sixth Paush, Sambat Era one thousand nine hundred and eighty.

W.F.T. O'Connor, Lt.-Col.
(Under Vernacular
British Envoy at the
translation of Treaty.)
Court of Nepal.

CHANDRA SHAMSHERE,
Prime Minister and
Marshal of Nepal.

Source: Printed and Published by the British Stationery Office in 1925 and available through internet.

3. THE TRIPARTITE AGREEMENT 1947

TRIPARTITE AGREEMENT AFTER PARTITION TO RETAIN GURKHA SERVICES IN BRITISH & INDIAN ARMY – 1947

MEMORANDUM OF AGREEMENT

Article I

At a meeting held at Kathmandu on 1st May 1947 between representatives of His Majesty's Government in the United Kingdom; the Government of India and Government of Nepal, His Highness the Prime Minister and Supreme Commander-in-Chief of Nepal stated that he would welcome the proposals to maintain the Gurkha connection with the armies of the United Kingdom and India on the following basis, If the terms and conditions at the final stage do not prove detrimental to the interest or dignity of the Nepalese Government, my Government will be happy to maintain connections with both armies, provided men of the **Gurkha Regiments** are willing so to serve (if they will not be looked upon as distinctly **mercenary**).

Article II

Discussions have taken place in Delhi between representatives of His Majesty's Government in the United Kingdom and of the Government of the Dominion of India and the points of agreement are embodied in the Memorandum dated 7th November 1947 a copy of which forms

Annexure I of this document, Necessary financial adjustments between the two Governments are still under consideration.

Article III

Further discussions between the representatives of the three Government have taken place at Kathmandu during which the Government of Nepal have put forward certain pertinent observations, on the memorandum of agreement referred to in the preceding Paragraph which are set out in Annexure II. In regard to these points, the representatives of this Majesty's Government in the United Kingdom and of the Government of the Dominion of India have replied as follows:-

Location of the Recruiting Depots:-

The use of the existing depots at Gorakhpur and Ghum has been sought by His Majesty's Government in the United Kingdom for a temporary period only pending establishment of their depots in Nepal. The wishes of the Government of Nepal have been noted and arrangements for the establishment in India of the Recruiting Depots required to meet the needs of the Gurkha units of the British Army will be settled between the United Kingdom and Indian Governments.

Desire of the Government of Nepal that the total number of Gurkha units to be employed in the Armies of the United Kingdom and of India shall be limited and brought down to the peace-time strength of 20 battalions out of which 8 battalions will be allowed to the British Army.

The representatives of His Majesty's Government in the United Kingdom and of the Government of Dominion of India have taken note of the wishes of the Government of Nepal.

The representative of His Majesty's Government in the United Kingdom has explained that the long trem planning of the British post-war Army has proceeded on the assumption that the Government of Nepal would be prepared to furnish sufficient men to establish the equivalent of an Infantry Division in South East Asia and he has received as assurance from the Government of Nepal that a final sucession on the question of recruitment of Gurkha in excess of 8 battalions at peace-time strength shall be left open until His Majesty's Government in the

United Kingdom have had an opportunity of considering the views of the Government of Nepal.

As regards the reduction of the Gurkha units in the Indian Army the Government of Nepal have informed the representative of the Government of the Dominion of India that the reduction should not be carried out immediately in view of the existing political situation in India.

Arrangements of the import of the foreign currency belonging to the Gurkha units of the 8 battalions serving overseas.

It is noted that the Government of the Dominion of India has agreed to afford all normal facilities in regard to the import of foreign currency belonging to these men (Annexure I. item 10). A reply to the specific point raised in this connection will be sent to the Government of Nepal in due course.

Article IV

The Government of Nepal being generally satisfied in regard to the terms and conditions of employment of Gurkha troops and taking note of the agreement dated 7th November1947 reached between His Majesty's Government in the United Kingdom and of the Government of Dominion of India hereby signloy their agreement to the employment of Gurkha Troops in the armies of the United Kingdom and of India.

Article V

In addition to the observations referred to above the Government of Nepal have put forward certain suggestions connected with the employment of Gurkhas in the armies of the United Kingdom and of India. These suggestions are contained in Annexure III of this document and the views of the two Governments thereon will be communicated to the Government of Nepal in due course.

Article VI

Note has been taken of the desire of His Majesty's Government in United Kingdom that prompt action be taken to ascertain in wished of the personnel of the 8 Gurkha battalions concerned as whether they desire to be transferred for service under the United Kingdom Government. With this object in view a questionnaire and Memorandum embodying terms and conditions of service have been prepared by the representatives of His Majesty's Government in the United Kingdom. These documents are acceptable to the Governments of India and Nepal. They will be issued to the personnel of the 8 units concerned as soon as possible. In accordance with the wishes of the Government of Nepal as well as those of the Government of India it is agreed that their representatives will be present with the 8 units while the referendum is being taken:

Article VII

The representatives of the three Government desire to place on record that their deliberations have been conducted in an atmosphere of cordiality and goodwill and are confident that the friendly relations which have existed in the past will be further cemented as a result of the arrangements which have been agreed for the continued employment of Gurkha soldiers in the armies of the United Kingdom and of India.

Article VIII

Signed in triplicate at Kathmandu this 9th day of November 1947.

ACB Symon (Sgd.)　　　　**Kanwar Dayasingh Bedi (Lt-Col.)**
(For the Government of　　　　(For the Government of
the United Kingdom)　　　　the Dominion of India)

Padma Shumsher JBR (Sgd.)
(For the Government of Nepal)

FOOTNOTES TO ANNEXURE III (NEPALESE SUGGESTIONS)
SECTION H
In this letter to the Maharaja of Nepal dated 7th November (1947) the terms of which were acknowledged and confirmed by the Maharaja on the 9th November Mr. Symon made clear that "Subject to the limitation as of finance and supply, Welfare facilities would be provided for Gurkha

troops on similar lines to those provided to British (United Kingdom) troops". In a Tripartite meting at Kathmandu on the 7th November Mr. Symon emphasized that the United Kingdom Government in no way regarded Gurkha troops as mercenaries and that they would form an integral and distinguished part of the British Army.

Source: *British Gurkhas (From The Treaty to The Supreme Court)* by The British Gurkhas Studies and Research Centre, Nepal.

A LIST OF THE GURKHA REGIMENTS FROM 1815 TO 2020

1 – The 1st Gorkha Rifles (The Malaun Regiment) Established as the Nusseree Battalion in Subathu in 1815, transferred to The Indian Army in 1947, and currently stationed at Subathu, Himachal Pradesh with six battalions.

2 – The 2nd Goorkha Rifles (The Sirmoor Regiment) Raised as the Sirmoor battalion in Nahan in 1815 by Lt. F. Young, followed the British Army in 1947, and disbanded in 1994.

3 – The 3rd Gorkha Rifles (The Kumaon Regiment) Established as the Kumaon battalion in Almora in 1815, transferred to the Indian Army in 1947, and currently based at Varanasi, Uttar Pradesh with five battalions.

4 – The 4th Gorkha Rifles was raised as the Extra Goorkha Regiment in 1857, transferred to The Indian Army in 1947, and currently stationed at Subathu, Himachal Pradesh with five battalions.

5 – The 5th Gorkha Rifles (The Frontier Force) Established in 1858 as the Huzara Goorkha Battalion, transferred to the Indian Army in 1947, and currently stationed at Shillong, Meghalaya with six battalions.

6 – The 6th Gurkha Rifles was raised at Chaubiaganj, Cuttack, in 1817 by Capt. S. Fraser, as the Cuttack Legion, followed the British Army in 1947 and disbanded in 1994.

7 – The 7th Gurkha Rifles was raised at Thayetmyo, Burma, in 1902 by Major E. Vansittart as the 8th Gurkha rifles and became the 7th Gurkha Rifles in 1907, transferred to the British Army in 1947, and disbanded in 1994.

8 – The 8th Gorkha Rifles (The Shiny Eight) was raised in 1824 as The Sylhet Local Battalion and became the 8th Gurkha Rifles in 1903,

transferred to The Indian Army in 1947, and currently stationed at Shillong, Meghalaya with six infantry battalions and a mechanized infantry battalion.

9 – The 9th Gorkha Rifles (The Khas Paltan) was raised in 1817 at Fatehgarh Levy and became the 9th Gurkha Rifles in 1901, transferred to The Indian Army in 1947, and currently based at Varanasi, Uttar Pradesh with five battalions.

10 – The 10th Gurkha Rifles was raised in 1890 by Lt. Col. C.R. Macgregor from the Kabau Valley Police Station, Burma as the 10th (Burma) Regiment of Madras Infantry and became the 10th Gurkha Rifles in 1901, transferred to the British Army in 1947, and disbanded in 1994.

11 - The 11th Gorkha Rifles was raised in the Middle East in May 1918 during WWI and disbanded in April 1922. The 11th Gorkha Rifles of The Indian Army was formed again after 1947 and currently based at Lucknow, Uttar Pradesh with six battalions, and a Territorial Army battalion at Darjeeling.

12 – The Gurkha Engineers – Established in 1948 at Kluang, Malaya, as a part of the Royal Engineers and became The Gurkha Engineers in 1960, and currently based at Invicta Park Barracks, the UK.

13 – The Gurkha Signals – Established in 1948 at Kuala Lumpur, Malaya, as the 'X' Brigade Signal Squadron and became the Gurkha Signals in 1955, and currently stationed at Gamecock Barracks, the UK.

14 – The Gurkha Transport Regiment – Established in Singapore in 1958 as the Gurkha Army Service Corps and became the Gurkha Transport Regiment in 1965 and currently based at Gale Barracks, the UK.

15 – The 1st & 2nd Royal Gurkha Regiments – With the amalgamation of the 2nd, 6th, 7th, & the 10th Gurkha Rifles, the 1st & 2nd Infantry battalions were established in 1994 after the British Gurkha Brigade permanently moved to the UK, and currently based at Shorncliffe Barracks, the UK, and Seria, Brunei.

16 – The Singapore Gurkha Contingent (The GC) – Established on 9 Apr 1949 in Singapore and currently based at Mount Vernon Camp, Singapore.

ANNEX 3

REFERENCES

Pageant of History Series – *Gurkhas* by David Bolt – 1967

Valor: A History of The Gurkhas by E.D. Smith – 1997

British Samrajyaka Nepali Mohora: Jhalak Subedi – 2012

British-Gurkha (From Treaty to The Supreme Court) by British Gurkha Studies and Research Centre, Nepal – 2002

Warrior Gentlemen by Lionel Caplan – 2009

Gurkha Warriors by Bob Crew – 2004

The Gurkhas by John Parker – 1999

Lahureko Katha by Himal Book – 2002

British Gurkha Pension Policies & Ex-Gurkha Campaign: A Review by Centre for Nepal Studies UK (CNSUK) – 2013

The Kukri – The Journal of The Brigade of Gurkhas – Editions 2, 3, 4 & 5

Gurkha Victoria Cross Reception Souvenir Copy 1994

Imperial Warriors by Tony Gould

Nepal, A Hermit Kingdom by National Geographic Society

Gurkhas: Better to Die Than Live a Coward (History Book 7) by Benita Estevez

Kukris And Gurkhas by Martina Sprague

Last Post: Indian War Memorial Around The World by Rana Chhina

The Invisible Force: Singapore Gurkhas by Chong Zi Liang and Zakaria Zainal

Kranji War Memorial – Singapore

Taukkyan War Memorial – Myanmar

Warriors' Association Malaysia (WIRA) – Ipoh, Malaysia

2nd Sirmoor Gurkha Rifles Log Book – Gurkha Museum

6th Gurkha Rifles Log Book – Gurkha Museum

7th Gurkha Rifles Log Book – Gurkha Museum

10th Gurkha Rifles Log Book – Gurkha Museum

The Gurkha Museum, Winchester, United Kingdom

Gurkha Memorial Museum, Pokhara, Nepal

Wikipedia: 1st Gurkha Rifles – https://en.wikipedia.org/wiki/1_Gorkha_Rifles

Website of 2nd Sirmoor Gurkha Rifles – http://2ndgoorkhas.com/

Wikipedia: 3rd Gurkha Rifles – https://en.wikipedia.org/wiki/3_Gorkha_Rifles

Wikipedia: 4th Gurkha Rifles – https://en.wikipedia.org/wiki/4_Gorkha_Rifles

Wikipedia: 5th Gurkha Rifles – https://en.wikipedia.org/wiki/5_Gorkha_Rifles_(Frontier_Force)

Website of 6th Gurkha Rifles – http://www.6thgurkhas.org/website/

Website of 7th Gurkha Rifles – http://www.7grra.com/

Wikipedia: 8th Gurkha Rifles – https://en.wikipedia.org/wiki/8_Gorkha_Rifles

Wikipedia: 9th Gurkha Rifles – https://en.wikipedia.org/wiki/9_Gorkha_Rifles

Website of 10th Gurkha Rifles – http://www.gurkhabde.com/10gr-2/

Wikipedia: 11th Gurkha Rifles – https://en.wikipedia.org/wiki/11_Gorkha_Rifles

Official site of Britain's Brigade of Gurkhas – http://www.gurkhabde.com/

Official site of Gurkhas, British Army – http://www.army.mod.uk/gurkhas/27784.aspx

Official site of Singapore Gurkha Contingent (GC) – https://www.gwt.org.uk/news/singapore-police/

Official site of Queen's Gurkha Engineers – http://www.army.mod.uk/royalengineers/units/41816.aspx

Official site of Queen's Gurkha Signals – http://www.army.mod.uk/signals/25300.aspx

Official site of Queen's Own Gurkha Logistic Regiment – http://www.gurkhabde.com/category/qoglr/

Official site of International Committee of the Red Cross – https://ihl-databases.icrc.org/ihl/WebART/470-750057

Official site of Commonwealth War Graves Commission (CWGC) – https://www.cwgc.org/

Blog of VK Kunwor – http://sirkukri.blogspot.hk/

http://www.bharat-rakshak.com/ARMY/

http://www.qarancassociation.org.uk/about/history

https://www.nepalarmy.mil.np/

The Gurkhas by Byron Farwell

British India's Relationship with the Kingdom of Nepal by Asad Husain

Acknowledgements

Without the help, encouragement, guidance and support of these magnificent individuals, it would not have been possible for me to complete this book, and I remain indebted to each one of them forever.

Professor Colonel Khin Zaw Naing Zaw and Madam Professor Colonel Kay Thi, Patrick Sharma, Dr. Zayar Htin Tin and his wife Ei Nwe Ni, Capt. Htun Tin, Myowin Vishnu Panthi, Lachman Neupane and all the seniors from the Gurkhas community in Myanmar. Dato R. Thambipillay – Founder President and Patron of Wira Association Malaysia and Dr. Niranjan Man Sing Basnyat, the then Nepalese Ambassador to Malaysia, Peter J. Karthak, Dr. Om Gurung, Padam Bahadur Gurung (Ex GAESO Chairman), Maj (Retd) Dalman Golay, Maj (Retd) Lalit Chandra Dewan MBE, Maj (Retd) Tikendradal Dewan JP (Chairman of BGWS), Gyanraj Rai (Director of Gurkha Satyagraha), Chij Bahadur Gurung, Bharat Gurung, Chandra Bahadur Gurung, Capt (Retd) Nam Sing Thapa, Lachhya Gurung, Rajendra Chetri, Hari Budha Magar, Capt (Retd) Rukmani Dewan O'Connor, V.K. Kunwor, Yuvraj Acharya, Tej Rai, David Gurung, Lt (Ret'd) Indra Bahadur Gurung, Capt (Retd) Tara Prasad Gurung, Nigel Rowe (Chief of Staff at GWT), and Gavin Edgerley-Harris (Director of the Gurkha Museum, UK).

A special thank you must go to my Nepal Mechi-Mahakali visit team – Chun Gurung, Lala Gurung, and Ramsing Lama – and those individuals who helped us during our long trip. Photographs used in the book are by Lala Gurung, except those mentioned otherwise, commissioned by the author.

My sincere gratitude goes to all the Gurkha veterans, especially those from WWII, who allowed us to meet them and shared their stories with us, and I genuinely believe that their accounts provided the soul that the book was missing before meeting them.

My sincere appreciation goes to all of these magnificent authors and publishers who were kind enough to give permission to use their works as a reference for this book: Zakaria Zainal, Chong Zi Liang, and Ethos Books Singapore for *The Invisible Force*; Jhalak Sebedi, Basanta Thapa from Himal Books, Nepal; Professor Lionel Caplan of *Warrior Gentlemen*; Dr. Chandra K. Laksamba from the Centre for Nepal Studies UK; Bob Crew of *Gurkha Warriors*; Tony Gould of *Imperial Warriors*; RW Press Ltd of the *Gurkha* series; and many more.

I would like to thank my in-house editor Victoria Giraud, my agent Anuj Bahri and Sarah Zia at Redink, my publisher Pete Spurrier at Blacksmith Books, fact-checker Paul Christensen, cover designer Cara Wilson, and finally the readers.

Heartfelt gratitude must go to my family members Lt (Retd) Arjun Kumar Gurung and Bibi Maya Gurung, Rajendra Gurung, Raj K. Gurung, Arbin Gurung, Pratima Gurung, Capt (Retd) Prem Bahadur Gurung, and all those who have supported me during this journey.

Without the help, support, and encouragement of my dearest wife Tina, my son Prabhat, and my daughter Smriti, this would not have been possible. Thank you so much. I love you all!

Tim I. Gurung
Hong Kong, November 2020

EXPLORE ASIA WITH BLACKSMITH BOOKS

From bookstores around the world or from *www.blacksmithbooks.com*

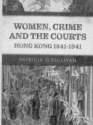